THE
MERCENARY

A Story of Brotherhood and Terror
in the Afghanistan War

Jeffrey E. Stern

PUBLICAFFAIRS
NEW YORK

PublicAffairs
Hachette Book Group
1290 Avenue of the Americas, New York, NY 10104
www.publicaffairsbooks.com
@Public_Affairs

Printed in the United States of America
First Edition: March 2023

Published by PublicAffairs, an imprint of Perseus Books, LLC, a subsidiary of Hachette Book Group, Inc. The PublicAffairs name and logo is a trademark of the Hachette Book Group.

The Hachette Speakers Bureau provides a wide range of authors for speaking events. To find out more, go to www.hachettespeakersbureau.com or email HachetteSpeakers@hbgusa.com.

PublicAffairs books may be purchased in bulk for business, educational, or promotional use. For information, please contact your local bookseller or Hachette Book Group Special Markets Department at special.markets@hbgusa.com.

The publisher is not responsible for websites (or their content) that are not owned by the publisher.

Print book interior design by Linda Mark.

Library of Congress Cataloging-in-Publication Data
Names: Stern, Jeffrey E. (Reporter), author.
Title: The mercenary : a story of brotherhood and terror in the Afghanistan war / Jeffrey E. Stern.
Description: First edition. | New York : PublicAffairs, 2023. | Includes bibliographical references.
Identifiers: LCCN 2022030983 | ISBN 9781541702455 (hardcover) | ISBN 9781541702479 (ebook)
Subjects: LCSH: Afghan War, 2001–2021—Personal narratives, American. | War correspondents—Afghanistan—Biography. | Journalists—Afghanistan—Biography. | War correspondents—United States—Biography. | Journalists—United States—Biography. | Arms dealers—Afghanistan—Biography.
Classification: LCC DS371.413 .S74 2023 | DDC 958.104/7092 [B]—dc23/eng/20220722
LC record available at https://lccn.loc.gov/2022030983

ISBNs: 9781541702455 (hardcover), 9781541702479 (ebook)

LSC-C

Printing 1, 2023

To Mom

CONTENTS

PART III: The Road and the Inn
(Our Story: 2011–2022)

A NOTE ON TRAUMA, MEMORY, AND MISUNDERSTANDING

THIS IS A WORK OF NONFICTION, BUT IT IS NOT A WORK OF INVES-tigative reporting. I have hired a fact-checker to help corroborate facts with sources, find errors, help me correct them, and, where the book deals in the experience of imperfect witnesses, help me faithfully represent perceptions.

There are parts of this book that depend on recall from one of two flawed human characters amid varying degrees of trauma. In some cases my contemporaneous notes provided some corroboration, as did other physical and documentary evidence, and occasionally other witnesses or news sources.

In other cases we can only call on the flawed resource that is wartime human memory. I believe the fallibility of memory must be compensated for in wartime memoir, or at least acknowledged. We can better strive for objective truth if we acknowledge frailty and bias. And while I don't think that needs to be a thesis—not every war correspondent needs to turn every defect of memory into argument—in this story, errors in perception were part of the point.

There were moments when, in real time, I believed I was resolving a crisis, only to learn later that I was exacerbating it; when I was certain a brother was OK, only to learn later he was suffering and I was causing trauma. This book's grandest ambition is to collapse some of the distance between two worlds by, at first, pointing it out.

To be faithful to facts when, more than anything I've ever written, parts of this book depend on my own memory, I have tried to avoid recasting myself in a flattering light. I've tried to be candid about my motives, which were not always pure, and about the grasp I had on my surroundings, which was not always as firm as I believed it to be.

Although I hope it feels like one, this is not a novel—I have not allowed myself to make things up when convenient, to take a few true facts and turn them into fictional events, or to turn a few true attributes into characters who are only mostly real. I *have* allowed myself—I've actually tried—to embrace the misperceptions I had in real time. The story is structured to highlight rather than run from them. When the storytelling in this book shifts from my own point of view in Part I to the other main character's point of view in Part II, those misperceptions are corrected. Or at least challenged.

I have used titles, as well as shifts in tense and style, to signal whose perspective—whose "story"—you're reading from. I believe it is not for me to determine whose view is truer. Only that they're different, and that they maybe didn't need to be.

Thank you for picking this up, and for coming on this trip with me.

"Go West, Young Man!"

—JANET RIES STERN, 2009

. . . *The rents are high, the food is bad, the dust is disgusting,
and the morals are deplorable. Go West, young man, go West
and grow up with the country.*

—HORACE GREELY, *NEW YORK DAILY TRIBUNE*, 1865

JULY 2011

Kabul, Afghanistan

AT THE TIME OF THE ATTACK, ALEX HAD BEGUN CARRYING A MA-karov 9 mm inside his belt. Safety on, but loaded so it was always ready to fire. Still, he often forgot it was there, each night remembering only when he undressed and saw the imprint the weapon had left against his skin. Most nights, he fell asleep with violence on his mind.

IT'S MIDNIGHT, MAYBE LATER. IT'S LOUD IN THE CAR, QUIET OUTSIDE. He flies past guard towers, barbed wire, and men standing, slouching, still, like they're not alive. Smoke outside the car, smoke inside the car. The girl in the backseat wears a face pale and made up, painted, her head covered in a way that's more suggestive, not less. A waxed rim of paved-smooth hair slips forward from beneath her scarf like a helmet visor. Her outfit assembled brightly, with care, though the young men in front look only forward.

A party on the move, they pass a bottle back and forth. The city blurs by and bursts in the mirrors, oil on canvas, not quite real. Smoke hazes everything. Light pools in puddles outside, groaning generators heaving power to naked bulbs, so hosed-down sidewalks seem to flicker. Alex drives too fast. Even before he was a Big Man, he drove too fast be-cause even before he was a big man—when he didn't know anyone but me, and I was nobody—the only way he could find pride was to break a rule and get away with it. Back then, there weren't really traffic cops.

1

Police worried about suicide bombers, or they were paid a little extra not to worry about suicide bombers. Reckless driving wasn't a crime anyone bothered with, and if it was a written crime at all, it was in an untouched book in the ignored drawer of some civil servant who had an office only because he was Somebody's Cousin. Today, Alex drinks, drives fast, and drives with girls and hashish in the car, not because he has something to prove, but because it's what he used to do, back when he did. He was a kid with bad habits and no money. Now he's a kid with bad habits and a lot of money. Now he's protected, a made man, a big man, a man with big friends—looked after. So at first he's not worried when something new flashes in the side-view mirror. Through the dark and the booze and the noise, the shape registers as familiar. A color, a pattern, a choreography, the way the weight of it shifts between its wheels. He *knows* that car.

Then there's the growl of an engine; tires screech. With a jerk, the new vehicle closes on his flank, and before he can make the judgment he used to make in an instant—it's too late at night, there shouldn't be other cars on the road, there should not be other cars going this fast—a window rolls down, and something metal telescopes out of the other car like an odd-angled antenna.

Alex feels percussion, a drumroll along the side paneling.

Orange flashes, a noise—"oh!"—like a question from the backseat. Only one girl is hit.

Now they're racing down city streets, Alex trying to weave, at speed, without losing purchase on the road. He's squinting to concentrate, clenching the wheel and trying to remember the route around potholes he used to know by feel. He used to feel these roads in the pads of his fingers on the wheel, a braille he's now forgotten. Now he has the window down, and he's shooting back, the Makarov bumping against his palm, and a friend next to him in the passenger seat is shooting too. The girl behind him is not screaming, she's dying, and it feels like an hour has passed before he's made his car a hard enough target that the other one pulls off and disappears, as though satisfied that a message was received.

In the sinking quiet that follows, Alex begins to wonder whether it's time to leave this place for good.

PART I

The Passenger

(Jeff's Story, 2007–2011)

CHAPTER 1

JULY 2011

THE ATTACK HAPPENED AS HE WAS BECOMING SOMEONE I WASN'T sure I knew anymore. A successful entrepreneur, an arms dealer with a heightened sense of irony, and before we reconnected. Before we stood together one night, years later, an hour west of Toronto in an ice cream shop lit up like a research lab. Fluorescent bulbs buzzing, Alex asking a girl behind the counter to write "Welcome to Canada" on an ice cream cake, then pausing, not looking at me, and telling her to add my name. Smiling with a mischief I knew well. And also with what looked like exhaustion.

His name wasn't really Alex. Alex was one of the aliases he used. His name was Aimal, but foreigners had a hard time saying it right. For a while he tried not fighting it. "Call me Email." People called him Email. Once, we agreed to trade names. It was mostly a joke, but it was helpful because he was working with my people, and I was trying to work with his. Then he just settled on Alex. It was close enough to his real name, the same number of syllables, and none of his customers ever asked how he ended up with a name they could say.

His role in my life, back before everything changed, was to drive me through a country being rebuilt quickly and secured slowly. Rising up and then strapped down, buildings growing behind blast walls, blast walls growing higher. "This is a citadel," a schoolteacher friend said, "not a city." Every year, a new glass-sheathed homage to progress shattered by shrapnel and gas from bombs that took down buildings and left in their place car-sized craters, waiting to fill with rain. Alex remembered the places where the roads opened; he absorbed them. He slalomed around rumpled concrete without thinking or looking, even at night. Keeping eye contact with me as we laughed about some grim thing or another, laughing at things we shouldn't have laughed at. Bombs were just occupational hazards for taxi drivers; the holes they left behind were not memorials for fallen countrymen, best not to think of them that way. They were just obstacles. What use is it to remember a building that once stood, or the people who fell with it? I'd ask for details—*What happened here?*—and Alex would jut his chin and turn the volume up like we'd both missed a lyric. For him, the city was an evolving series of roadside slowdowns to avoid. I sensed that thinking about it in this way helped him maintain his immunity to violence; I figured these were the calculations a driver learns when his city is a war zone and his livelihood lies in navigating it.

A driver fills his glove box with cigarettes to bribe soldiers. A driver judges his country's leaders by the roads they build. "Daud Khan was great man. He built roads, and they last forty years. Now you know the roads are not great but OK; now they make road, and one year, one half-year later, it's bad already."

The country was growing when I met Alex, but the progress was less a straight path than a swelling. Pumped full of money from different countries, construction projects emerged without pattern or reason. Foreign experts called it "development," but that implied a sense of order we didn't always feel. Instead, the way the country grew felt like a spill. A tide of concrete and rebar sludging along its path of least resistance, dammed and pooling in odd places. Progress was lopsided and uneven, but visible. *More* visible because it was lopsided and uneven. Roads were under construction forever, finally finished only to be shut down by the UN, by this ministry, by this or that embassy so visiting VIPs could pass through in their shiny little convoys. Alex would click his tongue. "Yah. Hold on, Jaff." He would touch my thigh to steady me. And then he always found another way.

CHAPTER 2

MAY 2007

Durham, North Carolina

I DIDN'T BELONG THERE AT ALL. I SHOULD NEVER HAVE GOTTEN ON the plane. I'd been propelled to war by a combination of naked ambition and overconfidence, a series of bad decisions met with favorable results. I was unprepared.

Ever since my father had me write letters as a child to earn time on my Game Boy, I had a place for writing wedged into the pleasure centers of my brain. Writing meant dopamine, and dopamine meant pleasure but also risk. My video-game characters didn't do much besides die quickly; Bart Simpson never made it past the second level in *Escape from Camp Deadly*. By fifth grade, writing assignments had me neglecting other work, and my one-page short stories spilled across notebooks in three different colors of ink. I played most sports left-handed and wrote with my right hand, but I wrote with my right hand like left-handed people write—with the pen tip pointing back at me. When it was my turn to read aloud to the class, there were long pauses I pretended were for effect but were in fact because my Technicolor scrawl was illegible even to me. I received few distinctions, but by college, as I found myself failing to compete with the glut of pre-law, pre-banking, pre-responsible classmates whose panning-out plans tunneled in on me, the one unoccupied lane was writing.

At college, at Duke University, probably a better school than I belonged at, we had a storied school paper I never managed to write for.

Instead, I took a single magazine journalism class, thinking "journalism" was getting to write while being less of a starving artist than whatever the Birkenstock kids were doing, and then I took a series of extraordinary risks that should not have paid off but did. I spent a week with a family of homeless men in an encampment near the train tracks for a story in the local hippie newspaper. The *Independent Weekly*'s editor swatted aside the half-cocked idea I'd come to him with and made me a life-changing pitch. Why not go see about the old red tent that had bloomed one night by the railroad tracks? The assignment launched my career.

I'd approached the tent cold. What other way was there? A man inside lifted the flaps and ushered me toward the one prized upturned bucket, a throne. I would win an award for a piece tracing their lives, though I was little more than a stenographer, sprinkling commas around stories they unfurled over malt liquor and street-harvested cigarette butts. I emerged from the story halfway in love with those men, wondering where the hospitality had come from. Mark, Concrete, White Mike. I thought the four of us would be friends forever. Even Concrete, even though Concrete hadn't spoken a word to me. I could tell he was kind. I could tell he cared about me; I couldn't tell why. I'd spent hours in a library basement with the microfiche trying to unearth a buried past, a two-tone scroll of 1960s Durham life. Drug feuds and violent crime whipping by, me leaned forward trying to violate his silence. I wanted to know what he didn't want me to know: who he really was, what his real name was, what exciting violence made him stop talking. He'd lifted the tent flaps for me, a gentle, silent soul welcoming me in, and I barged right by him looking for the private chambers of his past. White Mike—frail, hilarious, kind, nearly dying, and then deciding to enter rehab during our conversations. He invited me to his graduation from a halfway house. I sat in the audience and shook my head. White Mike, standing proudly in a full black-tie tailcoat, the only presentable thing in the donation bin. Looking like someone's butler, a monocle short of Mr. Peanut with an AA medallion. White Mike: he seemed to know exactly what I was thinking, and we beamed at each other. Later, he would come to my own college graduation party. My grandmother bought him an old Honda.

I kept having these strange, wonderful encounters. Studying abroad, I bonded with a stray dog while covering violent protests in an Argentine beach town. I found myself perched on top of riot fencing between police in tactical gear on one side and mulleted twenty-year-olds with Molotov cocktails on the other. Canisters of tear gas looped back and forth over my head, thumped out of riot guns, thrown back by protesters. The cops were trying to make eyes burn so people would leave, but I was so excited I wanted to scream.

I rode in a cattle car from Buenos Aires with a friend I'd made at a bus stop. A flower-peddling kid named Diego and his cohort of buskers, petty drug dealers, jugglers, and merchants of useless plastic shit commuting from a day working the city's clenched traffic. Passing a bottle of homebrew back and forth as we rode, legs dangling over tracks rushing by below. Diego brought me out to a violent slum he and his unlucky friends all lived in for a story on the cocaine trade. We spent a night poisoning ourselves and listening to pistols, and I fell into a new social circle. Low-level dealers and gentle addicts not yet fully decayed. Kids, young mothers, kids who were young mothers. I published a story in the *Buenos Aires Herald*, an English-language newspaper in a Spanish-speaking country, which was about my speed.

After my junior year of college, I tried to go legit. Through a family connection, I got an internship at *CNN Presents*, logging tape for a film version of Peter Bergen's *The Osama bin Laden I Know*. I thought I worked hard, but it was a running joke that I was the least-experienced intern they had. There wasn't that much for me to fuck up, though, and they liked me well enough. I had a council of tolerant bosses who took turns inventing tasks for me, and the youngest one was friends with a guy overseas who was serving as the Kabul bureau chief for a big newspaper. "Huh," the young boss said one day. "Griff is coming home." The detail burred on to me. I couldn't quite forget it. By my senior year of college, just as a slew of rejection letters from job applications began to arrive, I learned I hadn't counted my course credits correctly. While most classmates were coasting, collecting Phys Ed credits on the golf course, I had to overload both semesters like some hustling underclassman trying to triple major. It was obvious confirmation that I had a hard time following instructions and probably wouldn't do well at a job where I had to do that, which, as far as I could tell, was pretty much all of them.

By then I was nearing graduation and going nowhere. I wanted to write, kind of, and I had journalism experience, kind of, but hardly any training. I had a bad habit of getting close to sources, and I wasted a lot of time correcting editors on words they all coincidentally misspelled: DEK, HED, LEDE, WEL. Fuck—I knew nothing. No one would hire me. I figured, though, that maybe I could write if I traveled somewhere like that guy "Griff" had. Somewhere with a lot to write about. There were wars in Iraq and Afghanistan. I knew little about either, but I knew from eavesdropping on CNN producers that it was expensive to work in Iraq, and Afghanistan was still a little Wild West. I maybe didn't need so much money. Maybe I didn't need a security detail. Maybe I could wing it there. I had a fantasy of taking off on my own for Afghanistan. I knew it was fantasy. Beyond fantasy. I couldn't even daydream about it; I didn't have a palette to work from. I didn't know what the color of the place was, what things looked like there, aside from footage I'd seen in the edit bay a dozen times of bin Laden walking around on some rocks. Was that even Afghanistan? I wasn't sure my daydream was set in the right war zone, I had no idea what was there, and, starved of detail, it ran out of steam five seconds in— that slip in the film where you realize the scene set in some distant time and place was actually last year on a Burbank back lot, gaps filled by overdressed extras and plywood facades. I didn't really know how to get to Afghanistan and had no reason to believe I could pull it off besides, I guess, having already landed myself in a few hairy situations I'd managed to stumble out of unscathed. The logistics eluded me. But there was a good chance I was invincible. *Afghanistan*. Things filled out, details tumbled into place, and this wild idea of mine moved from a fantasy to a crazy idea and from a crazy idea to something actually worth a serious think.

I applied for travel grants and fellowships, was rejected by most and told I'd failed to correctly fill out the rest, and then somewhere near the end of my senior year I got to meet Richard Brodhead, president of the university. He'd somehow heard about my week with the homeless men. I wasn't talking much about the crazy idea of shipping off to war with no survival skills, mostly because I was superstitious. There were visa forms to screw up, plane tickets I might not be able to afford, a trough-full of broad-spectrum antibiotics I'd probably need if I was going to subject a weak tummy to whatever adventurous animal parts they ate in Afghanistan. But I must have mentioned something to President Brodhead about the idea, because later, at graduation, during his baccalaureate address, he told a chapel full of graduating seniors and their families, "As you write the story of your life, I hope you'll include some element of adventure." For a moment, I thought he might be addressing me personally. "You had the confidence to cross from known to unknown paths, and I hope you won't stop now." *OK*, I thought. *I won't.* "I know some of you who are going off to teach in places you have never visited; I know one of you who is going off to be an investigative reporter in Afghanistan . . ."

The room wobbled. Did someone else have that idea? Did he mean me? ". . . I know a person being commissioned as an officer in the Marines . . ." I still hadn't figured out how to get to Afghanistan; I hadn't even decided I was actually going. I shifted in my seat and understood that now, I had to.

I went to the bank to withdraw everything. The little money I'd saved working summer construction jobs in high school, mowing lawns, having a bar mitzvah, and publishing a few stories. I secretly called my parents' travel agent and foisted an ethical dilemma onto her lap, bought a flight through Delhi to Kabul, somehow secured a visa to Afghanistan, somehow didn't realize until a few days before departure that I also needed a visa to India, and somehow got that. It was like a video game in which I kept failing tasks and advancing to the next level anyway. A night in

New Delhi, then a short, what-the-fuck-am-I-doing flight from Delhi to Kabul on Air India. I tried to busy myself with two books, *Reporting* by David Remnick and *The Looming Tower* by Lawrence Wright, gifted to me by Bob Bliwise, my magazine journalism professor. But I wasn't reading. I was compulsively underlining as if stray pen marks might force information into my brain, and trying to look busy so no one would ask me what I was doing. I consumed everything put before me, including the traditional Indian soapy lemon water that made me very nearly hurl and that I learned years later was actually traditional Indian handwash.

I landed in Kabul without really believing it was Kabul, and headed to the person attached to one of two phone numbers I knew. Rory Stewart, a friend of a family friend. I'd never met or spoken to him, but he'd started a charity reviving old Afghan handicrafts and, now, apparently, housing wayward young Americans marching like wind-up toys on kitchen tables toward certain demise. Rory gave me a free room for a week, then two, and then an Afghan blogger named Nasim I'd found online helped get me set up with almost-free lodging at an almost-abandoned hotel in the heart of the city. I was the only guest until a strange European traveler showed up in the room next to mine, and I thought, *What kind of loser comes to Afghanistan on his own?* The whole thing was eerie. There were rumors the hotel owner had been killed in some kind of gang-related incident. I didn't know. What I knew was that the rooms were tiny, the location was central, there were two guests and no amenities besides two men who said hello and watched cricket, and a single exercise bike up on the roof. I went up there and felt so entirely alone in a terrifying and wonderful way. So untethered that anything might happen now, the part of a leap after your stomach has settled and now you're just flying. A wind blew. The muezzin sounded. One, then the other, then a dozen. A web of mournful voices, old men lamenting at each other over the rooftops. I watched old women in burkas down on the street hurrying home. I didn't know how I knew they were old.

I didn't know what I was doing. I was here to find a story and write it. How on earth could I do that? Nasim was gone now, he was helpful and kind but an island of a young man, off somewhere tending to his thoughts. I thought of the one useful tip I'd been given just before leaving America: if I found myself alone, I needed to call a company called Afghan Logistics. It had a taxi service that, for a flat rate of seven dollars, gave Westerners rides anywhere in the city with a reliable, English-speaking driver.

CHAPTER 3

EARLY SEPTEMBER 2007

WHEN ALEX ARRIVED TO PICK ME UP THE FIRST TIME, I FELT myself rushing to him. I didn't know why. He seemed totally in control, but he was skinny and slight, a mantis folded up behind the wheel. Jangly limbs shot off at switchback angles inside the car like he was part of its architecture. Thin, strong beams holding the sidewalls apart. The car smelled of dust and heat and stale tobacco, a little of old cologne, so slipping inside was like brushing up against a dark-suited bouncer, the sparkly crossing of a nighttime threshold into a pulsing, roped-off world. Breathless, floating excitement and chance, which notched up when Alex heard something on the radio, unstowed an arm, and reached toward the volume knob. I expected some chanty Middle Eastern thing, but instead a wobbly tin whistle squeaked out of the speakers, and then a beat so propulsive I could've sworn my organs woke up to dance. Some techno-inflected remix of a song I didn't know I knew at first, until a sped-up voice started tearing through lyrics I'd never heard sung this fast. *Far across the distance, and spaces between us*—a synth kicked in, and I remembered reading somewhere that *Titanic* was popular in Afghanistan. *You'rrrrrrre here, there's nothhhhhhing I fear*—this was going to be awesome. Alex put the car in gear and pulled off into traffic, and I knew he was someone I was going to turn into my friend.

We talked a lot but covered little of substance, and I didn't know why I liked him so much so quickly. I think it was because he was funny, though I found everything funny, because I was manic, because

I was in a fucking war zone and a speeding chipmunky diva was singing along with us. He didn't laugh when I told him I was trying to be a journalist even though I knew no one, didn't have an editor, had hardly any money despite the fact that Westerners all had money. He took me seriously. He listened, I think, though I wasn't sure because I spoke no Dari and his English was bad. I might have seen someone to save; I might have seen someone to save me. It was something like love at first sight. It felt like we were meeting each other at the exact right moment in both of our lives.

———

WE WERE MEETING EACH OTHER AT THE EXACT RIGHT MOMENT IN AN industry I was trying to break into. I climbed into Alex's car for the first time in the mid-2000s, just as news organizations began to think of their websites as more than just repositories for their print reporting. Hip young editors were poached from lifestyle magazines, and a herd of skinny-jeaned cool guys began a daily migration from their edgy Brooklyn habitats to the newish Manhattan skyscrapers. Given modest budgets and charged with finding cool new shit to publish. New bars were cool, street art was cool, war was cool too, and soon after settling into their cool new open-concept offices, all the hip young editors started receiving typo-ridden emails from a kid who said he was in Afghanistan with a fresh take on the latest violence.

With a lot of help from Alex and a little help from an industry at the exact right moment of its life/death cycle, I got to work.

———

THE FIRST STORY WAS AT GHAZI STADIUM, IN KABUL.

It was Ghazi Stadium where, before I ever came to the country, people had tried to heal with a soccer match between Afghans and the foreigners coming to fight and rebuild. It was a way to push aside memories of executions held there during the Taliban years—a ninety-minute hug for the cameras in the hopes that soccer would be enough. That was 2002, just months after 9/11. Back then, all there was was hope.

By the time Alex and I pulled up, five years after that soccer match, the stadium's brief honeymoon was over. It was back to being what it must have been fated to be: a coliseum for wars rendered in miniature. We were there for a holiday honoring the country's national hero, Ahmad Shah Massoud. Massoud was a controversial figure, though, revered by some for fighting the Soviets, then the Taliban, and mourned after his assassination at the hands of Al-Qaeda, just two days before 9/11. Americans liked him, the French liked him, the West generally liked him because he'd fought against all the people the West didn't like. But he was feared and hated too by civilians who'd suffered collateral damage at his hands and the hands of his men and, naturally, by the Taliban he'd fought against.

Here, as Alex and I arrived, was the president, Hamid Karzai, showing up at the stadium on a day when the Taliban's avowed enemy was being cheered. Karzai claiming the podium as a sovereign ruler seemed to be inviting chaos, and for me, that was reason enough to hope things might get rowdy. If the violence was unsubtle enough, I might have something to write.

We'd barely arrived before everything unraveled. Stones hitting walls or gunshots or both, and then stampeding acolytes. I'd found the flying sparks I thought I wanted, but in seconds I was in way over my head. I was an excited young man speaking none of the language as anger swelled up around me and began to tilt inward. Alex took my hand and yanked me away, pulled so hard I started running, and now we were skipping through people and over rubble, Alex leading me away from the danger I'd brought him into. He pulled me all the way back to the car, back into the comfort and heat and stale air of his little world and raced me away to safety, me giddy and drunk with adrenaline, becoming a chatty passenger as Alex went quiet, squinting for new routes through the city, as the city began to squeeze shut. He got me back safely, I wrote up a story and downloaded my photos, and published a piece tucked into a corner of *Esquire*'s website you had to really look for, but still: a piece by me, with Afghanistan in the dateline.

Alex and I became inseparable after that. I came to depend on him. I got a menial job to support my journalism habit, working as a glorified secretary at the brand-new American University of Afghanistan. It called itself "the only private liberal arts, not-for-profit, co-education university in the country," but as far as I could tell once I started, the university was a place for the country's rich kids to learn English and the world's lost souls to get faculty positions. I didn't mind. I liked the lost souls; some were interesting, and many were very kind. Anyway, I hadn't come to the country to educate people; this was a paycheck that came with housing. I heard a saying at the university I started repeating, that every foreigner Afghanistan attracts is either a missionary, a mercenary, or a malcontent. I was too young and unsettled to know about contentment, and I wasn't there to convert anyone. I was there to make a name for myself writing about all the worst things the country had to show me. The university itself was often brutal, but not in a fun or exciting way. Morale was low. Unlike nearly every other organization employing foreigners in Afghanistan, the university provided neither extravagant salaries nor much sense of purpose, since the students tended to be the least needy. There was a theory, clutched on to with white knuckles by some of us, that trying to bring a Western standard of education to the country *was* the Lord's work. That having a well-educated elite was a prerequisite to a country levering itself into the world economic system and developing a capable professional class, or something. What I knew was that people often seemed unhappy, their spirits weighted down most by the lack of freedom. We lived in a panopticon, a staff of poorly compensated guards watching our every move. We had to book grocery-shopping trips days in advance, and then we could go only if the time worked for enough of our colleagues since the university only had a few cars for the whole staff. The list of places sanctioned for us to visit shrank with each new Security Incident until it didn't extend all that far beyond the twice-daily drives between campus and university housing. We couldn't go anywhere without approval.

But for me, the whole thing was a little different. I had Alex. I had an escape from the Island of Misfit Toys. I was always just biding my time until something somewhere exploded, and I had my excuse to call Alex and go be my own young man.

Alex: friendly, talkative, clever, and always working. He somehow knew before everyone else when a bomb had gone off and where. I didn't know how he knew. I'd feel the window in my university-issued bedroom make a little comment, the building shimmying from an over-pressure wave, and I'd know to expect a call within seconds from Alex telling me exactly where the explosion was and when to be ready to go. He knew so damned quickly. He knew perhaps too quickly. He figured everything out, and all I had to do was find a way to slip past the guards who were posted outside my safe house. I slipped past guards whose jobs depended on keeping us safe, which meant keeping us from leaving.

Alex and I drove all over the city in those first few months. He wasn't like the "fixers" or translators other journalists had. He had no experience in journalism, but that was OK; I hardly had any either. We stumbled all over each other those first weeks, sometimes literally, once just after arriving outside the city at the site of a car bomb that had gone off down in a gulley. Police were keeping the crowd back, ignoring the flock of old men who'd already moved past them and begun to congeal into a viewing section tucked under the bridge, watching the mangled car as if they were waiting for a rain-delayed soccer match to finally start.

Alex and I hustled up to the makeshift police line, but I was over-eager, I stepped on his heel, and we went tumbling to the ground. Eyes veered from the car to these two strange young men who seemed to have chosen this of all moments to begin wrestling in the dirt. We clambered back to our feet, and Alex reached his hand out to shake mine like we'd only just met. I was confused. "What does this mean?"

He said, "It means we are not fighting." And he kept holding my hand, not letting go, as we moved closer to one of our many ground zeroes. He started doing that often, taking me by the hand or keeping a finger on my sleeve to make sure I was close, keeping hold of me as our tour of the worst the city had to show us picked up speed. We went to bombings, shootings, and protests. With his help, I published more stories. I wrote about visiting a minefield and being arrested while getting a haircut. I emailed editors ideas for stories I thought they might find sexy, or might make me look cool, and then I called Alex to have him figure out the details. And though I was on the make, self-focused and eager, I marveled at the way he moved. Nimble, slender, with bad posture, but quick and elegant as a pickpocket. Somehow hunchbacked and balletic at the same time, Alex was a dancer really, always in motion with his hands cupped over his mouth to light a cigarette. I marveled at the way he drove too, all the close calls, but his vision was measured on a different scale than mine. Zipping by cars within inches felt like near misses to me, but he was at home in the swollen current of vehicles squeezing between rivers and cliffs. Time and speed were arranged differently here, and maybe space was too. He was a superhero, able to think and move with ease when the world around him was frantic, hot, fast, and angry. Even the way he used the horn was so tactful that I laughed. It wasn't aggression; in his hands it was courtesy. A little percussive song to say, "Hey! Just letting you know I'm over here!" He drove not just by sight but by sonar too. And if he was a daredevil inside the car, he seemed to become more fiercely protective of me outside of it. When we weren't together, he started constantly checking in. Making sure I was still safe, I hadn't stumbled into some disaster without him, and sometimes giving little hints of places I might try to avoid today.

When a shooting had already happened, the bomb had already gone off, and we arrived at the scene of the crime, Alex could sweet-talk almost anyone. That was key because I had access to almost no one. I couldn't meet with important people. I didn't know any of them besides Rory Stewart, and anything Rory Stewart might want in writing, he'd write. He was a talented, successful author. And I knew Nancy Hatch Dupree. She was the one-million-year-old grandmother of Afghanistan, a frail and brilliant old lady who still drove back and forth across the Khyber Pass every year. She'd built a library in Afghanistan, knew more about the country than probably any other foreigner, and had literally written the (guide) book on Afghanistan. Her late husband had once taught at Duke decades before I attended, and the closest thing I had to an assignment before landing here was Bob Bliwise at the alumni magazine saying, "That sounds like a pretty weak connection."

I still had no publication behind me, no access to anyone important, so our beat became the people gathered near whatever the latest violence was. The intimates of the dead, the freshly widowed husbands, the early onlookers—little truths uncovered in the expanding radius of a blast wave. The old policeman trying to save children by whaling on them with wooden bats so they wouldn't gather into a tightly packed target for a second bomb. The theater owners, a quarter-mile down the road, sweeping up broken shards from a collapsed marquee, broom handle jabbing the last glass angles from poster boards of scandalous Bollywood dancers.

Alex handled it all without complaint. It didn't occur to me he'd have any reason to complain. We were adventuring. I needed him. I smiled and laughed. "I need you," I said, several times a week, and he never really said no to anything I asked of him. He asked for so little in return. Occasionally he asked for help getting to America, but I changed the subject, and he never pressed. Of all the people I befriended in this strange new country, he was the only one who hadn't ever managed to get out, not even for a weekend. Unlike the others, the students and bloggers, it seemed hopeless with him. What university fellowship would he qualify for? What think tank would want an Afghan taxi driver? I'd turn the conversation back to what I needed.

We'd park on the side of the road after a shooting or bombing, and he'd spend hours telling me in his broken English what people around me had been saying. He would twist in his seat and think of another way to explain something I didn't get. He was so patient. It didn't occur to me back then how frustrating it must have been for someone who depended so heavily on a quick tongue to have it tangled up in another language, one like English, with exceptions for every rule, a language of broken logic and false avenues. So we sat in the car, we smoked, we had the same conversation, again and again.

We saw terrible things. I was inoculated against trauma because I was high on adrenaline and friendship and because I felt so comfortable with this special sort of partner. Nothing touched me because nothing touched him, and he was always next to me. Alex *was* this country to me. He was the most important thing in it, and he was keeping me safe, and I thought nothing would ever happen to us so long as we stayed together. It didn't occur to me that it might be different for him.

CHAPTER 4

LATE SEPTEMBER 2007

EACH STORY WAS DIFFERENT, BUT THERE WAS A RHYTHM IN IT TOO: mark time until violence, then we speak. I got calls with him trying to hide warnings in casual conversation. "Yah, Jaff. How are you? Also, today please stay away from US embassy, German embassy, and Kabul City Center. OK? Thanks, welcome, bye."

I didn't know how he knew these places were likely to be hit. He just always seemed to know a little more than he should, and I thought it was better not to ask. An explosion, a shooting, an act of war. Alex would find out so fast I sometimes wondered if he'd expected the event, like he somehow knew ahead of time that an attack might happen in that neighborhood. I'd tell my boss at the university, "Attack in the west of the city, I have to go," and he'd say, "I've heard of no attack there." A few minutes later, cell phones around us would start ringing.

If Alex thought he could keep me safe, he'd pick me up. If I was at work, I'd have to convince my boss that it was OK, I'd be safe, I'd get my work done later. Then I'd have to convince the guards to let me out even though I wasn't in a university vehicle. I'd sign the little sheet that said what time it was, where I was going, what time I'd be back, though I never knew and had no idea either what to put in the "dest." box. "What's our destination?" I'd ask Alex. "The bombing." I'd scribble the time, and we'd launch ourselves into the city.

Alex talking, smoking, holding eye contact with me as he drives, making no-look circuits through Kabul. I laugh at something and grab his knee while he flies through conversation topics like he's constantly caffeinated, always in a lit-up mood. Always a mischievous smile, a der-vish. Working the wheel with one hand, bare left heel pulled up and resting on the seat, because why keep two feet on the floor when you need just one to work the pedals? Somehow revved up and nightclub cool at the same time. Only occasionally would he pull the throttle back on his giddy English to think a few steps ahead, an alternate route taking shape in his mind. Everything was a puzzle to be solved, a better way no one's thought of. It was like he'd figured it all out. How you drive at speed on the good roads to make up for time lost on the bad ones. How you try to separate yourself from the herd because a herd is a target. You never want to be boxed in if you're driving a for-eigner around, not if you're worried about bombs, since bombs are more likely to hit a bunch of vehicles clumped together and unmoving than one flying down the wrong side of the road. To him, there was no right or wrong way. Always looking for an angle, the route I didn't even see.

He figured out how to work intersections by feel; they all had their own fluid logic he ignored, applying his own. There were hardly any traf-fic lights in the city, so no one paid attention to the few that were there. Drivers regarded them as festive decorations for some foreign holiday. There were roundabouts with red-faced men standing in the middle waving ping-pong paddle batons at traffic, but they were amusement, entertaining drivers more than directing them. Their job seemed to be making extravagant spectacle of being frustrated that no one was lis-tening. They'd stand on planters and slice the air with hand signals of impenetrable meaning while city traffic encircled them, handling itself. Jerky conductors of mutinous orchestras. It was hard not to laugh.

Alex knew we needed to get to our destination quickly, and he was keyed into things like weight distribution; he knew how hard he could bank. He'd written his own scripture of little wisdoms I caught on to much later: That in the city, it's often better not to drive a car that's too nice or too clean because that's a tell, that you care, and you'll never win the thousand games of chicken it takes to cross the city. That it's the opposite when driving outside the city. He always stopped at a car wash before hitting the last checkpoints on the way back into Kabul, because if it's a run-down car that wins in the crowded city, it's still a nice one that gets you into it. A clean car commands respect at city perimeters; it looks less likely to be sacrificed for a vehicle-borne bomb dispatched by some huddle of insurgents out in the mountains.

He knew how to handle the asphalt quirks. The treads from dissected Soviet tanks unrolled across roads to serve as speed bumps. The shin-deep potholes. Take them at speed and you bust an axle, but slow all the way down and you invite a conference of beggars who assemble with entitlement, ardor, with dedication bordering on professionalism. The most ambitious of them weren't above lying down in front of your car, so Alex had a constantly updated terrain map of disturbances in his head. He knew where the clear lines through moonscaped roads were, he slalomed around potholes, coasted over speed bumps and gassed it down straightaways. He mostly avoided the avenues past the mansions, the "poppy palaces" owned by warlords and drug barons and harvesters of diverted aid dollars. US taxpayer money was in those mansions and in the one-ton armored vehicles that lumbered out from behind gates to worsen the surface. Armor-plated Land Cruisers emerged from estates carrying Big Men. With ten thousand pounds of ballistic-grade steel crawling over soft roads, they deepened ravines, which turned into running tributary systems when guards sprayed water to keep the dust down. The most expensive houses had accidental rivers running between them. Alex shakes his head. The wealthy wait for the government to fix roads that the wealthy have gullied into grade-school geology projects.

We'd reach the site of the bombing, the shooting, the standoff, usually before the bureaus and news crews. And by the time we got there, I was never nervous. His charisma kept it all adventure. There was no sense of solemn duty for me, no bearing witness to tragedy. What felt important was not informing readers about what was going on here, but getting published. Finding a way to wedge impressive vocabulary words into war reporting. If there was trauma here, it was a problem for later. We didn't feel it in real time. We were having fun, we were flying, the violence wasn't too much because it didn't seem real. It was a theme park ride with guardrails maintained by this new friend of mine. We couldn't be touched. There was a treasure map of exhibits the war had made for us to discover, lost jewels I could use to impress girls and web editors back home.

Alex would invent a parking space near the traveling carnival of emergency vehicles we'd meet at every bomb site, ready to redeem our tickets. We got our routine down to the point we could follow it without talking. We'd jump out of the car, and I'd unzip my backpack as we walked. I'd take out my camera and the impressive-looking ID badge I'd somehow convinced the NATO mission's media office to give me. The NATO coalition in Afghanistan was called the International Security Assistance Force, or ISAF, and "ISAF" was a hieroglyph almost everyone recognized, even those who couldn't read English.

I'd hand the badge to Alex. The badge said very clearly that I was MEDIA and should not be left unattended. It also said !ESCORT RE-QUIRED! in big red letters intended to keep me out of restricted sites, not let me onto them, but in Alex's hands it was whatever we needed it to be. He'd hold it up in front of whatever official-looking uniform had control of the site, sliding a finger to block the !ESCORT REQUIRED! part so only "ISAF" and my picture showed. If there was still resistance, Alex chiseled away at it with jokes or with lies about how important I was, until we were let through.

We observed, I took photos, I tapped notes on my BlackBerry. Alex laughed at that. To him, the clicking was just like old men and their *tasbih*, my little electronic talisman. But I found I could be more discreet dashing off shorthand field notes without looking down than I could waving a notebook in a source's face, announcing to everyone present, "There's an American journalist on the premises!" I didn't realize at first that it probably wasn't necessary, that it was Alex who kept the whole scene safe. There were always weapons around, usually someone with a rifle or a machine gun pointed lazily in our direction, and it took me months to recognize how Alex dealt with that. How he would cough and shuffle, make dirty jokes, and distract whoever stood between me and the story. While everyone's attention was elsewhere, Alex would shift his position and, without anyone noticing, find a way to put his own body between me and wherever the weapons were.

Then, only when I was safe, he'd set about finding someone to tell us what happened. I followed him around bomb sites and shootouts, trying to gin up artful ways to describe ghastly things and thumbing them into my phone while Alex led me to someone he somehow sensed could tell us what happened. He'd heel out his cigarette, and extract the story.

As the hip young editors in the midtown Manhattan skyscrapers began replying to more of my pitches, I started pulling all-nighters. Alex nabbed me a contraband bottle of nail-polish-remover vodka, along with little packets of instant coffee premixed with creamer and sugar. I had a little knockoff Chinese-made boiler that screamed "fire hazard" but got the job done, and I stayed up into the night slugging a nasty little cocktail that awled my cortex open so the words flowed. I sat at the desk in my university-issued room writing while the walls started to pulse and turn around me, voices coming alive in my head, fired by liquor caffeine and glucose, dispatching drafts to New York and cursing when the internet cut out. Thinking, all the while, *This story has to be perfect, this is the story that's going to make me, and I can't fucking reach the editor.*

The internet would twinkle on for a minute, then drop again when the power cut out, and I'd sit there willing it back on, running through edits so articles could be put to bed by close of business in New York, whatever uncivilized hour that was in Kabul. I'd try breathing exercises while coaxing bomb-site photographs through the narcoleptic internet connection. And if I finished, I'd try to stay awake, hoping an editor would send some closure, a "good to go, get some rest," which I never got, so I'd collapse into half-flexed sleep and have dreams of unease. Fleeing a disaster before a loved one reaches the rendezvous point, leaving them to some flood or spreading fire. Waking up an hour or two later to scratch at the internet, and hope to see my name. Then ride to my day job at the university.

It seemed an unsustainable way to operate, but there was enough excitement in the city, and Alex became so good at finding his way to it that a crazy thing happened. We laid the first bricks of a career. I could almost call myself a journalist, but with no support staff, half a translator, and no logistical help. *He* was all of those things. Alex was a one-man roving bureau: security, intelligence, ear to the ground, and source network listening for rustles in the dirt about the latest bloodshed.

We begin racking up stories: A story on the funeral of a tribal leader. Following dusty young beggar girls who drifted through mourners to see if grieving people are more charitable. Stories on every kind of car bomb, bombs in wagons, sedans, and taxis. Cars blown up in border areas, sometimes in just such a position that the report sounded off mountains, winged like a roulette ball around the bowl Kabul sits in, and made everyone everywhere think the explosion was just next door. We wrote about dwindling faith in the government's ability to keep people safe. Alex talked his way into interviews with people we were not supposed to talk to, or who I wouldn't even think to ask. Officials, kids, grumpy bystanders. We'd leave the scene knowing what happened, or not knowing what happened but knowing what it meant to one person standing on the fringes.

I learned that it wasn't worth thinking about how many people died, even though editors almost always asked. Everyone answered differently. Editors seem to like numbers, so I always asked once or twice, but it began to feel like every official, every agency, had a vested interest in the death count being high or low. There were always huge gulfs in the numbers. The counts reported in the local news often vastly outstripped what foreign publications reported. I sometimes asked for a count so I could tell editors I did, but then I'd let it lie because it didn't actually matter to me. I later learned that Alex hadn't quite understood that.

After a dozen trips around the city, coming into sniffing distance of the twisted, smoking metal residue of an accelerating insurgency, Alex and I had earned just enough favor with the New York web editors that we reached a major milestone: I started hearing pitches from *them*, rather than only the other way around. We'd made it. It was actually happening. I still hadn't been paid for any of the stories, but I had my university job to foot the bill, and Alex had helped me get web stories published by *Esquire, Newsweek, Time,* and *Slate*. This idea that I hadn't really thought would come together—*going to Afghanistan on my own?!*—was actually coming together. We were making me into a war correspondent, and for a moment the future was all possibility. Along the way, though, with so much focus on myself, my read on this partner in crime of mine had shifted, blurred, or maybe I'd never paid enough attention. There was one story we'd soon do that should have forced me to. It was a story unique in its savageness, even amid the circuit of grim sites we were touring together. It won me more attention than the others, but I didn't know, and didn't think to ask, what it did to him.

CHAPTER 5

OCTOBER 1, 2007

I was late to work at the university. I woke up too late for the convoy. University workers had to be shuttled from our guesthouses to work and back like schoolchildren. Except we were more difficult than schoolchildren. When we missed the convoys, we blamed drivers for leaving too early, and when we were down in front on time, we blamed the drivers for making us wait for colleagues. We held the drivers and our guards and all the Afghans looking after us in contempt for the noise and discomfort, for the dust and the distance from our loved ones and our fast food. Mostly we resented Afghans for enforcing the rules we had written.

That day, the convoy took off without me. It was a kind of day that was starting to happen, days I felt less like an aspiring journalist on the make and more like an underpaid loan officer, shuffling to a menial job in a dusty backwater. On days like those, I was more alert to discomfort. The aspects of war that were less sexy and more exhausting, the constellation of health hazards that manifested in boring ways. The decades-long massacre of trees here—for firewood and to deny insurgents hiding places—had brought on a country-wide drought. Kabul was constantly dry; there was dust in your eyes and ears, fossilizing in your nose. Blowing dust lifted shit from open sewers, so the air in Kabul had measurably high levels of fecal content. Sometimes we bleached vegetables because we preferred known poisons to exotic ones. Some foreign workers came to Afghanistan just for sanitation projects; some flew in just to plant trees.

I arrived at my desk late, after the convoy had gone, come back, and gone again. I was unshowered and bracing for a day spent warring with an office printer, trying to recruit someone from the skeleton tech-support crew to fix an endless procession of error messages trotting across the screen of a university-issued laptop imported from Lord knows where. My boss there was kind and brilliant and, in one forgivable way, narrow. He was Afghan but had grown up in the US and been educated there, and I think he hired me because, like I think Alex did, he saw someone in need of protection. And he also recognized the college on my résumé. He was a person for whom such credentials mattered, which made sense because back in America he'd grown up as an immigrant not only from a poor country, but from a poor country's poorest ethnicity. He'd come back to help rebuild Afghanistan, and I'd found myself in the unique position of being a foreigner with an Afghan boss when it was almost always the other way around.

He was a big soft hug of a man, a protector, and there was a sweet innocence in everything he did, with perhaps only two exceptions. The music he listened to—he had a weakness for raunchy R&B with overtly sexual innuendos, which he unfailingly missed—and slights to his ethnic group, which he unfailingly caught. When those happened, you could see the rage settling in; you could see it in his face, the tensing of his jaw, fists pounding the air. He became a child with a hundred-pound brain and hiring authority. I didn't notice until someone pointed it out that everyone he hired belonged to that same ethnic group, except for me. He had told me about his plan, but he'd spoken English without an accent, so I hadn't believed him. "There's so much ethnocentrism here," I said when I met him, lecturing him about his country after I'd been there less than a month. "It's refreshing to get to meet someone like you who's so open-minded."

"Yes, but—" he'd said, leaning forward, honoring me with an admission "—I come predisposed." He repeated himself, as he sometimes did. "I come predisposed."

In the office, my phone dinged. Alex's number strobed on the little screen, and a thrill went through me. I'd been in front of the work-issued laptop for all of twenty minutes, battling a million software updates the computer was trying to guzzle over a rickety internet connection, a demanding child creating problems for attention. "Yah, Jaff," Alex said. "Bomb blast near Baharistan Park. Want I should come for pickup?"

I looked at my boss across the office, firmly in the zone. Bouncing in his desk chair, earphones wired through his skull, air drumming to Ginuwine's "Pony" and struggling not to sing out loud. Errant lyrics broke containment as excited little squeaks. *My saddle's waiting!* Lips clenched, but he couldn't help it. *Come on, jump on it!* He'd once asked me about the lyrics, and I'd pretended not to know why Ginuwine was so passionate about horseback riding. I waved a hand across his field of vision; he pulled his headphones out and showed not even a flicker of disappointment. I'd been late to work, gotten nothing done, and the two of us were far behind on our tasks. He would have to answer for that, and I wouldn't. If I got hurt, he'd be held responsible. He would, on several occasions, come get me out of trouble I'd gotten myself into. All he asked of me was that I promise to be safe. I unzipped the backpack at my knee to make sure my camera battery was charged.

———

I WASN'T SURE HOW ALEX HAD HEARD ABOUT THE ATTACK, BUT THIS time, when we arrived, it was already being cleaned up. The target was a Ministry of Defense bus, and you could tell the explosion had been large by the radius of damage. I squinted and tried to guess the distance between the bus and the farthest shops where people were sweeping up glass.

More striking, though, was that the bomb had sent bits of flesh up into the park's trees, and now kids were hanging off branches trying to reach them. Alex explained that this was the country's children showing enterprise. They knew that families deprived of whole bodies would come looking for something to bury, and this thin lip of city park had just been transformed into a reliquary. Parts of a few dozen soldiers, janitors, cafeteria clerks riding the bus to the ministry, and some bystanders had been dispersed across the grass, through the wrought-iron gates, and up into the trees. A bag of stained leaves that a family might convince itself held trace amounts of a loved one would be a charm worth at least a few dollars.

I was at first surprised the children seemed so unaffected, but then, *I* felt unaffected. I was not horrified by callousness. In the moment it seemed only noteworthy, this interesting twist in commerce, not heinous, that children would exploit the grief of others for pocket money. Perhaps I felt that way because that's what I was doing.

As I shifted around for a clear photo of a climbing kid now pinned between branches, trying to shake a prize free, the kids on the ground were tugging on my sleeve, trying to show me Ziploc bags full of leaves with browned curls they said were body parts, while an old policeman waddled up with a wooden baton and started swinging at us. Alex pulled me away. "We have to go," he said; the crowd was too big now, and too many people in one place could always be a second target. "Come, Jaff. You have enough to make a report?"

"Actually, no," I said. I still needed to ask someone, really anyone, for a casualty count, just so I could tell editors. It didn't really matter who gave it; Alex could've given it to me himself. It seemed for a moment like he didn't hear me right, he looked to the side like he was turning something over in his mind, and then he nodded. "Yah, Jaff, OK, now I know." And we were back in the car, Alex's brow set, driving toward the military hospital. I didn't know where the idea came from; I figured it was instinct, Alex by now knowing what I was looking for before I did.

Once outside the hospital compound, he took my ISAF badge and made quick work of the checkpoints. First talking his way onto the compound, then into one of the central hospital buildings, then, somehow, up into a triage room where survivors lay unconscious. Exasperated doctors threw up their hands and pointed to men lying in strange arrangements. Faces freckled with shrapnel, splotchy and mustard-yellow with swirled Betadine and dried blood. Some had freshly shaven heads, one was crowned in gauze. Alex asked a nurse if I could take pictures, and the nurse shrugged like it wasn't really OK, but was the least of their concerns.

Years later, I might have hesitated. I would have weighed whether showing the public a true picture of war was worth violating someone's privacy. I would have been at best uncertain. More likely I would've walked out, knowing it wasn't my place to play God and that no potential shift in public awareness justified certain violation.

At the time, none of those things really mattered. I was there to impress editors. I was exploring a museum of other people's pain, it was all on display for me, and I was hoping to get credit for documenting it.

Alex disappeared for a moment, then returned, sidled up to me, and asked a question I thought I misheard. "Jaff, I get the permission. You want we should go to morgue?"

I wasn't sure where the idea came from. I figured it was some curiosity he had. That was Alex: cheerfully callous. Unaffected, like life just dribbled off him. I didn't know why we'd need to go to the morgue, but what self-respecting war correspondent shies away from bodies?

I lowered the camera, and we negotiated the maze of the hospital complex down to the ground floor, and then out across a lawn, toward a separate hutch.

There were no checkpoints for Alex to slip us through. It was quiet here; it was almost peaceful, at least outside. There were no guards stopping people from coming in or out, because why would anyone want to come in? And because it was a morgue, so few were coming out. The few soldiers there were there to identify bodies or to pay their respects, and we walked in almost unnoticed.

We entered a room with a smell of blood so strong that it was not only a smell but a taste too, the air in there thick and sweet with it. Iron and rust on my gums like it was leaking from my teeth, like someone had swung a pipe at me, and after a few more steps I knew why. On a table in a side room was a man laid out on a table, arranged in a strange geometry. Part of a man, really, a body transected diagonally across the chest. And from there it was like a slipping film reel. The body, the men standing around it, the blood on the floor. Alex there, then halfway out of the room, then gone. I knew I had to look, the way you look at an exhibit you've made a pilgrimage to see, but I also knew it was imperative that I look away quickly. I had a tactic by then to protect myself. You look at the grisly thing just long enough that the outlines imprint on your mind so you can trace it later, but not so long that the picture resolves into a human being. I suspected even back then that if you did that, you were done for. I looked for a moment and tried to describe the sight to myself, this fraction of body that had belonged to a man, a small man, I thought, though I couldn't tell for sure, and maybe he just seemed small because he'd been reduced by half. I remember thinking that in life this small man was gentle and kind. Then I looked away.

Alex, in his indifference, didn't have the same strategy. Why would he need one? I'd observed him before in front of murderous sights. Squinting, smoking, looking wherever he wanted. He was inured, I understood, by his two decades of war. One horror didn't threaten a calcified psyche like it could mine. And when I left the morgue, I found him outside with his shoes off, feet dangling in a stream. He was chatting with the religious-looking men in lawn chairs. He squinted up at me like something wasn't right—like he was worried about me. But I was fine. I was fine.

CHAPTER 6

DECEMBER 2007

IN THE WEEKS THAT FOLLOWED, SOMETHING SEEMED TO CHANGE in Alex. He seemed tired and sick. The company was short-staffed, and I knew he was working around the clock because whenever I called, he was always at the office. He was saving up his patience for customers, so he had none for anyone else.

We got together one evening, and he was sweaty and exhausted. He said he'd picked up a client near the attorney general's office just as everyone was getting off work. Policemen had fanned out to distance lesser people from the anointed ones in armored SUVs, and Alex's car was already too close. One of the policemen got in his face. "Why are you driving on this street? You can't drive here now!"

Alex ran out of restraint. "This isn't your father's street!" He said the policeman slapped him across the face, and in an instant Alex had the door open and was punching the policeman. He said he thought he broke teeth. There was blood, his or the policeman's. The convoy halted, and dozens of other policemen ran out of their vehicles at him. He knew people had been killed for smaller disagreements. He was surrounded, taking body blows from rifle butts, before a growing crowd shamed the police for unfair odds. "He's just one person!"

He'd made it out mostly intact, and tonight he's sore, spent, hot, but he smiles. "I think I quit driving now," he says. "At least in the day. Night it is quiet, and traffic is *little, little*."

Another afternoon he was taking me back to my guesthouse, and we got stuck in city traffic. A beggar with a patchy white beard moved between vehicles. He leaned against a sedan next to us. A passenger-side window rolled up. The beggar pendulumed between lanes until he reached us. He was hunched and emaciated. I waited for Alex to roll up his window, but he didn't. He looked the man in the eye and said something quick. The beggar's face released into a smile for just a moment, and he moved on. I asked Alex what he said. "Yah, Jaff. I tell to him, 'Sorry, brother. I not able to give. My luck right now is not better than yours.'"

<hr />

HIS LUCK KEPT GETTING WORSE. THERE WAS A FIGHT IN THE DRIVERS' barracks, and Alex found himself in the middle of it. Some of the drivers were mad at him for something, and at the same time his boss had accused him of stealing. A weapon, of all things. The story didn't quite make sense.

By the time he told me about it, he seemed so defeated I couldn't get out of him what exactly had happened. He came to the university listless and hunched, limbs folded over themselves, receding into his driver's seat as we sat together outside my office, and I tried to understand. He seemed to be saying he was fired because his boss had accused him of a plot to steal a rifle, and then sell it.

We took stock. He had no prospects, weak English, and no education. He had a sense of hustle, which I figured might be why the boss blamed him, but right now even that seemed to have left him. He was a shell of himself. The way he moved was different, arthritic and slow. I brought him inside and asked my boss for ideas. He pulled the headphones from his ears, and they sat together in the office, speaking in low tones, my boss's whole soft body leaned forward in a posture of compassion. I could hear sympathy in his voice, but it seemed there was nothing to be done. Alex had nothing to offer the university.

Afterward, Alex shuffled out of the office. I followed him out, and we sat together in his car again. A pulse rose in the distance. He pretended not to notice a formation of Black Hawks thumping past overhead, doing their violence to air. Burning fuel, $1,000 an hour just to be up there. Alex and I got along so well that I'd assumed he was a free agent like me, but now that he'd lost his job, I wondered who else he had to feed. Brothers, his mother, cousins? I'd never asked.

He piped up to say a few other drivers were fired too, and some of them were trying to launch their own taxi company, Zuhaak Tours & Logistics, named for one of the country's little-known treasures, an ancient citadel in the central highlands called Zuhaak built out of red clay, so the whole city seemed red. He could join them. They had a can't-miss plan: instead of seven dollars a ride like the old company, the new one would charge six. Alex turned to ask me if I would mind being there when he met with them.

I went on a weekend to his mother's house, where they all sat around to hash out details. But even when they managed to get the business off the ground, Alex just kept sinking. Now he was an employee of employees. They told him that because he helped them start the company, he was really like a partner, so once they had some success, he'd get paid from the profits. It'd be good for him, they said. But what it really meant was that for months, Alex wouldn't get a salary. He'd try to scrape by, working just for tips.

⸻

"GET READY FOR *DEREISH*," ALEX SAYS WITH THE DARK HINT OF A SMILE.

We arrive at a guard post in front of my guesthouse. It's dark, and we pull around a blast wall, flashing headlights at the guard. Instead of slowing down like he's supposed to, though, Alex hits the gas, drawing out a terrified little soldier who leaps from behind a turnstile and lands in a crouch with his weapon drawn. "*Dereeeish!*" the guard screams—*stop!*—in a voice that's almost feral. We've terrified him. Alex and I giggle like idiots and slap each other's legs.

Five minutes later I'm alone in my room behind guards and razor wire, with his stunt gnawing at me. He's starting to relish these interactions. He likes tempting people with power. He taunts them, with me watching.

I ask him about it the next day, and he doesn't concede, but he also doesn't entirely deny that he's interested in trouble. I've learned to study the way he answers questions like these. The way his mouth doesn't move but his face seems to smile, something not entirely in the eyes. He's changing in some way I can see but can't understand, and the way he talks about his future unsettles me. He says he wants to get out of Afghanistan so he doesn't *die like a fucker*. "Because life is short, my friend. If you are face-to-face with bomb blast before you have wife, you have no life. You die as some *fucking*." I wonder if not wanting to die for nothing is a step toward wanting to die for something. Maybe I've been resisting something apparent for some time now—that this new friend of mine could be going through some kind of religious awakening. I begin to hear him saying things I don't recognize. *Her father said, "If my daughter comes home at 3 a.m. from some wedding and is with drinking, falling around, you won't do anything." And I am say to him, "You are a fucking that I won't do anything; she will be my wife, and if she does that . . ."* They don't sound like the Alex I know. But then, I've only known him for a few months. He seems to me to be retreating someplace I'm not familiar with.

I see him in traditional clothes more often. He excuses himself to pray, which I've never seen him do before. Maybe these are parts of him that had always been there and I hadn't bothered to look. Or maybe it's just that everything's changing? Maybe something in the water, the country, the financial crisis we didn't quite realize was just then un-spooling across the world. Here, at least, everyone seems to be letting go a little. Here, the expats watching the war seem different from when I first arrived, more resigned already. A stranger I have drinks with at one of the expat bars speaks loosely of someone I met too, a beautiful woman with hidden things like elaborate tattoos in private places, a gift for holding hours of tequila, a daughter back home named for a char-acter in a sci-fi movie she'd watched while pregnant. A woman with black leather and advanced degrees, cool and smart and untouchable. "She had a breakdown," the stranger says. "They say she stole a jingle truck and took it all the way across a desert in Kandahar, away from the Afghan it belonged to and toward . . . nothing in particular." I ask if the story is really true, and the stranger leans his head back. "Yeah," he says, toward the sky, as if answering a different question. He didn't know, or he knew and didn't care. I left unsure, knowing only that trading stories about the downfall of others is a remedy here, like it is everywhere. You may be falling away, but there's some balm in knowing you lasted a little longer than someone else.

And there's more resignation on the street, as well. In Kabul, beggar women tap on car windows with more agitation, frustration, less mournful. More *don't you see me here?* In a voter-education book I worked on, the illustrator tried to draw cartoons of women in burkas, but they kept coming out as ghosts.

CHAPTER 7

MARCH 2008

I'D LIVED IN THE COUNTRY FOR SIX MONTHS, WORKING AS A FREE-lance war correspondent and a glorified secretary at the university. A family friend connected me by email to HR people at the *Wall Street Journal*, and I decided I'd pretended long enough. I wanted to go back to the States and try to be a real journalist, and once again it looked like my timing was lucky. As the financial crash began, Rupert Murdoch bought the *Wall Street Journal* and the rest of the Dow Jones company, put them under News Corp, and signaled there'd be an injection of cash. The few *Journal* reporters I spoke to said that their concerns about News Corp had largely been eased—concerns that Murdoch might try to control coverage or turn the *Journal* into a closer copy of its new step-sibling properties, the *New York Post* and Fox News. Instead, my new *Journal* contacts said, they were looking forward to an injection of capital to help them fill up the newsrooms and do real reporting, and it sounded to me like the Murdoch money meant even someone with unorthodox experience like mine might sneak into a newsroom, hidden amid all the inflowing staff.

Before I left Afghanistan, my university colleagues threw a going-away party for me at one of the Kabul restaurants that served wine and catered to foreigners. It was mostly my other Western friends there, but I knew Alex had to be there too, even at the risk of awkwardness. I worried he might feel out of place around so many people he didn't know, but when he got there that night, he looked fine. And it occurred to me that I'd rarely felt more welcomed anywhere, at any time, than I felt here, now, just as I was leaving.

———

BACK IN AMERICA, MY COURTSHIP WITH THE *WALL STREET JOURNAL* didn't pan out. I got a free trip to the Atlanta bureau on the Murdochs' tab, and Douglas Blackmon, the bureau chief there, took me out for a nice dinner and a nice conversation, spoke to me over cocktails like I was his equal, and eventually said, "I think if I hired you, I'd be keeping you from writing your book." A nice line, I thought, to soften the fact that he wasn't hiring me. I wasn't writing any book. He was, though—a side project he brought up only once, as if it were barely worth mentioning, but that turned out to be a ruthless, years-long, Pulitzer Prize–winning investigation into housing discrimination. That's what real journalists did, I thought—I was only pantomiming as one. I'd desperately wanted the legitimacy of working at a real paper. I wanted a livable salary, a life in my own country, my own apartment, to hear my own language at the grocery store. I wanted happy hour without strip searches.

The *Wall Street Journal* fell through, and I moved back into my parents' house with the little money I'd made at the university and the littler money I'd made pretending to be a journalist with Alex. I spent those months living in my old bedroom in Philadelphia, trying and failing to get a job in a contracting economy, and finally deciding it must be that I was hirable only in Afghanistan, where my kind old boss at the university was waiting for me. After three months in Philadelphia, I called him up to see if he'd like to have me back, and soon I was on my way back to Afghanistan. Back to the airport, hugging Alex, whipping through the city, feeling giddy and unbounded again, getting high on updates from his life. Back to my old day job at the university, but this time with a twist: the university's acting president had been splitting time between Afghanistan and America, where he was also a professor at the Thunderbird School of Global Management. Thunderbird had been flying aspiring Afghan businesswomen to its campus in Arizona for classes, assigning them mentors, running them through a special curriculum, and sending them back to Afghanistan better equipped to run their businesses.

Everyone loved the program, but it was expensive, so someone came up with the idea of trying to run the program *in* Afghanistan. Taking intercontinental plane tickets for each student out of the budget would free up money to reach more people. The idea was, in essence, to franchise the business school, adapt it for a country with low literacy especially among women, tailor it to local custom, and deliver it there.

Since I served no indispensable role at the university, I was tapped to be the project's agent on the ground. I had no experience in business, and the totality of my understanding about Afghan gender dynamics came from jokes Alex made and I sort of understood. I'd become part of a common breed here—foreigners getting foreign money doing jobs for which they were astonishingly unqualified. I started moving around the city to learn, meeting with people who knew what they were talking about so I could parrot the things they said and sound less like an imbecile, and my two pursuits—trying to build a network of women running businesses that our upstart program might benefit from, and reporting more on a now-expanding war—started to complement each other in strange ways. On a reporting trip out to a refugee camp, I saw people left exposed because the UN refugee agency didn't have enough tarps. Then, during a networking trip out to a bottling plant on the outskirts of the city, I stumbled across a wall of sugar sacks stacked like sandbags in the parking lot, shielded from the elements by a tent city's worth of UN tarps. It was important, a foreman said. Sugar is a very important part of fizzy drinks. There were things here. Opportunity, material for people to seize on. It just didn't always go where it belonged.

CHAPTER 8

JUNE 2008

By the time I came back to the country, Alex seemed to be emerging from whatever funk I'd left him in. It seemed like it may have had something to do with a girl he'd met, so I didn't say anything about the fact that from what I could glean, I thought he was headed for heartbreak.

He first met Fatima when she was working at the Turquoise Mountain Foundation, which he called "Turkish Mountain," and which was the same organization I'd stayed with for two weeks when I first landed in the country. It seemed to me that she didn't really take him seriously. That she received his courtship with good humor because she was a decent person and perhaps because she was uncomfortable with the status she had. She had a future he didn't, through no real achievement of her own. Her life was brighter just because her father had decided to flee a decade or two ago, and now she was a citizen of a European country. Alex had grown up fatherless and, as best as I could tell, poor. He never got to leave the country even for a vacation, let alone get citizenship anywhere he'd want to be from.

When I met Fatima, she seemed kind but reserved, like she wasn't serious. I wondered, in those first few days, if she was using him as penance. Or worse, as a kind of research. He was a gallery of her own country. Her exotic experience, a summer love to make half of her feel more authentic. An Afghan boyfriend—maybe the idea sounded nice, but I knew Alex felt that he needed a wife. I felt protective of him. If she had been stuck in the country like he was, she'd be the one looking to marry up.

He started bringing me to their get-togethers as a character witness. She'd grown up in the Netherlands, she was half-foreign, and I was proof that he already had foreign approval.

But when he was out of earshot, gone to get us mango juices or the quesadilla-like *burani* from street-side vendors, she leaned over and said to me, "Afghan men think that when they say, 'Hello, how are you, I am fine,' that's love."

Under the circumstances here, I thought, of course exchanging basic pleasantries feels like victory. And later, when he said he promised her I would come along if she joined him for a picnic, a day trip up to a mountain pass, I felt I didn't really have a choice but to wingman his underdog effort to woo a woman whose passport put her out of his league.

———

ALEX PICKED ME UP FOR OUR OUTING IN HIS BROTHER'S CAR AND A faded, tired-looking shirt. I nearly yelled. "You can't wear that! Here, hold on!"

I ran back into the guesthouse and grabbed my favorite blue button-down. I didn't know why I'd brought it to Afghanistan in the first place, but I wore it all the time. Still, in the moment it felt exactly right to give it away. I ran back out to the car, already seeing flashes of some future cocktail party, guests nodding along at my selflessness, "and then you gave him the shirt off your back . . ." He was standing by the car smoking, and I tossed the shirt to him. He shrugged and changed right out there in the street, and though he was taller and skinnier than me, it somehow fit perfectly. I grabbed his shoulders and beamed like a father on prom night.

We drove off and joked for a while, then found beer and picked up Fatima. We felt free. We made our way up toward the Salang Pass, away from the smoke and urgency of the city. We wove our way up into the hills, the hills turned to mountains, and Alex found a turnout next to a rope bridge across the water that led to a rock face that sped nearly straight up, hundreds of feet over a rushing river.

The Salang Pass was gray and cool and abrupt. The air and the water and the canyon angles all too sharp for pollution to linger, so it felt like a different universe. A clean and scenic place for a picnic, though here most things were touched by war, even if they're only grazed. These high points tempted militias back in the '80s and '90s. The armed parties were gone now, but they tended not to clean up after themselves, so our three-way date was a hike up hills not yet fully de-mined. Little slabs of paint on rocks marked parts of the hills that had been cleared—white for safe, red for maybe not safe—but rocks had tumbled and shifted, there'd been freezes and thaws, snow and rushing snow melt had since moved the painted rocks, so we crawled upward, thrilled by the risk of spring-loaded explosives leaping up to bring a messy end to the date. The knife edge of buried danger brought everything to life, everything more vivid, sharper; we were more alive than we'd ever been.

We climbed after Alex, following no path I could discern. He seemed to move not along but in between routes others had marked, paving his own way in big lunging strides. I was nimble too, but I couldn't move like him. He climbed faster; I found myself trying to stay at his heels. Hurrying over the boulders and between the painted rocks, catching and stumbling, but hurrying, even as it started to drizzle and the hillside slickened. The roar of the whitewater below drowned out our voices and seemed even to wash through our thoughts. We forgot that there were murmurs of war, that certain eyes would see immorality in this excursion, and as our clothes dampened and clung to us, it felt like the moisture came from river spray below and also from above. I slowed and breathed and closed my eyes, and realized that what it felt like was moving through clouds.

Alex pulled farther ahead. He bounded up boulders the way he drove: like he was born for it, a hunter becoming native in whatever territory he landed in. Using all four limbs, solving obstacles with barely a pause. That heat in his eyes. He turned back to check on me and to watch

Fatima slipping upward in fashionable sandals. She didn't complain. He stood on a boulder and squinted down like a conquistador. Proud, tired, accomplished, unsure what he was looking at. My soaked-through shirt flattened on him like he had no mass. Just spine and shoulder bones and a damp blue sail for a torso. Then there was wind and this odd illusion: the fabric seemed pressed not just into his body but through it like he wasn't there at all, like I was imagining all of it.

Fatima stumbled and let out a little shriek, and Alex's body coiled, but he didn't move. Touching was still too much of a trespass, so he held back and watched like he wanted to put a steadying hand on her elbow, but knew better. Her feet began to bleed. He kept a respectful distance. He went down to be closer to her but wouldn't offer a hand. "We should be married," I hear him say. "When your father comes to visit, he should meet my mother."

We climbed more. It felt like we were a hundred miles in the sky. Cars passing below were slow, tiny insects, and it was hard to know if we were hearing them or the water. We took photos, Alex giving Fatima bunny ears; Alex giving me bunny ears; Alex wrapping his arms around me in a hug he must have meant for her. He told her, "I kill myself if you don't engage me."

The spitting rain gave up, and we found a little plateau between boulders and colored rocks to unfold our picnic. Alex handed us each a hard-boiled egg, and we banged them against each other to see whose would break first. We laughed, Alex and Fatima smiled at each other, and I was starting to feel like I'd never been so comfortable in my entire life when a small boy appeared in the distance, skirting the hillside. Alex took out a cigarette, squinted, and tried not to engage. He was about to ruin it—no better way to turn a girl off than be mean to a child in front of her. I'd bail him out. When the boy got close enough, I gave a big idiot grin to draw him closer, pointed my forehead at him, and held some of our picnic out in my hand like I was summoning a timid animal. Fatima said something in Dari, and I saw a wince pass across Alex's face. The boy stood with us for a moment and took one of the hard-boiled eggs, but he didn't quite seem comfortable, and he left just as quickly as he arrived, shuffling off with his head down, like he was turning something over in his mind.

Alex held a smile, but it looked to me like he was troubled. He said it was time to go, even though we'd only just settled in. I sensed he had something else planned he hadn't told me about yet, or maybe it was just that he thought this spot wasn't private enough anymore.

We moved back down the rock toward the river, slipping between boulders. Fatima somehow survived the descent. Fatima wanted to see what the river was like, and Alex looked up at the rope bridge like he worried a detour might make us late for his next act, but his date was asking, so he obliged. The two of them rolled up their pants, waded into the river, found opposite boulders to sit on, and with rapids upstream and down, began splashing each other, letting the water do what their own hands couldn't. Alex relaxed finally, enjoying himself, at least for a moment unworried by whatever issue of timing had preoccupied him. I squatted to take photos, and again felt at home.

From the corner of my eye I saw a small convoy pulling off the road into the same turnout we'd parked in. It was noteworthy only because except for the boy, we'd been so entirely alone.

Then gunmen spilled out of the cars. Their mouths moved, but I couldn't hear what they were yelling over the current. They moved frantically over the rope bridge, and there was no one besides us they could have been coming for. They ran, submachine guns clanging against their knees. There was urgency in their movement—agitated motion as if something terrible would happen if they didn't get to us quickly enough. There was nowhere for us to go besides back up the mine-studded rocks, or deeper into the water, so we just sat there and waited for whatever was about to happen.

Soon the men had us surrounded. They yelled something I couldn't understand, but even without understanding, I knew we'd offended them somehow. Alex tried talking to them but didn't seem to be getting anywhere, and they kept closing in, tightening around us. Their hands were on our arms. Alex's and mine—they wouldn't touch Fatima. They dragged us back toward the swinging bridge, back across the water.

Then we were back in the borrowed car, but they'd commandeered it, squeezed us all in the backseat, and started driving us. Their trucks pulled out before and after us, and now we were in the middle of a convoy with escort vehicles, the wrong kind of celebrity. I didn't know where we were going, but I knew it was the wrong way. I knew we were heading farther up the Salang Pass, which meant farther from the city. Farther from safety. We kept driving and driving, dread settling into my stomach until we reached a desolate district police station. They parked us between a gutted tank and a crumpled car flipped over on its roof, wheel wells facing up, like a huge squashed insect. A parking lot and a statue garden, with relics from wars that had blown through here over the decades. Exhibits maybe meant to intimidate us, and we were dragged past them into a room where an officious man in a badge-less shirt sat down and considered us, working prayer beads in his hand. He said something in a low voice. Alex translated.

"Aren't you ashamed of taking an Afghan girl with this foreigner?" The officious man spoke of our indiscretions like a judge listing counts. He told me I'd trespassed. "It's *his* country, not yours, and you should show respect." I was a foreigner in his province, he said. I was a guest in his house.

I started to simmer. I felt some unstable energy, something like anger but even more combustible, anger mixed with entitlement. I realize that what I felt was *superior*.

"Who do you think pays for your entire office?" I said, Alex interpreting with his head down. "Your entire police force, all your vehicles? I'm a guest here, yes, but I come from *America*. How dare you hold me against my will? How dare you embarrass my friends?" Little icicles of rage knifed down my body. I hated this man. I hated this place. I was right, I felt righteous, I could have thrown a punch and been justified. I swallowed and tried to talk with spine. I wanted my voice to sound like a blade. Alex translated too softly, and still the man seemed to retreat when he saw I was advancing. I showed him my impressive-looking ISAF badge. I showed him my passport, from the country that freed his and feeds it now. I saw him look up at one of his deputies. I was *handling* this. I was sticking up for myself, for ourselves, a thing I'd never done before. I was coming out of my shell. Alex and Fatima would thank me later, and I'd say "No, it's nothing, get outta here, I was happy to do it" because I had what they didn't; I had knowledge of my rights. And I'm not sure why I thought that rights travel with you when you're in the unseen part of another country, but the restraints had broken and I was charging forward, Alex keeping pace in Dari next to me, and man, we're a team! I finished, Alex finished, the badge-less commander was silent for a moment.

I noticed Alex's hand on my knee, squeezing. Encouragement, gratitude—I knew what he was saying. I'd just given him the opening to get us out of there.

The commander didn't let us go right away, but I saw him beginning to retreat. He looked at Alex and addressed me. "I'm just trying to protect you," Alex translated, "from other conservative people around here. There are *others* who would take offense to unrelated women and men sitting together. I just mean to protect you since you are our guest." He said something else, and Alex signaled for me to get up first.

As we finally pulled out, my rage faded, the sense of triumph settled away, and what was left was just sadness for Alex. He'd been embarrassed in front of Fatima, and in front of me. He'd needed me to bail him out. The car was silent for much of the ride back to the city. Alex occasionally smiled, looked in the rearview mirror, and tried to make Fatima laugh to chisel away the shame starting to harden, a suitor trying to reclaim his cool after a spilled drink. But as we neared the city, just when it seemed he'd finally managed to correct the atmosphere in the car, we ran into more trouble.

There was a scrum of vehicles at the last checkpoint just before Kabul. Officers from various agencies orbited the slowing cars, ostensibly checking for terrorists sneaking into the capital. It was almost festive, the hysteria of anxious families trying to enter the big city and of security personnel on the make. Exuberant, just-hidden commerce, ten thousand transactions happening in the span of a minute. We were flagged down by a plainclothes officer from some branch of some agency, gesturing for us to roll down the window. He leaned down, looked around, and accused us of smuggling a prostitute. He stood back up. Alex whispered to me what the officer said into his radio. *Commander, I've caught some foreigners.* The officer considered our punishment, a hand on the car as if to keep us from escaping. He leaned back down, and Alex translated under his breath. "She's a whore, isn't she? The white guy is the foreign client, isn't he? And you," he said to Alex, "you're the pimp dirtying your own country's women."

I watched Alex keep his smile again, but could've sworn I saw his body slacken, as if something in him had finally, fully surrendered. He had no move here. No way to get us home safely and to also stick up for Fatima. He lowered his head, and they worked out a bribe. In the backseat Fatima tried to keep her own smile for the rest of the drive home, either blissfully unaware of what had just happened or else trying to let Alex believe she was. She seemed calm enough that I could tell myself she was not insulted. Maybe she saw the whole thing as part of her adventure. As I might have, except I was watching Alex still, that smile pasted on his face, but the light going from his eyes. As he drove us the rest of the way into Kabul, I thought I was seeing something beginning to break.

CHAPTER 9

JULY 2008

BACK AT THE UNIVERSITY, I PUT MY HEAD DOWN AND TRIED TO PUT the pieces in place for the women's business program. We hoped to reach beyond the more cosmopolitan women in Kabul, who had an easier time finding their way into programs offered by the West, and out into the provinces, where women tended to face more obstacles.

Our Mission Control was Thunderbird's campus back in Arizona, where a woman named Kellie Kreiser worked as the brain and the elbow grease behind the business school's most innovative charitable efforts. It was Kellie wrangling faculty to support us, Kellie dreaming up new ways to get exotic projects funded. Shortly after she and I started scheming together, she hinted at the potential of a big funder coming on board, so we started to build two different versions of the project at the same time. A modest one, and an aspirational one in case this mysterious funder came through.

It was months into working together before she let me in on the secret. She'd managed to get Goldman Sachs interested in the idea of an American business school translated for Afghan women. And despite the fact that Goldman Sachs was in the midst of a media feeding frenzy for its role in the financial crisis—or, maybe, because of that—it was interested not only in supporting us but also in launching a whole suite of similar partnerships between elite universities and partner institutions in the developing world. They were going to call it the 10,000 Women initiative. Overnight, I'd gone from a not-paying-the-bills freelance war correspondent to the acting Afghanistan director of an initiative that had one of the world's biggest investment banks in its name. I was twenty-four; I knew nothing.

But I was familiar enough with my little world. I knew by then that academic politics were fraught, war-zone politics were equally fraught, and that the two combined were probably capable of strangling even a project with the backing of Goldman Sachs. I wanted this program to succeed, so I spent the months before handing the program off hunting for ways to insulate it from university politics so that my successor, a person we'd chosen to *really* run the program in Afghanistan, might stand a chance of surviving the university with her sanity intact. I figured it was the lack of freedom that got to most people. Most people didn't have a boss who gave leeway like mine did or an Alex to emancipate them from their own guards. If the program was going to succeed, my replacement needed the freedom I had. So even though Alex was still just a scrappy kid potentially in the midst of some religious awakening, I figured our best bet was to put Goldman Sachs on his shoulders.

The partnership came with a separate funding source, so my boss helped negotiate with the university for my replacement to have her own mode of transportation, separate from the university's fleet of vehicles, and then I called up Alex to see if he could be on call for her when she arrived, like he was for me. He promised he would. He was now working full-time with the new taxi company, Zuhaak Logistics, and he promised he'd use the company to make sure my replacement was safe but also free. I figured that was about all I could do to keep the Goldman program going. A maybe-radicalizing taxi driver was the best chance for a major investment bank making its big gamble in Afghanistan.

CHAPTER 10

FALL 2008

HAVING BUILT OUT THE PROGRAM AND MADE WAY FOR A REPLACE-ment, I thought it was time to try again for a real job. The university had given me a home base, and the Goldman Sachs program was now in motion, but my housing was still barely more than a long-term youth hostel. I was offered a job at the Peace Dividend Trust, an out-fit I'd connected with during my listening tour of the city while trying to build a network for our incoming class of Afghan businesswomen. It was a Canadian organization whose mission was to keep more of the money coming into the country *in* the country. The idea was to help local companies win contracts that usually went to foreign ones. They were trying to slow what had become a seven-thousand-mile game of fetch in which, for example, American aid money was sent to Afghanistan for a new road, only for America-based companies to win the contract. A long transfer of funds from American taxpayers across the world and then back, into the coffers of a few American companies. Little of the money remained in the country it was in-tended to help.

Peace Dividend Trust was small, and I liked the mission even though—maybe because—I was part of the problem. I would be get-ting paid by an organization that was trying to keep people like me from getting paid, a job with a job description of self-eradication. I found the terms very generous. I was excited to start. But on a trip back to the US to visit all the people I'd now spend more time away from, I acciden-tally interviewed for a different position.

A family friend was working at the National Constitution Center, a grand, newish museum in Philadelphia, and I was told the museum had a new initiative to take its mission overseas. It would help new democracies through voter education, democracy building, and other Constitution-y things. I went in for a visit and thought I was just there as a favor, to share ideas and scroll through the old Nokia I used in Afghanistan, letting them copy down contacts. It didn't strike me as odd that they'd asked for a résumé first. It certainly didn't occur to me that I should review it before sending. I'd been out of college a year; my résumé still served mostly to advertise a tolerable GPA and the fact that I owned Microsoft Word. I'd had a job working construction during high school summers, but didn't really have marketable skills from it. I'd worn a tool belt and moved pieces of wood unhelpfully around jobsites, doing minor damage to pretty nice houses and learning words like "wainscoting" and "soffit." So it didn't occur to me that anyone would look closely at my résumé, or find it glaring that besides one summer at CNN, my only other entry under "Work Experience" was a college internship licking envelopes on the Allyson Schwartz for Congress campaign. I knew, but somehow forgot, that the CEO of the Constitution Center, Joe Torsella, had been the primary opponent. She won in what I later heard was, for him, a rather personal campaign. So I sat in his office, spending an oblivious hour holding forth on how much I knew about international affairs, and then Joe folded his legs, thanked me for coming in, and said, "We're thinking of bringing you in to hold a seminar on politically astute résumé writing." I laughed to demonstrate I understood grown-up humor, but didn't know what he meant until I asked my mother two hours later. She was keyed into politics, she was principled, she would know. And despite bungling the résumé portion of an application for a job I didn't even know I was interviewing for, I got a call a few days later from Hugh Allen, the senior director of special projects and government relations, offering me the position of international engagement manager at the Constitution Center.

Now, suddenly, I had two job offers, but it wasn't a hard choice. The Constitution Center would mean I'd get to live in America but maybe still visit exciting places. I'd get to go to bars without heavy petting from angry-faced security guards; I'd get to see pretty, dressed-up professional types without looking over my shoulder. If I played my cards right, I'd still get to travel to see Alex and the rest of my growing Afghanistan family, but I wouldn't have to *live* there.

And as if to confirm my connection with Alex wasn't going anywhere, soon after accepting the job I got a call from him. He was making a change too. He was starting his own business, and I realized a few minutes into his windup that he was asking me for a loan. He told me it was another taxi company, though something about it sounded a little different. He didn't specify an amount, which didn't surprise me. I knew he was proud, and it had to be hard for him to ask for anything. I figured this must mean he was out of his religious-awakening phase, if that's actually what it had been, or maybe I just didn't think about that at all. I wired $700 to a friend who was just then traveling back to Afghanistan.

A few days later I was walking down Market Street in Philadelphia, heading to my still-brand-new job, when I got a call from Alex. He sounded ecstatic. He was moved, he said; he was full of promise. He spoke as if I'd saved his life and lifted his entire family out of poverty. I smiled and listened, feeling like a player, like an adult. I was on my way to work in one city, closing a deal in another. I was Gordon Gekko in *Wall Street*, making moves, headed to my office while launching a friend's business on the other side of the world. Alex said I would be this new company's *owner*, laying on praise, promising me the vehicle of my choice the next time I visited along with a free place to stay whenever I wanted. His voice sounded lively again, like he'd gotten that edge back. I didn't question it all that vigorously. I didn't understand how $700 could make even a dent in a taxi company, given that a taxi company presumably needed cars, and cars were expensive. For me, $700 was a lot, so I just accepted my role as savior.

Meanwhile, now that I, apparently, owned a company in Afghanistan, I tried my hand at nepotism in Philadelphia. I tried to steer the museum toward the country that was becoming something like a second home to me. I wanted to shower my friends there with whatever spoils the Constitution Center had to give, and make sure I'd have sufficient excuses to travel back. My early efforts seemed to work: among my first duties was planning a fact-finding trip to Afghanistan with Joe Torsella, now my CEO.

Despite my résumé faux pas, Joe and I bonded. Here, inside the kingdom he'd built, 160,000 square feet of modernist limestone intended to serve as the nation's town hall, he was like a celebrity who would occasionally step down to your level of atmosphere, fix his stare on you, and ask a question as if only you possessed some key insight. As if there could be anything you knew and he didn't know. Maybe that's how he knew so much. Or maybe that was the politician's special brand of seduction. I was sure it wasn't, I wasn't all that worried, and I felt looked after. I wasn't worried about sharp elbows from colleagues who'd worked years to achieve the same size cubicle I had.

Like at the university in Kabul, here at the museum in Philadelphia I was a prodigal son. I followed fewer rules, did less than my part, and was given more leeway. I caused minor morale issues with junior staff because I didn't understand the wardrobe requirements everyone else had to abide by and because I'd been hired outside standard channels. I didn't know you weren't supposed to wear jeans on Friday, and I didn't know that it was unusual to travel with the CEO. All I knew was that within a few weeks of starting my new job in Philadelphia, Joe and I were driving through the night to catch a flight to Dubai, where we'd overnight before connecting on to Kabul. I was already going back. Only this trip wouldn't be another year in the country. We would be there for all of two and a half days.

I WAS TO LEAD JOE THROUGH A SERIES OF MEETINGS WITH POTENTIAL partners so that the museum might extend its mission to Afghanistan on its way to evolving from America's town hall to one of the world's town halls. The timing of our trip was fortuitous. Afghanistan was gearing up for its 2009 presidential elections, which would, potentially, be the country's first peaceful transfer of power. That made the elections important not just for Afghanistan but for the US and its allies too. Safe, normal elections would validate the whole American-led adventure there, and insurgents would surely try to disrupt them. Perhaps there was a role for my new employer working in voter education or forming some kind of democracy-related partnerships.

I'd lobbied for us to use Alex's company when we landed. My company. I was overruled, and we opted instead for Blackwater, a notorious private security contractor. The Devos family, as in Betsy Devos, the family behind Amway, the worldwide multilevel marketing company, were big donors to the Constitution Center, and Betsy's younger brother, Erik Prince, was Blackwater's founder. Joe would be holding high-level meetings, wearing a suit, and looking the part of visiting dignitary, so my security proposal of "look too stupid to be threatening, and let Alex keep us from getting killed" made the board fidgety.

It was strange to travel with an outfit I'd railed against privately. I had a journalist's knee-jerk suspicion of successful companies, but especially one so easily cast in the role of villain. I considered them mercenaries cashing in on violence, and now I was depending on them for safety. In the time I'd spent in Afghanistan thus far, I'd rarely felt personally targeted, and when I had, it was only because I'd made an obvious trespass or done something extravagantly stupid. But during those two and a half days traveling with a Blackwater team, I started to absorb their worldview, which seemed to be that every vehicle you weren't in was definitely full of terrorists trying to kill you. Women shuffling down the street in burkas carrying babies were also hiding high-caliber Rambo guns, and every hand you couldn't see had a thumb on the detonator. I'd driven down these same streets before with Alex, but it didn't feel like the same country.

Still, during our lightning-quick trip, we managed to hit every entry on a packed calendar. We met with the minister of the interior, with a small organization that published educational magazines, with a friend of mine who dealt in handmade carpets, and Joe even came out to the western slums of Kabul with me. We visited Marefat, a coeducational school I'd become attached to during my year in the country, and he toured the grounds with its founder, a dynamo of a man named Aziz Royesh, always smiling and full of mischief. Joe took to him, I think, putting his arm on Aziz and laughing as class let out, running kids bounced off their legs, and it started to get dark. Just off-camera, giant Blackwater men kept their sunglasses on and clicked their radios at each other like nervous, chirping birds.

And even though I wasn't allowed to use Alex's company—my company—I asked him to host a dinner party at his house for Joe, since Joe's birthday happened to fall right in the middle of our blitzkrieg trip. The Blackwater guys weren't thrilled about Joe visiting a local they didn't know, but I pretended to be unintimidated by them, stood up tall, looked them right in the chest, and insisted, which didn't really move the needle, but then Joe insisted, which did.

———

I'D TOLD ALEX I WAS COMING WITH A VIP BIRTHDAY GUEST, SO HE found a bottle of wine somewhere and surprised us. I was proud when he presented it to Joe. We sat on the floor and ate course after course appearing from behind the curtain, and then Alex took us out on the roof for cigarettes and a view of the mountains. He told Joe to look at the one with all the antennas. That was TV Mountain, Alex said. That's where some of the first bombs were dropped when America invaded after 9/11. Joe listened. I was proud of how Joe showed my friend respect. He did that thing, coming down to our level. This friend of mine who was, as far as Joe knew, basically just my taxi driver, Joe treated as an equal.

But I was also preoccupied because Alex seemed different. Like there'd been another change I'd missed. He was relaxed, but in a different way than I'd seen before. Relaxed like he was in control. He'd thickened out, calmed down. He seemed less like the adaptable hard-luck young man trying to ride whatever wave rose before him, and more like a chief with some mastery over his surroundings. It could've just been that he seemed older. That in the time since I'd last seen him, he'd reached that point somewhere between adolescence and adulthood. The hairpin turn where even a few months can change a wiry kid into a rounded-out man with a jaw and some mass to him. Slowed-down confidence replacing the sparky aura of boyhood. I wasn't sure. But there was something.

And then there was something else, a new mystery. When Alex and I went walking after dinner, Joe back at the house calling home, a kid slipped out from behind a tree with what I could have sworn was a machine gun.

It was dark, so at first I dismissed it as just me, the hypervigilance I'd caught from the Blackwater guys. But when I looked at Alex, he was staring straight ahead with such rigid focus it almost seemed like he'd seen the kid too and was trying to keep me from noticing. The figure slipped back behind a tree. I saw light glint off metal, and I turned to yell, but Alex grabbed my arm. "Shhh," he said. "Don't worry."

And then he said something strange. "He works for me."

CHAPTER 11

AUGUST 17, 2009

THE TRIP WENT BY TOO FAST. THERE WAS ONLY A MOMENT TO dwell on the strange way the evening with Alex ended. Alex had a kid with a gun working for his company. My company. Did I have kids with guns working for me?

But once back in the US, there was plenty to keep me from worrying about whether I was a warlord by proxy and what was going on with Alex. Anyway, I had a tendency to worry about minutia, not the important problems I should've been dealing with, like a lease I'd signed but couldn't actually afford or the fact that I was maybe employing child soldiers.

I spent the next months crouched over my desk in the basement of the Constitution Center, working mostly on a shiny new partnership. It turned out Joe really was moved by his meeting with Aziz, and the coed school out in the slums of Kabul, so Hugh Allen and I came up with an idea. We'd partner with a charter school in Philadelphia near the museum. Students from the two schools would work together across the world, remotely, learning documentary photography and getting to know one another online. They'd work on themes—women's rights one week, "democracy in action" another—and then, after a year, we'd launch exhibits simultaneously in both countries, at our museum and at the National Museum of Afghanistan. Each object in the exhibit would be not a single image but a pairing. An Afghan student's photograph mounted with an American student's, a Kabul madrassa's towering minaret, sun shining on glazed tile, set against the towering Comcast corporate headquarters in Philadelphia, sun shining on high-performance solar-reflective glass. We won a grant from the US State Department to fund the whole project, and I started planning another trip to deliver cameras, computers, and money for satellite internet. I'd be traveling on the State Department's dime, but the money was funneled through the museum, so I could travel the way I wanted to. I'd ditch the gaggle of burly mercenaries and ride around with Alex, even if I still wasn't sure what exactly was going on with him. I tried not to think about that.

I timed the trip to happen during the country's 2009 elections because what better occasion to launch a democracy-related project than during national elections? But also, the elections promised to be exciting. There were bound to be fireworks, and if I was there anyway, I might find something to write about.

When Alex picked me up at the Kabul airport, I felt excited like I always felt when first landing back in this familiar place, excited mostly to see Alex, but also already hot and worn out. I'd used the paid-for travel and some vacation days to tack on some extracurriculars, peeling off before Kabul to venture up into the contested Kashmir region between India and Pakistan, where I'd found a version of Alex from the area to help me get around, and covered rising violence. I'd carried all the US government-funded equipment with me up into an erupting front, hiding it under my hotel bed and going out to befriend soldiers and separatists. I spent ten days trying to decipher the violence there, then got back on a plane from India to Kabul, muscling out article drafts on a creaky tray table with the lift of mini whisky bottles and bottomless airplane coffee, flicking my eyes a few times each minute up the bulkhead that housed all the US government-funded tech. By the time Alex and I were hugging in the arrivals area in Kabul, I was desperate for a shower, a Gatorade, and a few days of sleep.

Instead, we stashed the equipment at a guesthouse and left Kabul, driving down through the desert into Jalalabad to profile one of the presidential candidates having a campaign rally that day.

It hadn't been too hard to pitch the story. The candidate was a novelty with no chance to win, but still interesting to American readers. Born in

Afghanistan but an American citizen, a PhD from Columbia University at that, who now looked to be playing dress-up. I was to write a story about this strange creature, whose name, Ashraf Ghani, was known better in Western academia than in the country he sought to lead.

We drove east from Kabul, Alex and I both exhausted and hungover. I'd spent the night before drinking alone on a plane, and Alex said he'd spent it drinking at a cousin's wedding in Kabul while he waited for me. He'd managed to score some liquor, so he and some friends siphoned it into 7 Up bottles and drank all night. "A small boy wanted some soda," Alex said. "His mom asked if we could give some for her son. We had to say, 'No, we don't want to share soda.'" Alex smiled. "Yah, Jaff. I met a girl at the wedding and gave her my business card. In dream she call me."

After that, the humor began to fade. A shared second wind from our reunion burned off, and before I could figure out a way to ask what exactly happened on my last trip—that kid with the machine gun—we both lulled back into a kind of sick weariness.

We drove past Camp Phoenix as a giant Chinook helicopter settled toward the ground, a storm cloud changing the light. Its tandem rotors sucking up dust, making a show of it. Outside the camp's walls, damaged Humvees and armored personnel carriers sat on top of flatbeds serving as gurneys—mighty machines wounded in ambushes, lamed by bombs heeled into roads. All these beasts lined up in plain view along the road, an offer of steel and vulcanized rubber. Alex said he chose the worst vehicle he could find for the drive. Expensive vehicles attract attention, and today he wanted to avoid second looks. It made sense at first, but now we're driving through the desert without air-conditioning. We stop when we can to buy Mountain Dew and Carabao from boys selling out of cargo containers so weathered and brown they seem like part of the landscape, like they've been here for eons, left behind when some prehistoric tide went out and left behind desert. The boys standing in front of the beached shipping containers, examining us as if they're guarding the fossil record. The drinks go warm in minutes. In half an hour, Alex and I are impatient, sweating, still not talking, and we're in this state when we catch up to a military convoy.

Alex begins following too closely. His forehead glistens. It occurs to me that I've rarely seen him sweat. Up ahead, the soldiers in the vehicles hang out of the turrets and smile until we're right on top of them, and then their faces change. Their weapons swing toward us. Alex keeps smiling. We stay with them around blind curves, dips and rises. The soldiers in the follow vehicle look at each other, then us, then back at each other, holding fingers to mouthpieces and updating someone somewhere about the rusty old sedan following too closely. No one wants to shoot civilians, but who the hell knows what the guy driving a car bomb looks like right before a car bomb goes off? Alex hasn't stopped smiling; he looks manic; he's tempting the men in the turrets. For the first time maybe ever my safety isn't his priority, and I'm grinning like an idiot so that if they can see through the windshield, I'll look too stupid to be threatening.

The convoy turns off the road, and we keep going. My shoulders unclench. More blind curves and near misses with three-axle trucks on a road the Soviets wedged into the rock face back when the candidate we're going to see was doing his dissertation in America. The road is narrow with a long way to fall, and as we move around corners, green funereal flags appear from behind rocks as if they're moving, not us.

———

AFTER THE CAMPAIGN RALLY, HALFWAY BACK TO KABUL, ALEX AND I stop at dusk to swim in a river. It's been a punishing day, both of us sweating and sick, but when we walk down to the water, we lose our view to rising riverbanks. For the first time since I first came to this country, I see no visible signs of war. It's like going back in time. Five or ten steps to the water and it's forty years before, when women in Kabul wore miniskirts and Americans came for the dope. I'm on a journey now, in a lyrical mood. We've crossed a threshold into a time before the Soviets came, before holy warriors started shooting at them, before foreign governments started giving guns and money to the Afghans they liked the best.

Downriver, two young men stumble up the rocks toward us. "Salam," they say, smiling and wading gracelessly into the water. One stays near the bank with the water at his shins; the other pushes off and fights the current, swifter than expected. He begins to struggle. His mouth clenches, and he throws his head back to keep his face above the water and gulp at air. What a foolish way to die this would be, in a place with so little water and so many other ways to die available on land. He erupts into frantic splashes, grabbing at the surface, and I can't think of a way to save him, but I find that my mind isn't working that fast to find one.

He makes it back to the riverbank laughing, and wrestles in the water with his friend. Alex goes back to the car to get the pistol from the armrest.

Alex won't swim, but he wades into the water, keeping the weapon cradled at his chest. He doesn't look at the boys, but I know him well enough to know he's keeping track of them. Even when he faces away, they're blinking on an internal radar screen that he's constantly checking.

He says he doesn't want to stay in one place for long, and he doesn't like the idea of traveling here after nightfall because Talibs will climb up on jagged ridges every once in a while to drop RPGs on cars, just to remind everyone they're there. As we leave the riverbank and head back toward Kabul with the sun setting, we pass men who, in the thinning light, take the faded colors of their cars and the rocks they fish from. It seems they've been there forever. It seems they will be there forever.

CHAPTER 12

AUGUST 19, 2009

ON ELECTION DAY, I FIGURE ALEX WILL ROLL OUT THE RED CAR-
pet, take me to anything I want to see. But at first he doesn't even show
up. I heard there was a shootout at one of the polling places and want
to go see what happened, but when I call the new company, one of his
brothers comes to get me. It seems strange. I try not to be insulted.

We get to the polling place near a police station and find a woman
in a burka writhing on the ground. Putting herself down in the dirt before each vehicle that emerges from the police station gates. It's hard
to tell whether she's grieving or protesting, but whatever she's doing,
it's violent and disturbing. A crying boy tugs at her arm. It seems like
he's trying to pull her up, then like he's trying to pull her out of the way
because cars keep bursting out of the gates, quilled with men who stick
out of the windows and laugh as if the woman is immaterial, a soccer
player hamming it up for the refs. The guards watch her, I watch her, I
look at Alex's brother, he seems unmoved.

He does some asking around. He's not as good at it as Alex. He
learns two Talibs were holed up across the street, hiding in a house
still under construction, where they waited to strike. This morning,
some of them attacked the police station, but the fight didn't last long.
One Talib was shot, the other was chased back into the house, where
he detonated a suicide belt too soon, so no one was hurt. Except for
the bomber, who distributed himself all over the empty interior. The
police took his top half inside, couldn't really find his legs, and had
since stopped looking. But when they fanned out into the surrounding

houses to see who knew what, they came across this woman's other son with bullets in his pockets. He's been detained all morning.

As the woman cries and screams and throws dirt at the guards, I see a flash of color; her palms are stained with ink. Not the blue dye everyone who's voted has on their finger to make sure they don't vote twice, but red henna, the elaborate lattice women get on wedding weeks. She was celebrating something last night; this morning she writhes and screams. She doesn't seem entirely present. Everything seems off, something uneven. A cool universe ignores a burning coiled specimen. It's like I'm imagining her, so unmindful is everyone around. Or maybe it's because her grief seems exaggerated or because no one can see her face. The misfiring question that keeps occurring to me is how someone can be so bold and be hiding at the same time. And still, no one seems to notice her. Except that one little boy, crying and tugging at a blue mass.

Alex finally emerges from whatever hangover kept him from helping this morning, and we tour more voting sites to see if anything newsworthy is happening anywhere until, by evening, we're driving west into the slums to Marefat, the school I'm supposed to be working with, which is itself a polling place. The students scramble around taking photos with their new cameras. They're excited; they take to it instantly. There's an excitement here in the slums. Kids thrilled that their classrooms have been colonized by democracy, to them still an exciting mascot rather than an experiment that has to work. It's different from the polling place near the police station. Maybe even the opposite, and there's something troubling about that too. Two different worlds, at least, in the same city. Elections mean different things to everyone and to some people seem to mean nothing at all. Alex seems distant.

When the sun sets and the voting is over, giant Tupperware boxes full of ballots trucked from Marefat's dusty little campus off to some important place, we retire to the headmaster's residence near the school, and I sit next to Aziz as he receives guests. We talk absently about the elections, the elders all weaving some kind of elegy. Their old rooted memory from civil war wraps around everything. I try to keep up. They talk about the ophthalmologist, Dr. Abdullah Abdullah, who, they say, has a decent chance but is a silly man, too stained by his role in the civil war to lead. Ashraf Ghani, the candidate I wrote about down in Jalalabad with Alex, doesn't even figure in our conversation. In these elections, Ashraf Ghani will barely register in the polls, even though in five years' time, he'll win. As the others talk, Alex looks toward a window like something out there has his attention.

Talk homes in on a long-shot candidate from Aziz's ethnic group, a man named Bashardost, who someone says is like Gandhi, someone else says is like Hitler, and someone else says is like Mao. Aziz calls him "mob-ocrat" over and over as if repeating it might make us know what he means, and anyway, best to vote for Karzai because the devil you know, and so on. The evening progresses, Aziz's women cast shadows like finger puppets moving across the wall, we recline more, Aziz eases into an essay casting his country as the *Titanic*, the ship moving toward its fate while everyone concerns themselves with the irrelevant scandal of Jack and Rose. That's perhaps what these elections are, Aziz says, just a distraction. Alex is quiet. He looks like he has something else on his mind. I think this conversation is a little academic for him. Plus, he likes *Titanic*.

He doesn't want to leave me there, but he's clearly somewhere else already, so I insist I'm fine. I shove him off, and the rest of us spend the night there next to the school-turned-polling place, debating candidates until city power cuts out and it's too late to go home, so we shine phone lights at each other, talk more, sleep some, and wake up expecting the country to somehow announce its change. We look around, Aziz and I and all his followers, for something to claim the moment for itself, but everything is the same. Elections happened, the Earth spun, the gray sun is out, I need a shower.

CHAPTER 13

AUGUST 23, 2009

On that trip, in the days after the elections, Alex talked more of wanting to get out of the country, like some vague threat was forming on the horizon. I couldn't think of how to help him. I still didn't know how to explain his value to anyone besides myself. I didn't think he could get a scholarship to study: he had little in the way of formal education, and I figured his written English would disqualify him from college in America. I couldn't see how to fit him in any box, besides as the person who kept me alive for a while. The person who helped someone else who didn't fit in any box start a career.

At the same time, he didn't seem desperate. He'd started the company, and a year in, it looked to be going well. Maybe very well. He paid the wages of twelve people and said he was proud they could support their families. He still didn't have one of his own. I still didn't quite understand how he paid for all those cars.

There was more and more I didn't understand about him. We took another nighttime walk down the street near his mother's house, and again, kids with guns stepped out to walk next to us, though this time they didn't bother to hide. I still didn't know how to ask. I didn't know exactly what I wanted to ask. He'd been absent during the elections, like it was all a show that didn't concern him. I'd seen him growing angrier and angrier with American soldiers and Afghan security personnel who worked with them. I'd seen him taunt them all. I knew that collateral damage from American attacks was increasing, Afghan civilians were being killed in growing numbers, and an American president was ordering more and more drone strikes. Maybe all of it had finally pushed Alex over the edge. I was confused, and I didn't know how to broach the subject. Was he becoming sympathetic to the insurgents? Had he joined the Taliban? How do you ask that? "Hey, brother, pass the rice. Also, are you a terrorist now?" I loved him. He was my brother, and I felt he always would be, no matter what. So what happens now? Do we part ways? Do I have to resign myself to the fact that we may now be on opposite sides? He'd launched me, he'd protected me, he'd fed me in his home. If I accepted hospitality from my country's enemy, did that make me a traitor? Or maybe, probably, I was overreacting.

He tried to get me to start carrying a gun. As if it was only now that I needed one. Maybe it was an honor thing. If we're becoming enemies, maybe honor dictates that you make sure your enemy has a chance. Or maybe it was trying to show me that no matter where our allegiances went, no matter which side either one of us was on, the safety of a friend is sacred. Sitting in his living room, he took out a Makarov 9 millimeter, pressed it into my palm, and winked.

To make me feel better about accepting it, he said don't worry; he'd just bought himself a new Beretta outside Bagram Airfield for $1,300, and he likes it better. "With this one, the recoil is *little, little*. It never go off by itself." He moved it around to demonstrate, waving it at me.

I told him thanks, but no, I'll cause more problems than I'll solve with it, and hand the Makarov back. He slips it into his waistband. A few days later, I'd mostly gotten over the notion that he was going through another worrying change. It was just the heat and me, a place and time doing things to my imagination. He drove me to the airport like he still insisted on doing. Always the last one to say good-bye, no matter which side I was on; he was telling me, I think, I'd always be on his. He wanted to make sure the end of my trip was as safe as the rest, as he always had. He slowed for a checkpoint approaching the airport compound, and a soldier leaned down into the window, inspecting the inside of the car. Alex translated. "Yah, Jaff. He ask me if you have a weapon."

"No," I said.

The soldier looked around the car again slowly, squinting, and then settled his gaze on me. "Why not?"

CHAPTER 14

LATE AUGUST 2011

Philadelphia

THAT WAS THE LAST I SAW OF ALEX FOR A LONG TIME.

After two years at the museum in Philadelphia, I left for grad school. I wanted to read and talk and write papers about interesting things. I was an anomaly, an applicant not from a country at war but who'd been to war, but who wasn't a veteran. There weren't that many of me. On the strength of an unconventional background, I'd snuck onto the admission rolls of a few schools. I'd applied to some of the known programs and also one at Stanford, a pinnacle for things like engineering, not as much for international relations. They had a newish program, and Stanford was *Stanford*, a website splashed with terracotta and palm trees. Undergrads called it The Farm; others called it an academic spa. It was worth a look, even though it was less likely to shunt me into some fancy foreign relations job.

My mother came out to California with me to visit; we rented a hatchback and afterward drove partway down the Pacific Coast Highway to mull what at the time felt like a major life decision. I hadn't actually wanted her to come. She was a complicated person, we had a strained relationship, and I was often uncomfortable around her. She'd flown across the country with me, for me, and I knew there was brutality in treating her with indifference. I hated myself for being like that, but I was like that anyway. I wasn't interested in what she might be going through.

We pulled over somewhere down the highway around Big Sur, and she took a picture of me standing on a rock looking out at the Pacific and pretending I didn't notice her taking it. Later, when it was time for me to decide whether to make an impulsive move to California or make the more conservative choice of the established East Coast mainstays on Gothic quads, she made sure her vote was known. She gave me a photo of myself looking out over the Pacific, blown up to poster size, with a caption in big white letters that read "Go West, Young Man." And I did.

It was a foolish choice; it was exactly the right choice. The Stanford program attracted the kind of person ambitious enough for a graduate school with a big name, flexible enough to try a program that couldn't guarantee higher-income jobs to compensate for loan debt. I met curious, bright, young, service-minded people from Brazil, India, Bulgaria, Indonesia. From America, bankers who'd survived the crash, some who made too much money and were ready for a phase change into a lighter or heavier substance. And I also met a friend, Kathy, who'd danced in and out of journalism jobs like I had and who decided to take the summer between the two years of the program, when we were all supposed to get internships, and go work for an upstart news outlet in Afghanistan.

She didn't know anyone there, so I took it upon myself to help make sure her adventure was as safe as could be, but also successful. And of all the friends I still had in the country, people I knew would care for Kathy as their own, the most important was still Alex. Whatever was going on with him, he was still the one I'd trust the most to keep a friend safe without straitjacketing her.

But another strange thing happened. I couldn't reach him. I'd taken for granted that he would be there, waiting for me in Afghanistan, whenever I wanted him, no matter how much time had gone by. I had three different numbers for him. I called and called and couldn't get through. Then Kathy left, and for weeks I kept trying to reach him. With growing confusion, which switched to frustration, then resentment, then worry, and back to resentment. *Wasn't it MY company you started?*

One of his brothers answered a few times, and said Alex wasn't available, but gave no explanation. They all knew me. They all constantly told me how important I was to the company, how their home was my home, their cars were my cars, so why wouldn't they let me speak to my friend?

Kathy left to navigate the country on her own, and finally, one day late in the summer of 2011, my phone rang with a hidden number. I picked up, and an operator announced a call from a detention center in Edmonton, Canada. I didn't know anyone in Edmonton, Canada. The operator asked me to hold.

Then Alex's voice came on the line. "Yah, Jaff. It's me. Here I am in Canada now."

PART II

The Driver

(Aimal's Story: 1992–2011)

CHAPTER 1

1992

Kabul, Afghanistan

AIMAL IS SCARED.

He's a child just old enough to know that these things he sees might become things he sees later, in his imagination.

He should look away, but this strange violence, the fire and noise, is happening just as he's reached the age of fierce wonder about the world. Biology and history have conspired to shunt incomprehensible images into his memory. His neighborhood exploding and he's at just the age when a child's instinct is to look at everything, when it's hard to accept not understanding things. He opens his eyes at everything; he doesn't know he should close them.

The civil war years are bad. Holy warriors fight around his house, Sayyaf and Gulbuddin, Massoud and Mazari and the rest. The names of storm systems drifting into the city and flagging on the mountains, aiming violence at each other but killing civilians instead in the streets. Some actually aim violence at the ground where the civilians go about their business; some warlords turn up the soil because it still holds trace amounts of communism, a pollutant requiring fire and violence to purge.

Down below, Aimal smiles at customers in front of his family's shop. Not a shop but a garage door he and his brother Naheb lever open sometimes to let some cadaverous passerby in, to pick at the aimless inventory. Seven years old, and Aimal keeps it open, more or less, through the fighting. Sometimes for just minutes at a time before warlords perched on the mountains that ravine his city start lobbing rockets at each other again. Sometimes the men up on the mountains fire rockets for sport, or because they have them, or because they haven't in a while. A bored fighter up on TV Mountain hiding somewhere under all the antennae up there, launching a rocket for some noise to break up the day.

Once, a bus pulled in front of the store and picked up a pretty girl he'd practiced his wink at. Already, at eight now, a flirt. The girl boarded the bus, the bus grunted into gear, coughed out a black puff of diluted fuel, and then crumpled and keeled like a dumb game animal. The girl dead, the bus sniped by some strong type of bullet. Metal squeezed bodies inside, and Aimal didn't bother going close. This had been his clientele.

Another day, Aimal is keeping the shop open through the hours when the rockets are falling in clumps like some aspect of astronomy. He's in the basement being bored, listening to the familiar whistling of metal through air, and he hears a crash and a thud that sound closer than usual.

Upstairs, a rocket had torn through the store while Naheb manned the counter. It came through the roof, passed a few feet from his ear, crashed through the wall behind him, then through the neighbor's wall, and lodged in place, some strange tumescence, Naheb waiting for it to detonate. And then when it didn't—when the rocket just sat there, sticking out of the wall like it was waiting for someone to say some-thing—Naheb took off running. Aimal sees his panicked brother crash into the basement and can't help collapsing into laughter, Naheb stand-ing like some painted bride, powdered in the crushed flower stems and dried mud the family fashioned the house from and easily pierced by a Russian-made dud. Naheb orange over white, suddenly an old man. An *older* man: Naheb is already a grown-up to Aimal, Aimal the youngest and Naheb the next youngest, but he is the one brother who is around, so when their father was killed, it was Naheb who slipped in as the first in a series of not-quite father figures Aimal would try on and discard. Naheb his partner in crime, Naheb with his bad luck, his good luck, never killed but almost killed, again and again. Playing volleyball in New City Park when a rocket fell near the court and the lights went out for him, then he woke up to everyone but the coach lying still, like he'd missed a drill.

———

WHEN THE TALIBAN ARRIVE IN AIMAL'S NEIGHBORHOOD, THE ROCK-ets stop; there's no more fighting. No buses with pretty girls dying in front of him.

Soon there is no food. Aimal scrounges where he can. His brother learns calligraphy and tries to start a printing business. Printers and copiers are hard to come by, so the "printer" is just Naheb and his tired right hand. Hunched over paper, writing signs as fast as he can. He offers himself up to the few businesses and NGOs that can find some way to justify paying. Aimal watches Naheb write bizarrely ornate advertisements for mundane things. Sweeping, triumphant script for a sale of old clothing. And then, finally, Naheb gets his big break when an NGO hires him to write two hundred metal signs for a sanitation project. Aimal watches his brother get to work applying his intricate script to shitters, until he runs so far behind he enlists Aimal to help make a dent.

Aimal, nine years old, with a reverence for the art of the deal. How to manipulate his environment to squeeze coins from a city without any in plain view, and a few scattered calories from a city without food. He walks around thinking of a story a friend told him once, made up, probably, but one he loves anyway: a wily employee drives his boss to frustration by always scoring a little more money than others thought possible. A little cleverer, a little more thought-ful, than everyone else.

One day, in this story that Aimal hears once and then—submerged in the boredom of life under the Taliban—recites to himself again and again, the boss takes it upon himself to teach his wily employee a lesson. The boss visits every market in the city to find the cost of calligraphy. He returns from his excursion and summons his employee. "Go get a sign made for me," he says. "It'll cost you one coin per letter."

Off goes the wily employee to the marketplace, where he finds a cal-ligrapher and asks how much it costs to make a sign. "One coin per let-ter," the calligrapher says, "and don't bother trying to find a better deal." The employee shrugs. He says, "Fine, I'll have two letters please," and hands over two coins. He says he wants the letter *Yeh*—and here, that first time, Aimal's storyteller started scratching in the dirt with a stick:

$$ى$$

The wily employee says the second letter he wants is *Qaf*:

$$ق$$

So together, he wants:

$$ڠى$$

The calligrapher in the story takes the money and gets to work. Just before he closes the circle on *Qaf*, the wily employee says, "You know, you don't have to close that circle; I'll spare you the effort." The calligra-pher shrugs. The employee says, "And would you mind putting the dots *here* instead of *here*?"

It makes no difference to the calligrapher. It's the same ink no mat-ter where the dots are, and the same effort. "Sure, why not?"

But by leaving the circle in *Qaf* open and moving the dots, what the calligrapher has written is actually no longer just two letters. Instead, the two letters

$$ڠى$$

have become a word, a *three-letter* word, a common name, Ghani:

The wily employee had seen something his boss had not: that the only difference between that three-letter word and those two letters written next to each other was the arrangement of a few dots and a small part of a circle. The employee has compensated the calligrapher fairly for his time, his ink, and his effort, he's fulfilled his duty to his boss, he's cheated no one, but he's outsmarted the market. By looking past the rules that apply to everyone else, he's turned two coins into not two letters, but three. He won by solving a puzzle no one else even saw.

Aimal holds on tight to this story. He's inspired by it, the neatness of it, and he goes around looking for other games most people don't see. Usually, he decides, if you look where others aren't looking, if you pry open the space between the buyer and the seller, you find something meaty for yourself. Even if only a little dignity.

IN THE GARAGE, PORING OVER THE SIGNS FOR THEIR NGO SANITATION project, Aimal knows they have no chance to fulfill the order. It's too much, two hundred hand-painted signs. They need a shortcut. They need to solve a puzzle no one else sees.

They go out walking, looking for a hint, and find themselves near the hospital. Like they often did during the Taliban years, they pick through the garbage. There's not often anything of value in the trash because the whole city has learned to beak through waste, a city of vulture eyes hunting for untended specks of protein.

Naheb pulls an X-ray out of the trash. Evidence of some internal war trauma some patient didn't understand and discarded, but the brothers have found their answer. The X-ray film is thick and sturdy. They bring it home and blade the NGO's name and "sanitation project" as well as the project number into the film, curling the knife around a stranger's bone. They place the carved X-ray over sheeted metal, daub the paint over it, and finish twenty signs a night. With their makeshift stencil, they've quartered the time. They fulfill the order.

For Aimal, this one small puzzle—helping his brother write signs for toilets that foreigners are building in the villages—is enough to fuel his mind. He wants more. Life is boring, and he's tormented by the acid feeling of a stomach gone days without food. But foreigners, even when he doesn't see them, mean challenge, chance, some money, food.

WITH A LITTLE EXTRA CASH HE SHOULD'VE SPENT ON FOOD, AIMAL'S brother gets hold of a rusty old satellite dish. Aimal aims it at the sky and basks in the colors beaming down at his forgotten corner of the world. They come up with a dance, Aimal and Naheb, how they catch the microwaves just after the sun goes down, when the Talibs can't see. They wire the dish to the television set inside and watch. A soccer player, a breast, an explosion, a moaning coil of body parts that excite Aimal for reasons he doesn't understand, snow. Naheb sends him back outside to aim the dish through the starving grapevines hanging over the yard. "Try to the right. Slower. Go back!"

Out in the yard, the dish comes up to his waist, so Aimal learns to twist his hips an inch at a time, aiming his crotch at the stars so many nights that he becomes an expert at finding the signal. Inside, at night, the family becomes close, absorbing the world like sustenance. Aimal, his mother, his siblings huddled together the few nights they have power, bonding on Schwarzenegger, Bollywood, pornography, propaganda, and news. Others go off to sleep, but Aimal stays up communing with packeted data coming down from the entire large universe, disturbed only sometimes by his mother's early-morning laughter. Aimal turns to see his mother leaning on the doorjamb in her nightclothes, watching him. A boy kneeling before the TV and trying to sound white but making only high-pitched falling silverware sounds. "My dear, are you trying to speak Chinese?"

He gets angry, gets over it, he loves her. Every night that they have power, Aimal goes out fishing for a signal. Every morning after, he goes out just before sunup to hide the dish so Talibs won't see the fatherless family falling by the eyeballs into sin.

But so many mornings, he barely has the strength to lift the dish. There's no bread, and sometimes not even tea. The tea leaves reused for a week are so bleached from re-steeping they can't muster color to shade the water. Even the tea has given up. Grapes won't grow. The Taliban are exuberant in their rules but seem unable to feed people. Aimal knows he has done something to earn this fate for himself and his family, but he isn't sure what.

He looks at his mother's face.

Even at ten, he can't bear the kindness in her eyes. Widowed young with an armful of children and no education. Her husband murdered by they still aren't sure who, a mystery they agree not to speak of. It had been war, so people had been killed. So many burdens. Aimal is a burden. She wouldn't be able to handle knowing, so he keeps it from her: Aimal might be starving to death. A neighbor walking by with *halwa*, sweet and thin, and Aimal can almost taste it from the window. A blade in his belly. He goes to the stall where some charitable man is handing out the sweet street food for free. The smell drifts, a funny insult to the air. Sugary and smoky, caramel in his nostrils, it triggers hope in his gut, and he's just to the front of the line when he hears, "Sorry, brothers. Halwa is finished."

A poor old man sees him, and Aimal knows what he looks like. A skeletal jangle of dangly limbs and open gashes, arriving too late for the handout. Aimal scrunches his face to keep tears in their place, and the poor old man says, "Boy, will you try mine? It's different from what I'm used to. Tell me if this one is good."

But Aimal can sense the man is trying a kindness on him, and he feels a liquid chill, something he'll later know as pride. He shivers. This is what he's come to. Taking food from the hands of a poor old man.

"No, no, I'm OK." Then, he feels himself starting to shake, his whole body rebels, he forces himself to say, "I'm not hungry."

But the hunger infects him. He's cold even when it isn't cold. The scrapes on his knees don't heal like they're supposed to, so he carries the hunger with him, on him.

He will deal with the hurt. He'll keep it inside him. He'll use it, there must be a way to use it, as fuel. Fuel like the Talibs have to run their generators, generators the Talibs have even though the Talibs are connected to hydro and have power all day and all night. He can smell their generators running on some foul-smelling fuel that poisons the air. So he can too. He will use the hurt like some noxious thing to power a change, brighten the lights. His mother starves. He'll find a way. He curses himself. *Do something.*

WHENEVER THERE'S POWER, THEY FOLLOW THE SAME ROUTINE WITH the dish, hiding their dirty habit from the Talibs roaming nearby as close as the next-door neighbors. The next-door neighbor is a senior Talib minister living with his wife and kids, working down the street at a place that seems like a Judgment Factory where the people are shamed and all the creative punishments are handed down.

Aimal decides his job is harder because the family's withering grapevines draped over the garden are blocking the stars. Even though they hold a suggestion of food, he has priorities now. He climbs up with a handsaw and hacks away a dish-sized opening so the foreigners he's trying to summon won't get caught up in the vines. A hole big enough for Bollywood and Hollywood and the flashes of pale American breasts and square-jawed white newsmen in suits, but not so big that the Talibs he can see from up there on the roof will wonder about his strange-shaped harvest. And when he sees his neighbor, the Taliban minister in charge of the Taliban Judgment Factory down the street, Aimal smiles at him and winks, and knows he has the camouflage of youth. He knows Talibs see him as corruptible but not yet old enough to be corrupt. The Taliban minister smiles back. Aimal knows he can move with impunity.

He can't feed the hunger, so he tries to distract himself from it. He mans the family store when it's his turn, but no one has money to buy anything. He closes up and adventures. He walks down to the Taliban's Judgment Factory to watch the women being frog-marched in for their sins, wondering what they look like beneath their burkas. He watches men being led in for final judgment presented before Aimal's neighbor, the old Taliban minister, who decides whether they'll be jailed for listening to music or watching profanity or have a hand removed for using it to steal.

There is fear in those years, but more than fear, and as much as hunger, there is boredom.

He starts going to school for a few hours a day, but in school nothing happens. Class is never learning, no puzzles to solve. No kids with backpacks like the ones from the dish having interesting conversations about girls while slamming colorful lockers. No math or science because the Talibs think math and science contradict the Quran, so even school is mostly just sitting on the floor with a teacher flitting between rooms like a trapped bird banging around for an open window. The boredom and the hunger together feel deadly, and the longer it goes, the less energy Aimal has to be respectful toward the Taliban. Their year in power stretches to two. Food doesn't get easier to find. He sees the Taliban as parents who offer nothing but punishment. Elders undeserving of respect. Maybe elders don't deserve respect simply for being elders. From the dish he knows other countries have governments that give people things. Other governments hire people to help put out fires. Other countries have fathers who ask sons what they want for breakfast and then make it for them. It awes him.

From the dish he learns just how poor he really is. It makes him see, when he looks around, how many people have better corners of life carved out for themselves than he does. And what have they done to deserve it? Even close by, when he walks into his neighbor's house and jokes with the Taliban minister's family, they seem just like his. They've accomplished nothing his family hasn't. So why do they have a father and he doesn't? Why do they have electricity every night? Why are they connected to hydro when his family relies on a rickety old grid the Talibs never bothered to fix?

He grows more resentful. He gets bolder as the regime goes on. He plays with the Talib's kids, jokes with the Talib minister—he's unafraid. Hunger drains his reservoir of restraint; he doesn't have the energy for it. So he just talks to elders as if they're equals. His respect for boundaries atrophies. His fear that the Talibs will see that he's outside with the satellite dish at night lessens. So what if they do? He roams his neighborhood, walking into neighbors' houses without knocking. He looks for diversion, novelty, so he'll forget his stomach at least for a moment. He walks into the Talib's house one day to ask if the kids want to come out and play, and he sees brown bodies draped in colorful fabric gyrating on a TV screen in the living room.

There's a breathless moment before he registers that the Talib has a television. The Talib's wife is watching some blasphemous Bollywood soap opera. The Talib's wife too slowly scooping up her clothing, leaping to her feet, fumbling to switch the television off but too late. Aimal has caught her. He feels a strange thing; he's a young boy with a surge of power he shouldn't yet have. It isn't anger—perhaps a bit of anger—it's mostly something foreign, something new, an interesting twinge in his chest: *opportunity*.

CHAPTER 2

1993

Montana, USA

WHEN I WAS IN SECOND GRADE, MY FATHER PACKED UP THE TOY-
ota, and we set off west for Montana. A week on the road, playing *The
Odyssey* on tape. I asked questions incessantly. My father was mostly
patient, never quite regretting that he'd committed himself to a week-
long inquisition, longer if there was car trouble. *Why do we have to
drive so long?* Because Montana is on the other side of the country.
Why are we going to Montana? Because your mother . . . *Why is it on the
other side of the country?* We stopped at the Corn Palace, we stopped
in the Badlands, we wondered at the hundreds of miles of breadcrumb
signs for Wall Drug, and we arrived halfway into *The Odyssey* at our
destination: Livingston. Thirty miles from a place called Four Corners,
thirty miles from a place called Story, home of nothing but a dream
my father had of finishing his book, which was in fact already finished
and which was not really a book at all but a medical text he had to
peer review. Back in '78, my mother read a *Town & Country* article
about a dude ranch called Sweet Grass and wanted to go west, so over
the years my parents turned the big empty state into their playground.
Now that my father had a sabbatical, Montana was where they set up
camp. But it was on my father's sabbatical, somehow—somehow, in
venturing to this frontier of ours—that I first encountered larger-than-
life luxuries. Our little rented house had a waterbed, a living room
above the bedrooms rather than below, a hot tub, and in the front yard a
satellite dish that could turn on a motor and that, to my barely four-foot

frame, seemed big enough to reach other star systems and also the Philadelphia Eagles. From the front door, houseless plains stretched as far as my imagination went, a huge empty slate serrated by mountains that in the mornings woke with us and stretched their bodies into the clouds.

We fished, we tried hunting, I saw guns fired for the first time. My sisters and I enrolled in the local school. I excelled next to kids who came to class only after hours of early-morning labor on family farms and ranches—kids who even at my age had responsibilities. I was an ardent rule follower. I joined a school initiative selling candy bars to raise money for something or other, and when my teacher asked if I'd like to try writing something that sounded like "S-A" that not all the other kids were "quite cut out for," I felt like I'd arrived. I followed a workbook with prompts that ushered me into paragraph-long compositions, most days feeling the work was my reward for having done what I was told. I did my assignments, I remembered the pledge of allegiance, I stood erect, I put my hand over the side of my chest with my heart and not the empty side, I honored my flag while overtired ranchers' kids goofed off. I made friends, a special one I spent entire days with. Vincent: the nicest person I'd ever met, whose sturdy mother belonged to some kind of cult. Even on weekends we'd frequent the school playground to ride our bikes on the ice, make our bodies into vehicles, fling our hands out and turn our jackets into sails. We'd catch the wind that funneled down the eastern slope of the Rockies, across Livingston and to us, driving us across the slickened concrete like frontier Jetsons.

We'd spend hours in his family's double-wide, which somehow seemed huge to me even in a part of the country where everything was huge. My mother decided it was time for her own family's religious awakening, inspired, I think, by the sense of belonging Vincent's mother took from her cult and also her bowling league. My mom rediscovered Judaism. She took to spreading awareness like a civilizing force. She was surprised and delighted when she discovered that the local library had only one book on Judaism. She began holding clinics on how to make menorahs, which she did not know how to do. Our upside-down house filled with misshapen globules of hardened clay that held candles at all angles like some comic-book predator's misaligned jaw, another one each day, until our mantle looked like a specimen display of goblin dentistry. It didn't stop her, more and more of them arrived, as if we might atone for our lapsed practice by the sheer tonnage of deformed Judaica.

There were no synagogues there, and we wouldn't have gone to them if there were. We missed family events, an uncle's engagement, surely some bar mitzvahs, and my mother began to show discontentment that would lead her, later, to wander further from us in ways I wouldn't understand, and would discover only when an early, aggressive dementia had so enfeebled her that certain family secrets had no choice but to leak out. Back then, we were just a Jewish-ish family having an adventure.

When I was bullied on a school bus, not for any of the things I was actually insecure about but just because the bully was a bully, I was thrilled. He reached forward and cuffed my ear, then reached forward again and flung my head into the window hard enough to make noise, not hard enough to hurt, not really, or perhaps it was adrenaline. My older sister, sitting next to me, rocketed out of her seat like someone pulled an ejection lever. She went through some kind of flash mutation into a different kind of matter. She leaned back over the seat and stormed into the bully with clenched fists, and I learned what violence in real life was like. I was energized. Everything was outside, my own battle with mental illness that was not yet florid, but I was seeing enough to know, in some perverse way, *this is what I want*. Something in me vibrated, keeping beat with the violence. I wanted a life where force was exerted outside, in an arena. I wanted to go someplace with shots fired and punches slung, force and resentment released in explosions, not held and compressed, to test the soundness of a mind. That night we turned on the TV, which triggered a motor on the dish, and outside the mighty thing turned, but I still shook. I shook with purpose, even as we browsed the hundreds of channels, looking for one that might connect us to something outside.

CHAPTER 3

1996

Kabul, Afghanistan

BOUNCING OFF THE BLADE OF AN ANTENNA 22,300 MILES UP, thousands of hours of information shine down on Aimal all night long. Invisible light vibrating as packets of data that Aimal reaches up and grabs. Not just some nights anymore, but every night. Because he's found an angle, he's solved a puzzle no one else saw. He made a deal with the Talib next door, an eleven-year-old kid standing with the Talib and the wife caught red-handed with forbidden soap operas. *I'll tell everyone*, Aimal said, *and everyone will know what hypocrites you are.* Adults hadn't known quite what to make of the kid's extortion, but Aimal had a proposition. *Or*, Aimal said, *we can make a deal.* He made his calculated gamble. "We have a dish."

He didn't wait for the Taliban minister to fake disapproval.

"You're just watching the same cassette over and over," Aimal said, "but we have as many channels as you can imagine."

With a splitter and a cable running from his living room to the Talib's house, Aimal could provide the Talib's family all the content in the world while they sat in the secrecy of their own home. All Aimal wanted in return for his silence, and his gift of a thousand hours of programming, was for the Talib judge to let Aimal wire into his power panel so Aimal's family could have 24/7 electricity too.

Now Aimal consumes as much as he wants while one house over, the Talib watches whatever Aimal is watching because Aimal controls the receiver. Aimal, twelve years old, controlling information flow to the block, to the Taliban.

Now with city power, Aimal every night dips his hands in the current of foreign lives, and one day, in his classroom, in real life, a foreigner walks in.

Aimal rubs his eyes. It's as if he himself, from such ardent nightly focus on foreign places, has summoned the visitor down to Earth. A white person from an NGO. A foreigner, offering something. Aimal doesn't know what exactly; it doesn't matter; he wants it. He wants to be with *them*, to put his heels on the dish and climb up the waves into space and then down again to the white world, white girlfriends, money, cheesecake, tall women, pride. The foreigner asks anyone who could use some help from the NGO to raise a hand, and for a moment Aimal forgets his burgeoning pride. The other students know etiquette prevents them from admitting they're poor, but for the moment, all Aimal can see is opportunity. *Everyone knows we're all poor anyway.*

He's seen what his classmates haven't. He knows there's more to life in foreign lands, where boys have their own bedrooms and have girlfriends and their dads who never died of anything violent and who come to them in the morning and say "Son, do you want cheesecake or pancakes?" or something like that, and a chorus of invisible people say *awwww*, and there are so many options of what to eat it's sometimes hard for people to decide. He raises his hand.

The NGO is a revelation. They teach him a trade, feed him, and give him things to bring home. He learns to make men's clothes. They teach him the simple way the fabric falls. He takes to it, though the women's clothes are too much. He can't negotiate the million cuts and darts to make the fabric fold over a more complicated body; the female form holds too many mysteries. But working with all the fresh fabric, he begins to imagine himself in finery. Walking down the street in the clothes he makes for others. Starched and scratchy but brilliantly clean. It's strange to be so close with clothing like that, exotic objects, each one fashioned from the same kind of fabric, rather than his own things sewn from a thousand patches. Now, he looks out at men who wear dresses with collars that stand upright, twinkling metals sewn into the chest, and feels he is actually the same species as them. So why is he not like them?

With the foreign NGO, he learns what it feels like to provide. His brothers are too old for a program meant to keep young boys from idleness and violence, so it's him, the youngest rather than oldest male, who comes home once a month with seven kilograms of cooking oil, a sack of sugar, and a bag of beans. A surge of pride each time he arrives with supplies for his mother.

And the foreign NGO teaches students the rituals of Islam. A gesture to the Taliban so the Taliban won't worry too much about the NGO leading children astray. Aimal learns from infidels how to be faithful. They teach him the *duas* for difficult times, how to come up with a vow when he's in need. *Oh, Allah, by the power of Muhammad, if you let me pass this test, I will pray a hundred ra'akats under the name of the prophet; I will donate to charity . . .* The NGO tells him this is the most powerful kind of prayer, the one he's most likely to need someday. They tell him to remember it.

When the NGO teaches each student a different specialty of Islamic ritual, Aimal draws the straw for funeral rites. They teach him how to wash the body and wrap it just so in the *kafan*. He memorizes the prayers and verses you use to send someone on their way. *Forgive this person his sins so he can enter heaven with you.* He learns all of it, and takes to it, and it's as though they also know he might have to deal with death one day too.

———

He remembers the lessons. A year goes by slowly, but a little less slowly. Then another year, and another. A fraction of childhood passes. The way home through his starving city hasn't changed, but it feels different now that he's doing something with his days. It's still a familiar trek through a forest of gaunt-limbed bodies, and he can read the creases on faces. All these wandering ghosts less connected to the foreigners than he is, until one day, as if by a snap of the fingers, he suddenly can't read anyone at all.

Out on the street, a slow-breaking wave moves through the crowd. Squinting eyes but hiding meaning—like everyone all at once knows something he doesn't. He stops someone on the street. "Explosion in America," the man says. "People are in trouble."

Aimal is confused. *Here* people are in trouble.

At home, his brother seems stricken by the news. Aimal asks, "How far is America?"

Naheb tries to explain in a way that Aimal might understand. "It's . . . well. By car, if you want to go to America, it would take . . . at least a week. Driving day and night."

Neighbors begin to arrive quietly and slip through the door. By now, the rumor has seeped across the block that Aimal can speak the language of frequencies. Today is different, though. On all the channel numbers he knows by heart, there are only movies playing. Behind him in the living room, as he fiddles with the receiver, he hears gasps and whispers, and now Aimal understands that everyone has been fooled. They haven't seen as many movies as he has. They think what they see on the screen is real.

It's real, one of the neighbors says.

Whatever has touched people out in the street has them in its thrall inside too. They've all gone stupid. The dish is picking up a movie. How can they not tell? It couldn't be more obvious: the movie on the screen takes place during the day, but all you have to do is look out the window to see that in real life it's night.

Aimal changes the channel to show the *actual* news. But . . . strange: it plays the same movie.

He tries another channel. The same movie again. Every news channel, almost every *channel*, shows the same movie, and Aimal begins to feel haunted. Naheb comes to his side and whispers to him what no one ever has: *Aimal, dear, in different parts of the world, right now, it's a different time of day.*

Aimal tries to comprehend, but gasps from behind him crash into his thinking because one of the buildings is sort of kneeling down like it's done with all this. *All that dust,* he thinks, as a tidal flow of debris swells up from a building slipping down the screen toward the family carpet. *Dust like we have here.* His neighbors cover their mouths in horror. *Why do you care so much? This is dust like we have here.* Outside, Talibs are celebrating; they've begun singing.

CHAPTER 4

FALL 2001

THE NEXT WEEKS ARE THE MOST WONDERFUL OF HIS LIFE.

The dish no longer shows some foreign world but, miraculously, his own. What a strange and wondrous thing, that his forgotten corner of the Earth is being shown to America, to Europe, to Africa, to itself. He has a feeling like a family growing. Even for a reason like explosions, his home is leaking its qualities around the world. Sharing its dustiness. He goes out at night and adjusts the dish, wondering not what strange new land he'll visit today, but what the world will learn about his. It feels like he's waking up; it feels like life is about to start.

And if life is about to start, the moment of creation arrives suddenly, as a light pulsing off TV Mountain. So bright that night turns to day, and so long that when the accompanying thunder booms across the city, it's like the sound has come back to collect something the explosion forgot. A boom so loud he doesn't just hear it; he feels it with every sense, in his belly and his shaking legs. Sound that moves things, removes the dish from his grasp, relocates his mother. She was standing next to him while he set up the dish and is now on her back, somewhere else. The Americans have arrived.

They must have cut the hydro line because everywhere is dark. When power comes back and he fires up the dish again, Aimal learns that one of the pilots dropping those first bombs was an American woman. He imagines her: tall, pale, he imagines the flight suit, he tries to stop imagining, *be respectful*. The bombing continues. Talibs scatter, their celebration cut so short that Aimal finds it funny. Death becomes

95

less tragic. He sees a pile of Taliban bodies burned in the street by some kind of weapon. A splash of color near a barbecued leg. Aimal recognizes the color as cash. No one goes to take it because the punishment for theft is amputation and the people don't know the Taliban are losing power, though people are starting to know. He has never seen Taliban bodies before; the Talibs always retrieved their brothers quickly. Now no one does because the Talibs who would've retrieved them are scared, or running, lest some tall blonde woman with a bust pressing against a flight suit comes in a plane from America to blow them all away.

More and more Talib bodies litter the street. Near vehicles and outside safe houses in Aimal's neighborhood, Talib bodies are some strange mushrooming species he's never seen before but now sees everywhere. He picks his way down the streets until one day, soon after the bombing begins, he hears a commotion from the horizon, and a procession of trucks comes rolling down into the city.

His countrymen are coming down from the hills, riding behind the American bombs to drive the Talibs out. They come shouting, cheering, playing music from speakers—real music with instruments, not just chants—and Aimal has an idea.

Music.

Music and movies will be legal now, won't they? There will be a release, a countrywide sigh. Aimal is an expert on entertainment after spending the Taliban years in nocturnal study. He imagines a renovation to the family's poorly stocked shop, converting it into a rental business.

Soon, the Taliban are gone. He hears the closest gunshots. Hiding fighters up in the trees of New City Park, picked off like game birds. He hears the thud of their bodies on dirt.

Aimal begins feeding the demand. Hawking *Rambo* and the Arnold movies and the bootlegged Bollywood numbers to people who want to blast it from car speakers. To him, the city seems to be rejoicing, and he's a kid making a small cut for his mother off the joy. A lesson learned: a good salesman doesn't need to convince people to buy something; a good salesman just needs to find what they already want and give it to them.

HIS CLIENTELE GREW. HE MADE FRIENDS WHO LIKED HIS HUSTLE, hearing Aimal had the latest Bollywood soundtrack to bump from their Corolla windows, throb the *Mashallah* decals on rear windshields. Kabul shook. A friend named Nasir came by, a cousin of a neighbor, not quite family. He smiled at the boy's pluck. Nasir was a kindred spirit, picking his teeth and enjoying the spectacle of Aimal upselling his patrons. A bit older than Aimal, Nasir always had cash to burn, cash that he'd procured from some unknown place older boys went. When they played poker, Nasir took adult-sized risks—like he knew he could always make more if he got cleaned out today.

Finally, Aimal got too curious to avoid the rude question: "What do you do to get all this money?"

Nasir smiled. He'd only done what Aimal had done: taken a leap into a new market. It was just a bigger, better market. He dealt the cards, and they sat atop upturned boxes in the store: American money was pouring in, right? You've seen it. Soldiers and spies and preachers of various faiths. Preaching the gender stuff, "economic development." All arriving with fat American paychecks. "Brother, you wouldn't believe the foreign paychecks." They get bonuses just for being willing to come to our shitty little country, and one thing the foreigners always needed was a ride. "Brother," Nasir said, pushing his stack to the center, "people with a taste of that foreign money are buying cars like you wouldn't believe." Anyone with cash. Cars for themselves. Cars for their friends. Cars to turn around and sell for a little extra. Cars a better sign of status even than a house because a house can show status in only one place.

But, Nasir said, here was the catch: foreigners didn't just come with a lot of money; they came with a lot of fucking rules too. Whole systems of dos and don'ts they were trying to lay over the country. It's not like before. Foreigners must not like buying and selling things; they make it so fucking hard. "Cars aren't like bootlegged Bollywood DVDs, brother. Now, you want a car? You need it to be registered, taxed, inspected, titled." Steered along a whole elaborate scavenger hunt. Rich people want cars to drive and sell and look at in their driveways, but don't want to spend days crisscrossing the city for signatures. Nasir flicked a toothpick at the door. "That's where I come in," he said. "And, if you want, where you come in."

Nasir hooked him up on a trial run with a dealer moving a dozen vehicles at a time from Iran, and Aimal set out on his first ministerial treasure hunt. A seventh grader driving unregistered cars around the city, trying to navigate a maze of new rules. Getting permits and tax forms and signatures from offices all over Kabul. He was immediately overwhelmed. He'd hardly started on his first job before he had to pull over, touch his fingertips to his forehead, and start sketching out a map for himself. He was learning the routes in a way he never had before. Places he'd never been in his own city. He was finding out how a Western government worked, or tried to.

The swirl of American rules twisted into choke points, stations manned by gate agents with their hands out. Bribes were required, and some sneaky unseen bureau was already on the case. Nasir told him the rumors: someone sending undercover agents on mini-sting operations. Giving cash bribes with tracked serial numbers and busting anyone found with the marked bills. So what to do? A kid like him with no weight to throw around couldn't get a vehicle registered without paying people off, but cash bribes were dangerous. He needed an untraceable way.

It took only a day to figure it out: top-up phone cards. He bought a few and slipped them into documents he was handing over for signatures. The only way an investigator could trace the payment would be by the number beneath the silvery latex strip, which was hidden until the bribed official scratched it off to top up his cell-phone minutes, and then the card was thrown out anyway.

He got to know a map of important people, the ones who'd look out for him. In the office that signed off on customs forms, gave permission to get a plate number, *and* approved all necessary requirements for registration, the boss took a liking to him. "You're the youngest person I've seen here!" He took Aimal, young and harmless looking, into his office and signed Aimal's fistful of registration forms without bribe or cajoling.

He smiled. "Here. Now you can go home early." And he did. Aimal still had school.

For six months, the registration boss signed titles for Aimal without any bribe, and then, suddenly, like a parent pushing a coddled child to stand on its own, he stopped. A curtain dropped across his face. "It's time to start paying."

Now Aimal had to go see the secretary like everyone else. Wait in line, pay the bribe, get his forms back. Wait in line all over again, to see a man who had been his guardian but was now just a leech. Aimal needed another angle.

The next day, he arrived at the office but stood off to the side, studying a line of people taller than him inching forward. Walk into the secretary's office to pay their bribe, walk out, walk across the hall, wait for the boss. A constant zombie drone, and it occurred to him as a flash: a step was missing. How did the boss know who had paid the bribe and who hadn't? There were no phone calls between the secretary and the boss. No walkie-talkie in the offices. No way for the secretary to tell the boss, "OK, Aimal's paid, and his forms are in order. You can give him your signature now."

Was there a camera system? The registration boss watching the secretary's office on a TV screen? None that Aimal had seen in the boss's office. There was something going on out of sight. *Qaf, Yeh, Ghani*, they were playing a game no one else noticed. He went to the secretary's office to pay the bribe, but this time he kept his sunglasses on. He pretended to be distracted by a phone call, stood up, and walked to a corner of the room. "Yes, General," he said on the phone to no one. "I'm here in the office now. No, General, not until later. I'll stop first at—" He pointed his head toward the window but peered from the side of his sunglasses over the secretary's shoulder, as the secretary looked through the forms, slipping the top-up phone credit card out of the stack and into a drawer, then tracing over the text with a pen, reading along to make sure it was all filled out correctly. "OK, General, I'll be there—" And then, just like that, he saw it: the slightest flick of the wrist, the pen just barely touching the paper before the secretary flipped to the next page.

Outside the office, Aimal took his sunglasses off, brought the pages nearly to his nose, squinted, and sure enough, there it was: a tiny mark, impossible to see if you weren't looking for it and almost impossible even if you were. A tiny blue dash, hidden up against a letter.

When he walked into the boss's office and handed his forms over, the boss skimmed the pages, stopped for a moment on each one, and checked—Aimal now understood—for that tiny blue mark. When he saw it, he knew the bribe had been paid, and he gave his signature.

The next day, the secretary made a tiny checkmark, in green, on a different part of the page. So: they changed the code each day.

Aimal went home, rifled through the cobwebbed boxes of unsold inventory from the old store, found a retractable ballpoint with six different ink chambers, and brought it with him to work. He had five vehicles to register the next day, but in the secretary's office, he handed over the forms for just one. He paid his top-up card bribe for one vehicle. Then he walked out of the secretary's office, went down a hall and studied the application, looking for the code. He found a tiny green crescent near the bottom of a page.

He used the green ink chamber to make tiny crescents on the other four applications and then waited in line for the boss's office. When the boss flipped through the pages, he saw the code marked on all five applications, believed the bribe had been paid on each, and gave his signature for all five vehicles.

He'd found the angle, the unseen game. He'd played it so seamlessly that he saw a second revenue stream. He could offer other agents his services, offer them a cheaper way to get their signatures. If they didn't ask how, they could pay him half what they paid the secretary, and he'd get their applications signed. Each morning, he went to the secretary's office, paid the bribe for a single vehicle, went outside, found the nearly invisible code, copied it on the applications for the rest of the vehicles he was trying to register that day, and on applications for anyone else who'd paid him the smaller bribe.

It didn't take long for the boss to realize the bribes were drying up. He couldn't figure out why. The volume of vehicles kept increasing. His profits should have increased too, but they'd leveled off, then fallen. He fired the secretary for skimming, then fired another secretary.

It took him months to stumble on the notion that it must have been one of the applicants behind the missing funds, and longer still to suspect the kid he'd taken under his wing.

"You come here and take my money!" He shoved Aimal into his office, grabbing at his pockets looking for pens. "Where are they? Why do you have so many different color pens?"

"Because they smell good," Aimal said. "Because I'm a student."

"I'll send you to jail!"

"For what crime?" The temperature rose, but words came easily. "For what crime, brother? Tell me what crime is it to steal from a thief?"

Aimal was unintimidated, but he knew it would now get harder for him to operate here. And just as the boss of registration learned Aimal was cutting into his take, Aimal learned that Nasir, still his partner and his introduction into this racket, was cutting into the government's. Nasir had started volunteering to pay the taxes at the bank, which was strange since he was the elder and Aimal could have done that busy work. So one day, Aimal followed him. He found out that Nasir never actually went to the bank. Instead, Nasir stopped in a parking lot with a copy of the bank's stamp he somehow had, and applied PAID marks himself.

Aimal didn't like it. This was wrong. It was too dangerous, and it was immoral. Aimal had been stealing from a thief. This was totally different. This was stealing from the government. This was stealing from the people, really.

He tried getting in Nasir's face about it, but Nasir didn't care what Aimal thought and had no plans to stop. They were flying too close to the sun. Meanwhile, the halls were growing ever more crowded with pushy citizens attached to the swell of vehicles crowding the city's already overstretched roads. A system designed by the Soviets for a population of a half million was now facing almost three million a year as émigrés flooded back into the newly liberated city. He needed to move on. He called a friend from the neighborhood who also had some kind of car-related job. Over energy drinks and cigarettes, the neighbor got to talking about what exactly he was doing. He was a driver, he said, for a particular kind of company. "I'm working with the foreigners," he said. "It's nice, man. I learn English more. And they give you tips. They don't scream at you much, as long as you don't ask too many stupid questions. On the weekends, when these people go for parties, we pick them up, and sometimes they give us fifty-dollar, hundred-dollar tips. You make more in tips than your salary." For seven dollars a ride, the company drove foreigners all over the city, so the cars couldn't be too old, they had to be clean, and the drivers had to speak English. That would be an issue, but he'd picked up enough English practicing in front of the dish, and he could fake the rest with body language. He'd make it work. He had to. A chance to work with the Rambos and the Arnolds. The large Americans who'd left behind their large, beautiful, American girlfriends and their flexible kind fathers and their big diesel cars to come here.

His neighbor got him a meeting with Muqim Jamshady, the company's owner. Muqim issued a series of quizzes. Aimal did well; by now he knew the streets, and he had a pocket full of shortcuts. Muqim explained his incentive structure. Drivers got to keep their tips, and if Aimal made enough, Muqim would add to the tip money himself. He incentivized good customer service. He would compensate drivers who had ideas to make the business better, and the best drivers would get to drive the nicer cars. The only rule was not giving personal cell numbers out to clients: we're here to serve them; they shouldn't think of us as their friends. Other than that, drive safe, be good to the foreigners, get your share of all the foreign money they're coming in with.

Aimal could hardly contain himself. *God must really love me*, he thought. *I've arrived*. What better job could there be? Besides, he could tell that Muqim was the kind of boss to look after his employees. All that was left was a clerical matter. Muqim said, "Just let me check your driver's license."

It hadn't occurred to Aimal that he needed one. He hadn't heard of such a thing before the Americans came, and in all the time he'd been driving around the city registering new vehicles, he'd been too young for a license. Anyway, it was the vehicles that needed all the documentation. No one had asked for *his* documents. "I forgot it. It's not in my pocket right now."

"Well, next time, bring it, and we'll get you started."

Aimal thought of Nasir and his forgery. After two days, he'd added three years to his age and had a passable driver's license. He was ready to meet the foreigners.

CHAPTER 5

2006

As the NATO coalition expanded and the number of foreign troops rose to 50,000, then 65,000, the number of foreign NGO workers grew too. More foreigners meant more passengers unable to take regular taxis because they couldn't speak the language, and because they were scared. More companies like Muqim's sprang up, some trying to serve foreigners the way Muqim was, some sending cooks and guards to safe houses. A hundred new hustles emerged, but Aimal was learning the life of a driver. Watching the other drivers, learning their habits. How when French people called, all the drivers had to go to the bathroom at the same time—the line on the French was that they were proud and bad tippers. How when someone called from the growing archipelago of bars catering to deep-pocketed foreigners—L'Atmosphere, Taverna, Crazy Eight, a whole nightlife flowering behind blast walls—all the drivers leaped up from their mats. L'Atmosphere was the bistro where locals wore black suits and served wine. Crazy Eight the one where the Chinese girls got drunk and did sex things for money, sent the foreign soldiers out to the cars excited, liquored up, loose with their cash, and you could score a big tip from a sated American. Sometimes the drivers drove the girls too, back and forth to their boardinghouses. Sometimes the girls seemed to be having just as good a time as the men, sometimes they seemed at least as drunk, and if Aimal was called to Crazy Eight to pick up the women, sometimes there was a bonus in that. Playful fingers, the shock of cold hands slipping under his belt. "Sorry," in accents as thick as his. "No money for trip."

He came to appreciate those girls, the eight or nine of them moving in procession to the restaurant every night like miners to the cage at shift change. Coming out soiled but flush. Happy and elastic, or else needing to distract themselves from a toxin they'd been exposed to. He came to adore them. They treated him like a foreigner. He felt honor around them, a mutual respect. They were symbiotes in this evolving habitat, the girls far from home, and the drivers like Aimal, two families looking after each other. But the girls sometimes seemed so drunk and wired that they didn't know what they were doing. Shy and quiet on the way in, giddy, released on the way back.

When he was dispatched to drive foreigners back and forth to the bars, the luster of being around them shone bright. Even if he had to sit, parked outside one of the new bars, sometimes for hours, waiting for the foreigners to finally come claim the car they'd called. And even though when they did, they weren't always like the Chinese girls. Some were as kind, but some treated him like a feature of the landscape, an append- age that came with the car. Like he had nothing better to do than wait for them to finish a fresh round inside. Or worse, some of them treated him like he was part of a conspiracy to inconvenience them, guilty for the homesickness they must've felt, and for all the inefficiencies of a culture they didn't get. Like he was to blame for the frustrations of a language barrier, as if he wanted to not understand them.

But he could take it. Because even then, even when they were rude to him, they were *foreigners*. They were allowed to be rude. They'd stepped off the screen in his living room and into the seat behind him, and he was light-headed with his good luck. His dreams were coming true. He was flying high. He wanted the bigger tips, the nicer car. He wanted to meet as many foreigners as he could. He wanted to absorb their foreign- ness. His quarry was the night; he was the best then. Less traffic, and though there were hardly any streetlights, he didn't need them. He knew routes by feel and timing. *About 10 seconds at about 60 km/h until the turnoff.* He learned how to work the checkpoints, even though the security branches were touchier at night.

He learned that even police smoked hashish, pulling from the herb to keep them awake but relaxed. He decided everyone needed some way to get high in this country, maybe in life, even police, but liquor was too hard on their salary. He learned where the best hashish dealers were and where the worst dealers were, he learned which bodega had a secret stock of Russian beer hidden under ice cream in the cooler, and which shop on Flower Street had the knockoff Johnnie Walker in the back, how you asked the florist for "something foreign" and got an elaborate bouquet, big and colorful enough to hide the bottles in the middle, and he learned the little intricacies in how people acted when they didn't know they were being watched. To the foreigners, being watched by an Afghan didn't seem to feel like being watched at all. If you got the foreigners misbehaving, if you got them loose, they sometimes produced opportunity.

Aimal was out on a night run one weekend, working a gig with one of the other companies, ferrying drunk foreigners from their safe houses to a party and back, when the radio crackled to life. Another driver, Barialay, had picked up a couple of soaked-through soldiers from Crazy Eight. Barialay was in a frenzy; he came over the radio incoherent. Screaming about the sexed-up foreigners in the back of his car: "Boss, boss, boss! This fucker is poking me! They're trying to touch my ass!"

Aimal dialed the radio down because Barialay's was octaving up and Aimal still wanted things comfortable for his passengers, but he listened as the boss came over the radio clipped to Aimal's hip. "Don't scream. Don't scream at them. Don't say anything to them. Stay quiet. They're just drunk."

Barialay was hysterical. "No, no, boss. They're touching my ass. I don't care that they're foreigners; I'll punch them in the fucking face!"

"Barialay, calm down. They probably have weapons. Be the nice guy. Everything will be OK."

A beat of silence. Aimal reached down and thumbed the volume up a notch. "Barialay: *OK*?" More silence. "Barialay?"

"Boss, boss, this fucker is . . ." and then *BOOM*, an explosion over the radio that every driver all over the city listening in knew was a gunshot, too loud to be a small gun.

The boss's turn to be frantic. "Barialay? Barialay?" There was no answer. "Barialay? *Answer!*"

The radio was silent, all the company's drivers around the city waiting for Barialay to come back on and say he was OK. Aimal went dead silent. The foreigners in the back of his car were quiet too, picking up what they needed to.

The boss came back on, but with a different voice, like everything had changed. "Everyone. All drivers. To the America base. *Now.*"

Aimal U-turned and gunned it in the other direction. The foreigners in back protested. "Whoa, wait! Where are you going?" He ignored them. He didn't know what the plan was, maybe to gather forces and show strength. Though what strength would a few unarmed drivers in Corollas show at an American military base?

When Aimal arrived at the base, Barialay's car was there—perhaps a good sign? Aimal got out and went to the driver's side, and found Barialay, still behind the wheel, unmoving. Aimal reached for his shoulder, and Barialay's eyes twitched. Stunned into silence, but alive.

Aimal poked his head in the window. The inside of the car was pungent with the smell of gunpowder, a surge of cordite in a confined space. Thick enough that it hurt his nostrils, and he thought it might be poisoning his friend. By the floodlights coming off the base, he could see two holes in the roof next to Barialay's head. Two bullets had passed within inches. Maybe Barialay had gone deaf. He'd been that close to having his head blown off.

Other drivers started arriving. The boss arrived. From the base, an American officer emerged, held out a hand, and whisked him inside.

Aimal began to worry.

What happened now? Would they try to shut him up? Would they take him to Guantanamo? Would they execute all of the drivers to be rid of the evidence?

A few minutes later, the boss emerged with a thick envelope in his hand, the American a few steps behind.

The American asked for Barialay next.

Aimal tried to shake Barialay from his stupor and help him to his feet, shoving him with enough momentum to make it toward the base, the American's hand reaching for the small of his back.

When Barialay emerged, he was enlivened. He could hardly stop talking. "These white people shook my hand. 'Sorry, brother. Sorry, sorry, accept our apologies.' Then they gave me this money." He showed the wadded envelope, and Aimal had a strange thought: *I wish someone would fire a gun near my head too.*

CHAPTER 6

EARLY SEPTEMBER 2007

THERE WERE OTHER THREATS. IT WASN'T JUST DRUNK FOREIGNERS mishandling weapons and nearly lobotomizing their drivers. The Taliban, it turned out, weren't entirely gone. The country had gone a few years without hearing much from them, but President Karzai and the Americans looking to Karzai for guidance kept trying to attack them, even the Talibs who'd given up and disappeared into outer provinces. Now, as if riled from hibernation, they started to attack. Security everywhere was beginning to deteriorate. The foreign armies were less and less able to maintain stability. Aimal started to hear of Talibs blowing themselves up just to kill the people around them, or blowing up cars while still inside them. Even born into war, Aimal hadn't seen that kind of thing before.

And still more foreigners came. They came not just to fight but to work, build, proselytize about their better religions. To teach their better medicines and their more modern systems of government, make money, give money, and bear witness to their own largesse. Some coming as little more than tourists for a spectacle, the sights and sounds and vigorous traffic of a country changing so fast that parts of it felt foreign even to the drivers working its streets every day. Aimal was energized every time he hosted a new foreigner in his car, even though there was a little riddle in each of them. Why leave a place like America, Canada, why leave Europe to come here? Why on Earth leave a place with no dust and no violence, where most people had fathers and most fathers cooked breakfast? Why would anyone be *here* unless they had to be? Muqim sent him to a public event where foreigners were due to show up for some incomprehensible reason: a public celebration of a martyred holy warrior. The one with the ridiculous nickname, "The Lion of the Panjshir." A legendary enemy of the Taliban, supported by America and beloved by some people from the Panjshir Valley but hated by others, by those who lived in the Kabul neighborhoods he helped lay waste to back during the civil war years.

Why celebrate HIM? Aimal thought. *All he and his ophthalmologist deputy did was destroy my city.* And why do it in a showy public event at a big stadium? Wasn't that inviting trouble? Wasn't this just a taunt to the stirring Taliban, who were already starting to launch attacks—wild, new kinds of attacks?

But this was a national holiday, and President Karzai was due to make a rare public appearance. *Oh well*, Aimal thought, driving toward the stadium to pick up two foreigners Muqim had assigned him. *Karzai is as much the foreigners' president as he is ours.* Aimal got as close to the stadium as he could but couldn't find the foreigners he was supposed to pick up. He called in to the dispatcher, who handed him over to Muqim.

"They're by the gate," Muqim said.

"*I'm* by the gate. I don't see them."

"Park your car and go into the stadium. You have to find them."

Aimal wedged the car near the stadium off a main street, got out, and walked toward the stadium, but just as he got inside, he heard the *pop pop pop* of small-arms fire. Then yelling, and then all hell broke loose. People running in all different directions, more gunshots, or were they rocks hitting concrete? People started to stampede, Karzai was whisked off the stage, Aimal was picked up by the wave of escaping bodies and driven a dozen yards back out of the stadium. He tried to swim his way against the current. He had to find the foreigners. There was yelling all around him, and the press of bodies surging with its own purpose. If foreigners waiting for Afghan Logistics got hurt, he'd be in trouble, Muqim would be in trouble, the company would be in trouble. He jumped up and down to see above the mass, swinging his head and scanning the sea of bodies for white faces, looking for color that popped against the crowd. Left, right, above, up in the stands. The crowd shifted, and he was carried farther outside the gate, past an eddy of people massing around the entrance. All the while trying to lock onto the face of each person flung from the stadium. And as he was driven farther and farther away, he zeroed in on a face a shade paler than the rest, a hundred yards from the stadium looking lost and kind of homeless. Someone who didn't belong. Aimal tried to claw his way out of the crowd.

This guy's white.

He breaststroked over torsos and necks to get closer.

But not *white* white.

As Aimal neared, he felt a curl of resentment. He was in danger because of this person, and this person didn't even look that special. Not a Rambo, not an Arnold—not some square-jawed specimen like Americans from the NATO coalition bases and Aimal's nights with the dish. *He hardly looks different from me; how come he has all the luck? How come he gets to travel and have documents and probably had a dad who asked him whether he wanted pancakes or cheesecakes every morning?* "Hey," Aimal said when he got close enough to me, "you looking for the taxi?"

———

AIMAL CLICKED THE RADIO TO GET MUQIM. "I DIDN'T FIND THEM, BUT I got a different foreigner. Tell the other driver to get the other foreigners."

Around him, chants were starting to get ugly. *Fuck Americans!* But they were chanting in Dari, and standing before him, I clearly had no idea what they were saying.

Muqim came back over the radio: "Who do you have?"

Aimal turned to look at me. He clicked the radio back on, replying in Dari, "I don't know. A white dude. What do you want to know? He's a white dude who looks American, so I'm taking him."

The chants got louder; people were starting to notice us. The crowd pulsed forward. Aimal clicked the radio again, but as he tried to speak to Muqim, I interrupted. "Hey, man, can I ask these guys some questions?"

Aimal tried to be polite. "No," he said, "this isn't the time for that."

Around us, he could sense the temperature rising, close to tipping into outright violence. He could hear it in the chants. He could see I had no idea. I wasn't cooperating.

"We have to go, *now*," he said, and clicked back on the radio. "Muqim, I've—"

"Why?"

Aimal put the radio down. "This *not* the time for questions!" He tried to get back on the radio. "Muqim, I—"

"Wait, why not?" Aimal turned to me. *Who the fuck is this guy?*

"Sir, we have to get to the car. We have to leave because if something goes wrong, then God might save you, but I'm not. I can't fight a hundred people for you." *Fuck it.* He clipped the radio to his belt, grabbed my hand, and yanked. "Run!"

And now we were skipping over boulders, Aimal gliding easily even in his sandals, our hands slipping apart and reaching again for each other, him checking to make sure I was still with him. Finding his car, helping me in, and zooming off before I had the door swung shut. Aimal checked the rearview, checked on his passenger, but focused mostly on the road: he knew he had to get clear of the stadium area before a security cordon came down and cars trying to escape were stopped or shot at. He peeked out of the corner of his eye at me. I looked like I was in shock, frozen like Barialay after the shooting. He'd get in trouble if he delivered a passenger in shock, so, engine revving, Aimal tried easing me back into consciousness. He tried to get me talking, then immediately regretted it. I began peppering him with questions. What happened? Why were they shooting? Who was shooting? Who are you? How do you know English? By the time he pulled up to Turkish Mountain, I had glommed onto him like a drowning man. Afghan Logistics had other clients he had to get to, people around the city waiting for rides, but this one foreigner was insistent. I had more questions; I had an idea.

"I'll pay you for two rides. Tell them that I needed you to take me somewhere else." Aimal sighed. He could use a cigarette anyway.

We sat there for another hour. Talking, me not letting up. I had end-less questions, so many that I wasn't done even when the pretend ride had to end. I reached into my bag and tried to give him a hundred-dollar bill. Aimal felt a stab to his pride. Why did Americans think Afghans only save people for money? *What did he think I was going to do? Leave him to die if I didn't think he'd pay me extra?* But it would be too rude to refuse, and anyway, he was beginning to feel something special may have just happened. The endless questions had shifted from annoying, noise and desperation, toward feeling like genuine interest. He knew a white guy couldn't actually be interested in *him*, but it felt special. He felt noticed, even if the white guy wasn't *white* white.

This connection was beginning to feel like it might not have been an accident. And this didn't feel like just another client. This one seemed needier than most. Maybe they'd see each other again. He knew he wasn't supposed to give out his phone number right now, and maybe it was the adrenaline or maybe it was the extra nicotine, but he felt like breaking the rules. This one was different, after all; he might get himself killed without Aimal's help. And he was more *familiar*. It turned out that not all Americans were made of bigger, better stuff than Aimal.

Aimal took the tip money home. He'd give it to his mother to hold on to. He had an idea of what to do with it.

CHAPTER 7

LATE SEPTEMBER 2007

AIMAL DROVE AWAY FROM THAT FIRST, STRANGE MEETING, THAT near miss of an escape, thinking, *We're not all that different, him and me. The same blood moving through us*. Why had he exalted Americans? This foreigner was still sacred because he was a foreigner, he was a guest, but he wasn't some lofty being, no man-God like the ones on the dish.

What he *was* was an inquisitor. Endless questions while Aimal tried to focus on the road, and now that an American had his phone number, Aimal realized he'd only invited more. He'd made sure to explain that he couldn't respond personally to requests for rides. Those still had to go to the company dispatch, but this new American didn't seem to get it. Or just didn't care that Aimal had rules to follow. Aimal started getting calls at all hours asking for rides, as if Aimal had no other life and didn't need sleep. Questions about this or that blast. "Sir," Aimal pleaded, "please to call the *dispatch* number, and ask to *dispatch* if you want for I should be driver."

But even annoyed, Aimal still took pity because this was a foreigner trying to make news reports all by himself. Aimal knew from other clients that foreign reporters were supposed to have entire bureaus supporting them. Translators, security staff, photographers, drivers—they were supposed to be teams. This was just one confused-seeming kid trying all by himself, and Aimal found he could relate. Aimal decided, *screw it*, he'd try to help. He'd do what he could, he'd find a way to keep it secret from his company, and when

I asked him, "If you hear about things happening, can you call me?," Aimal decided he would do that too. He would use all his accumulated knowledge of the capital city shortcuts for this new guest, an underdog without the support his peers had, just like Aimal was. He'd deploy his gift for seeing the game unseen by most, for talking and talking and talking until locked doors gave up and let him through. He would do what he could to keep me safe. And to help me fulfill my wild mission, however impossible it seemed.

FIRST, IT MEANT KEEPING AN EAR OUT. IN THE MORNINGS, AT THE barracks, Muqim woke the drivers to wash themselves, pray, wash the cars. Then he gathered them together and shared whatever security rumors he'd heard.

It was in these briefings that Aimal learned how connected his boss was. But then, of course Muqim was connected; he had to be in order to run a business here, especially this kind. Muqim's company cocooned foreigners in a brief moment of home and charged for the privilege. The whole proposition was viable only if it kept them removed from even the notion of violence. So Muqim held frequent meetings with officials from NGOs, with different government representatives, with people from security and intelligence services, and sometimes with traditional-looking people who came by the office. Muqim knew so much about potential threats that Aimal wondered if he might have a way of getting intel directly from insurgents. A businessman could speak to all types of characters without the bureaucracy that slowed government agencies, and Muqim often seemed to have a read on threats that was at least as good as the more official services. Muqim kept the drivers updated about threat chatter so they could prepare safer routes for their passengers and avoid certain neighborhoods, but Aimal started to pay special attention to those neighborhoods. Because he knew I was a kid alone competing against big publications, and because he knew I wasn't cut out to survive in his country alone. He'd started to worry about me even when I wasn't with him, this lost child who could stand oblivious in the middle of a riot and ask, "Can I do some interviews?"

So after the morning briefing, Aimal started excusing himself from the drivers' barracks, stepping outside for a cigarette, picking up the phone, and breaking his boss's confidence to read me in. "Yah, Jaff. How are you? Also, today please to stay away from US embassy, German embassy, and Kabul City Center. OK?"

"Wait, *why?*" Always with the *why*. "How do you know? Can we go? Where's the threat from?"

If an explosion had already happened, the threat already mostly past, Aimal heard about it first because he'd been focusing on that neighborhood already. And because when he wasn't driving, he'd started sitting in the room with dispatchers. At any given moment the company had drivers all over the city. The dispatch room was the central node of what was in effect a roving, street-level intelligence service with eyes and ears nearly everywhere. The foreign militaries tried to predict threats, foreign spies plied their networks, and the NATO coalition would soon use aerostats—high-tech tethered blimps packed with sensors, floating above the city—but no one had better intelligence than the taxi company Aimal happened to work for. Between Muqim's businessman ability to meet almost anyone, and the wheeled de facto data-collection network constantly circling the city, Aimal found himself not just perfectly positioned to keep me safe. He could give me a leg up.

His thinking evolved. He didn't want me near danger by myself, but as long as he was with me it was OK for me to make my reports; he knew he could keep me safe.

If Muqim told the drivers about a threat no one else knew about, or if Aimal overheard something while sitting with the dispatchers, he'd step outside, call me, tell me to call dispatch right away and ask for Aimal. He'd hang up with me, snuff out his cigarette, step back inside, and pretend to be surprised when the dispatcher said, "We have a call from a customer in Area 3 who wants a ride but only wants to go with you . . ."

"Weird." *Grab a radio from the dock, the keys, head out before more questions.*

And then he was racing through the streets before authorities could start shutting them down, meeting me at the guesthouse, me hustling out with a backpack and a giant camera, and then we were off again. Aimal unpocketing every accumulated shortcut for me. Dialing up his favorite techno remix of "My Heart Will Go On" as we raced toward our violence, summoning up the map he'd drawn and then memorized back when he was registering vehicles for rich people. Carving out the quickest path through a crowded city grinding to a halt, save for him and his guest, this one shooting comet. Driving by sight and sound and sonar, using all lanes, he felt young, but he'd been driving since he was younger. Since seventh grade he'd been coevolving with a car so he knew it like his own body. A map of its angles and muscle memory. This was just an extension of his arms, swerving out into oncoming traffic, twirling around the hapless rotary traffic cops waving their red ping-pong paddle batons, and then inventing a parking place near whatever smoking rubble he knew would be there. Delivering his passenger to the tragedy, revved up and excited, before the other foreigners with their bureaus and big cameras and those big puffy things attached to their microphones could arrive.

He began a months-long tour of the city's grimmest exhibits with his strange new needy guest, and for a while the stress of looking after me kept him looking away from the extraordinary forces tearing apart his neighbors. Bodies that looked like his brothers, parts of bodies that could have been parts of his brothers. He found himself less reluctant to take tips. After his fourth time taking me to some awful thing I wanted him to take me to, we began our now familiar dance. Wrestling against a passenger trying to shove twenty extra dollars in his breast pocket. "I'm your driver. Ride is seven dollars! Please, I cannot to accept. This is shame to me."

"No, no, you're not *just* my driver. You're like . . . a partner, right? You're doing the translating; you're finding the stories. You're doing like four things. I'd be an asshole if I only paid you for one of the things. What way is that to treat a friend?"

And fireworks went off in his chest. That word—*friend*. Why did it fill him with pride? An American, a real foreigner, calling him a friend. Did that mean I *liked* him? Maybe even respected him, for more than just his forced smile with security guards and his shortcuts? Could that be true?

Aimal tried not to get his hopes up. It's easy to *say* the word "friend," after all, but just saying it didn't mean all that much. And still, he was filled by the pride that comes from being seen by the people who matter most. So he decided he didn't mind so much that I complicated his life. That I called his phone constantly. "Who's that?" Muqim asked, when he caught Aimal on the phone, sitting in the dispatch room.

"My mom."

Other drivers gave me rides sometimes, when Aimal was already out with another customer, or when Muqim purposefully sent someone else, as if trying to suss out what was going on with this one client. In the barracks they started to joke. Just like they kept scouting reports on groups—the French were undesirables, the people from the NATO bases were the prizes, the night trips to Crazy Eight were the holy grail—they had nicknames for individual customers too. The big colonel they drove around was Colonel Buffer because "buffer" was their word for subwoofer and the colonel had a voice like a trunk-sized speaker. This one, though, the one who clung to Aimal like a child was the *Afghan-American* because he acted stupid like the Afghans and didn't seem any more sophisticated than they were. This one wasn't some blond specimen raised on roomfuls of food. They made fun of him back in the barracks. Wiry, dark, and frowning like them. No better than they were, really, skinny and kind of ragged looking. Poorer-seeming than other foreigners, but somehow still always tipping, and tipping Aimal the best. I made fun of their English, but I made fun of Aimal's the most, and one day he decided I made fun of him because I was trying to help him get better, so when I laughed in his face, he got goose bumps and said thank you.

Once Aimal decided he could start accepting tips, he told his mother he was saving for something special. He decided not to keep any of the money for himself. He gave all of it to her to hold on to, while he tried to build up the courage to ask me something he worried I'd find offensive. Or threatening, or gay, or aggressive.

But I kept asking for him to pick me up, and his worry wouldn't survive so much exposure to someone who seemed to need him so much. Now that we were seeing each other several times a week, he began to feel that perhaps it was not just this one American, but *Americans* he was actually not so different from. Proximity to this version that came in a more accessible form, and sat next to him in the front rather than the back, gave him a confidence that verged on invulnerability. So once he'd saved up enough tip money, he asked his mother if, should I accept, Aimal might invite me over for dinner. She looked at him like he was a schoolboy with an out-of-his-league crush, walking himself into a embarrassment.

"He won't feel safe in our house," she said. "Why would an American want to come to *our* house? He may think you're taking him here to kill him. He may not think it's professional. Aimal, dear, you're his employee."

He'd been over all this in his head already. He'd worried about those things and settled them. And *he'd* provided all the money, so it wasn't really up to her, was it? He was even paying for the cooking oil. He insisted. She shrugged.

———

WHEN HE FINALLY SUMMONED THE COURAGE TO MAKE THE INVITATION, a strange thing happened. To him, I seemed not just willing to go, but proud to be invited, *touched*, even eager. Aimal felt honored. He took his mother out to Butcher Street the next day, and together they spent all the tip money he had on the finest mutton, lamb, the healthiest-looking chicken. It had to be the cleanest; he couldn't have his guest getting sick. His mother and sister disappeared into the kitchen for two days, hunched over lamb-infused saffron *pulao*, the dumpling-like *mantu*, and sweet pistachio-flaked *firini* between multiple trips to the bodega for a fridge full of soda. *How much do Americans eat?* They needed double that amount, triple; they'd bankrupt themselves if they had to, making it look like they were wealthy.

And when the momentous day finally came, Aimal bringing an actual foreigner into his house, I slipped my shoes off, slipped on the communal indoor sandals, and Aimal thought I actually seemed OK. Not disgusted. Smiling the whole time. Was I already drunk? It felt right. Maybe we *were* friends. Aimal felt just a sliver of shame that he could only afford to invite me once; he wanted his mother to prepare three feasts a week. If he'd known I would accept, that I wouldn't be afraid . . . Aimal needed to drive more, make more tips; he needed to show I was welcome in his house and it wasn't a hardship to have me. He tucked me into a comfortable corner of the floor, carefully assembled a small wall of soda cans for me to choose from, and couldn't believe it. We waited for the women in the kitchen, and I watched TV in the sitting room with him. The same room where foreigners on the television had distracted him from hunger and boredom during the Taliban, and it was like one of those foreigners had come through the dish, crawled through the wires, and leaped off the screen into the room. Aimal looked at the person he'd brought into his home. *I might be capable of almost anything.* His mother called to say the first course was ready.

CHAPTER 8

OCTOBER 2007

THE INSURGENCY WORSENED. HIS LIFE WAS CHANGING AT THE same time the war was changing. Aimal gained a friend, and the war became a war. The capital city became a coliseum with the Taliban, terrorists backed by Pakistani intelligence, old awakening insurgent groups, and new insurgent groups all showing off. A competition for how many pounds of ammonium nitrate and daisy-chained antitank mines you could sneak into the city and detonate.

Aimal mostly listened to it in the dispatch room. The sound of his city being reshaped by explosive force, in the hiccupy voices of other drivers calling in, trying to keep it together. They stuttered, and there were long pauses. Half the story, and Aimal's mind applied the other half. He pictured things. The drivers' frightened, staticky chirps yanked up memories and shot color through them: dead Talibs on the street when the Americans first came, the thudding of their bodies next to the bigger trees. A bus ferrying a dead girl past his house, blackened bodies blocking a route from school. Off-duty drivers slept next to him, the lights were often dimmed, and that made it easier to see.

Most customers wanted to stay away from the violence as much as he did. But if he was to be a friend to his new friend, he'd keep running up against it. This new friend who wanted Aimal to come along and watch. Faces pressed up against the glass, prying his eyes to let the horror in. But he had to do what his foreigner asked. He couldn't say no to the foreigner who knew his name, as much as he wanted to. He couldn't let a foreigner get hurt on his watch. Some of those reports

Aimal helped with slid off him, but sometimes, in trying to answer a call for help, he made mistakes he regretted forever.

———

THERE WAS AN EARLY-MORNING FARE BACK TO TURKISH MOUNTAIN, dropping off another foreigner. Polite and forgettable. Up into a neighborhood spotted with mansions where the Sikhs and Hindus used to live. It was already hot that day, hot even with some of the city still asleep. Already gritty like the country can get, the air like sandpaper on his finger pads. Dust gets into your eyes, your clothes, the hinges of your glasses. It hardens in your nostrils, and the river collapses. As if it slipped underground to hide from the heat, leaving behind a scrim of trash down the middle. The country browns, brightens, bleaches. People squint against the sun and the dust and scratchy rooster yells that seem a feature of the heat, hacking up something dusty from their gullets.

Traffic was just beginning to pick up as Aimal headed back to headquarters, while a few miles away, I was arriving at the university, fiddling with the wall-mounted air-conditioning unit, opening my laptop, and listening to my kind boss across the office trying not to sing Ginuwine lyrics about aggressive sex.

Aimal drove down around a traffic circle toward an old cinema, and just ahead of him, a Ministry of Defense bus neared a bus stop and began to slow. By now, fully morning, reluctant bodies moving along commutes. The bus approached; people moved toward it.

On the bus, a man who wore a military uniform but who was not in the military shifted, and slipped a finger toward a detonator.

Behind the bus, Aimal's car drew closer. Just a hundred yards and closing on the now stopped bus, eighty, seventy, and then, for just a moment, Aimal suffered a strange lapse in memory. He forgot entirely that it was the holy month of Ramadan. He forgot he was fasting. The heat and his thirst were blinding him, and he pulled from the crawl of traffic to the side of the road, and stopped the car. He waved down a street-side vendor selling energy drinks and cigarettes.

He turned the car back on, pulled back into traffic, and in that moment, before he had a chance to register that he'd just stopped to buy provisions he couldn't use, the bus in front of him rippled. The air went black. Metal and body parts shot through the sky; so much smoke and dust that for a moment it felt like the explosion had shattered even the structure of time. Earth slipped through daylight and skipped right into night. The sun vanished, and it got so dark Aimal thought it was possible he'd just been killed, then knew he'd survived even though he couldn't hear anything. Instead of the sound—the ignition crack and the roar of gas—his head filled with a basic computation running on repeat at high speed: *an energy drink saved my life; an energy drink saved my life.* He'd never before been so close to a bombing. A bus exploding from no rocket or mortar, violence where nothing came from outside. As the spreading smoke uncocooned them and the midnight lifted, wails began to rise from people meeting their altered bodies. A swell of realization dominoed down the avenue, this was real, people needed help, and Aimal knew what he needed to do. He picked up the phone and scrolled to my number. "Yah, Jaff. Bomb blast near Baharistan Park. Want for me to pick up? Call to Afghan Logistics and tell that I should come to get you now."

He raced up the hill and across the city, already close to the university when the call from dispatch came in, then together, with "My Heart Will Go On" thumping, raced back to the site of the bombing. He watched his charge jump out and try to find good angles for pictures, immediately fixated on the street kids scrambling up trees, and Aimal kept an eye on me while trying to gather details he knew I'd ask for later. He tracked shifts in the audience around ground zero. People left; more people arrived. He read their intent. He kept his eyes on their eyes.

An old policeman came with a bat to try to disburse people.

A convoy arrived, and Aimal recognized the minister in its middle car. Guards got out and tried to clear the gathered people. Aimal saw a man lunge to pass through them, slinging himself against a brace of their interlocked arms, and yelling when they wouldn't let him through. "Hey, motherfucker, that's my mother. Let me get her!" Aimal checked my status: I was saying English things at kids. I was oblivious to the growing commotion. A guard pulled a gun, the man reached out to try to slap him, and Aimal saw the aftershocks of this attack were now beginning. There would be more violence soon. He needed to protect his guest; it was time to leave.

"Come, Jaff. You have enough to make a report?"

"Not yet, no." *Shit.* There was a commotion from the crowd, a swell and fall of noise, and from me he thought he heard ". . . to know how many people died."

Now he faced two opposing priorities. He needed to get me away from danger, but he needed to get me more for the story.

He tried to think. Was there a way to do both? He had an idea. "Do you want we should go to hospital?" Away from the roiling situation here, and maybe no one would know about the dead better than the hospital.

I shrugged. "Yeah, sure. Let's do that." Aimal had me in the car leaving the bomb site as more people began to gather, racing back across the city to the military's hospital.

The hospital compound wasn't a challenge; it yielded too easily. He showed my NATO coalition badge when he needed to, sleight of hand to show "ISAF" and block the rest, quickly finding his way onto the grounds of the military hospital, then up to the floor where the wounded were being treated. Many of them already resting, heavily anesthetized, or just dying. Aimal left me to browse while he hunted down the information I'd asked for, but none of the doctors knew the number of dead. They were busy with the patients who still had a chance. It occurred to Aimal that maybe the best place to find the number I needed wasn't the place where people were dying, but a place dedicated to the already dead.

Aimal walked over to me, pulled me from a patient's bedside. "Do you want we should go to the . . . what's it called? The place with the bodies?"

"The morgue? There's a morgue here?"

"The morgue. Yah, Jaff."

He watched my face twitch to the side and flicker with confusion, as if he wasn't helping me get exactly what I'd asked. But I nodded.

Down the stairs and across a green quad, and now that he was looking for it, he found the morgue without problem, a low-slung, nondescript building. He saw traditional-looking old men sitting in white plastic lawn chairs, threading *tasbih* beads through their fingers. He knew they wouldn't be a problem. He saw soldiers and guards, but could tell they were distracted. With little resistance, he found his way inside, me at his heels, and almost immediately recognized his error.

The scene inside assaulted him. The first room off the hall had an examination table with several people gathered around it, and lying on top of it was a part of a man. The body like a piece of discarded equipment, a giant severed power line with all its colorful tiny wires exposed. This was not right; this wasn't natural. The image flew at him, and he could feel it lodging in his brain and kicking him back, a toxin spreading through his body. Images of other bodies he'd seen spilled through his mind. Why had he come here? His brain began to shut down. He felt the contents of his stomach lurching; what had the predawn meal been a million hours ago before fasting? A worm swirl of acid shifted in his stomach. This thing, cut in half diagonally across the middle, could have been his brother, his father, him. His people didn't care about his people. He needed to stay and protect me; he needed to leave immediately; he needed to run away from here so fast that this grotesque thing would suction out of his head in the slipstream and leave him alone.

He made it outside just in time. He fell to his knees by the stream and began to convulse, expelling the contents of his stomach, his body trying to rid itself of a poison. But he sat up afterward, dry-heaved a little more, and the image was still there, a strobe light shouting at him from the inside. He tried to wash the vomit off his pants, his legs. Any residue of what he just saw. He took his shoes and socks off and washed his feet. Maybe praying would help. He prayed. He remembered the duas and the vows from the NGO when he was just a kid, but he couldn't shake free of what he'd seen, and then there was a commotion nearby.

A convoy arriving, someone high up at the Ministry of Defense. As the man approached, guards trying to scatter all the smaller men, Aimal recognized him: the defense minister's spokesman. They drew near him, and Aimal tried to muster an excuse to stay near the morgue because he couldn't leave his passenger stranded. "There's an American in there," he said. "I'm his translator."

The big man didn't seem to hear. "Son, you have to eat. You have to drink water."

Aimal looked down. "I'm a Muslim. I won't break my fast."

"Your fast is gone. Break your fast. You need water."

The man left, but the image stayed. It was gathering force, a monster summoning its minions. He knew this day would haunt him. He would dream about this day for his entire life. Naked, pale, bones. A small man exposed, a triangle of body from groin to shoulder blade. The idea lingering in the back of Aimal's head, maybe lingering in the fragile heads of most of his friends, heads that could peel open with a little metal. A thought that came rushing up like bile. He resolved, quietly and to himself, to not only become a big man in his country but eventually, one day, to leave it. And then there was a shadow over the stream, the sun shifted a bit, and he looked up. He squinted to make out the figure. This time it wasn't the minister's spokesman; it was me, nodding, like everything was fine.

CHAPTER 9

DECEMBER 2007

AIMAL WAS GOING ROGUE, FAVORING ONE CLIENT, AGAINST COMpany regulations and maybe against what was best for him. And still, his knowledge of foreigners from all that time with the dish locked him in as a core part of Muqim's team.

Muqim looked after him; Muqim asked him to stay longer hours. Aimal felt a bond of trust between them. He seized on Muqim's policy of compensating drivers for good business ideas. He thought about how to sound with foreigners, what body language to use. He channeled the Indian movies smuggled from Pakistan and brought his Afghan-American friend to mind; Aimal always knew how much to joke. How to seem familiar but not too familiar. He learned how to make foreigners feel like they had a friend, but a friend they were comfortably above, and how to make trivial tips seem life changing. He already knew how to make gratitude seem genuine and how to make the foreigners in his car feel that if they were strangers in a strange land, they were at least somebody's savior. He was becoming more confident in his standing at the company.

From confident, perhaps inevitably, to underappreciated. The drivers were beginning to grumble. There was more and more opportunity in the country, and how much was Muqim making? Aimal's salary slid from feeling sufficient to kind of meager, actually, given his skill with the foreigners. With so much foreign money swirling around the country, why shouldn't the drivers get a bigger piece?

When Barialay came across a US military–issued rifle someone left in his car—like the universe setting things right for him after nearly getting brained by a drunk soldier—he saw possibility. He didn't tell Muqim right away; he told Aimal and some of the other drivers first. A rifle like that was easily worth $10,000 on the street—maybe $15,000. A hundred times their monthly salary, and the guy had just *left* it there? What if instead of trying to return it, they found a way to sell it?

To Aimal, it was an inch over the line, more an outright crime than a clever puzzle solution. He liked ideas he didn't think would hurt anyone or, at least, wouldn't hurt anyone who didn't deserve it. This wasn't his hustle.

As the drivers moved the weapon around to different hiding places, still figuring out how exactly to sell it, Aimal overheard drivers discussing another idea. Two of his friends had begun talking about starting their own taxi company. They'd call it Zuhaak, after an ancient "Red City" in the country's central highlands built out of red clay. If Muqim was getting all the foreign money and they weren't, why not just turn themselves into Muqim? They invited Aimal in on this plan, too, and this time he saw the moves unfold before him. Another taxi company meant another way to earn. And the two drivers planning to start the new company had senior positions at the old one. If they left their jobs, those positions would open up, and Muqim would surely choose Aimal for promotion. For Aimal, the move was obvious: encourage the drivers to start another company he could drive for and, meanwhile, take their positions at the old company.

But before Zuhaak got off the ground, Muqim found out about the rifle. He flew into a rage: this could ruin his company's reputation. "If foreigners think we're thieves, we're finished!" He waved his arms and, on the spot, fired all the drivers he thought were involved, saving Aimal for last. "I didn't expect this from *you*," he said, bringing Aimal into his office. "I *relied* on you. I thought you were my brother. You were the one I trusted most. I love you, Aimal," he said. And then he looked at Aimal and breathed deep, like he was thinking about something else, his face cast in a strange aspect that seemed off for this moment. "But I can't trust you anymore. You're gone. Get out of here."

Aimal saw red. *I didn't steal the rifle! I've done nothing wrong; I didn't even want to go through with it!* This was Muqim standing on his undeserved podium and spitting down, like everyone else in this country. *Fuck him.* Aimal's thinking went frenzied again, that jet of adrenaline ignited by a slight. He saw the boss of the registration department whining about losing bribe money; he saw soldiers waving him off the road. He saw all the people better than him because he was only a poor Afghan kid who'd never been to a foreign country. *"I thought you were my brother."* *Motherfucker, I'm not your brother. I will bury you, Muqim.* He left the office already thinking about revenge, but soon, as it often did, the wrath gave way, receptors emptied, and he was left with the hangover. Now there was just dejection and worry. How would he ever feed himself and his family now? He was desperate again. Back to the street, kid, hardly any higher than the mud puddles from the morning wash downs. He needed help. It would be too much shame to ask me, but, then, I had said we were friends. So maybe we were friends.

Aimal called, and on the other end, a distracted-sounding voice invited him to the university. Aimal took his brother's car to see me, and I told him there was good news: my boss had agreed to meet with him.

My kind, jolly boss sat him down and made his face serious. He leaned forward, making a display of taking Aimal's concerns seriously, and asked him how he was feeling, if he was OK, how can I help. He told Aimal to wait. He left, came back, and just like that, he'd already secured Aimal a job as a driver for the university.

Aimal perked up. "Driving the Americans around?"

It wasn't quite that. "You'll be driving the local staff. The Afghans who work here."

Worry spilled back. He knew how that would play out. Being a driver for other Afghans meant being their servant. They'd make a display of being superior to him. It would be too big of a fall. He tried to keep the disappointment from his face. He'd just dug himself deeper. His foreign friend had tried to help him, and he was too proud to accept the help being offered, so now he was jobless *and* ungrateful. He decided he wouldn't say anything to me about it, and maybe I'd just assume that my boss hadn't been able to help.

Aimal walked out to the car thinking about next steps, me walking alongside him. Maybe he could just use his brother's car occasionally to drive a foreign client or two. If he could find some foreigners who wouldn't mind the shittier car and the intermittent service, he could make a little money that way.

He sat in the car and thought in silence for a while, trying to think of what to say. He knew he needed to ask another favor. He summoned the nerve and blurted it out before he lost it. "Would you help find some foreigners who might need private driver?" He couldn't bear to make eye contact. He kept his locked eyes forward as he asked.

"Why not start your own company?"

Aimal felt knocked back. *Is he bullshitting?* Now he turned to look, to see if this was some kind of joke. I looked earnest.

"You know the system. You know the streets, all the shortcuts. How the business works. You know how to deal with clients. What's stopping you?"

Aimal held the idea in his mind for just a moment, examined it. Then dismissed it. *Yeah, but where are the cars? Where's the money? Where's the office?* It couldn't work. You couldn't just start a business. Aimal turned the car on. He needed to be alone, too much shame for one day.

As he drove home, though, the idea remained with him, turning over in his mind. Afghans would laugh if he said he was starting a business. For now, he'd latch on to Zuhaak, help his friends there, and maybe it would turn into something real. He reached the New City neighborhood, parked the car near his mother's house, and got out, thinking that for now, there's no chance, but maybe, one day, if fortune favored him . . . because after all a foreigner thought he could—and before he got to the door, a group of young men slipped out from a shadowed alley and angled in on him.

"What the fuck did you do behind our back?" Drivers. He recognized them: the other guys Muqim fired.

"What the fuck are you talking about?" But in an instant he saw what they saw. The drivers had all been fired on the spot, and Aimal had been brought into Muqim's office.

"You snitched, motherfucker."

One of them grabbed Aimal's collar. He scanned their pockets for protrusions that might mean guns or knives. The others closed in.

"Hey, fuckers," he said, his shirt pushed up his chin—and now, as the words came out, he had a flash of realization: Muqim's odd expression just before letting him go. "He fired me too."

The hands around his collar loosened. They stepped back; charged muscles slackened. They looked at each other. The violence in their eyes subsided, for the moment at least. But they seemed to realize, all the fired drivers at once, that there was nothing left to do but try to get Zuhaak off the ground.

CHAPTER 10

MARCH 2008

Aimal knew no foreigner would stay in this country for-ever, no matter how close he let himself believe we'd become. Closer, he sometimes thought, than half a year should have allowed. So he wasn't all that surprised when he was invited to a going-away party. A dinner gathering mostly for white friends at Old Lebanese, one of the restaurants for foreigners. Aimal had never been inside. He'd been outside a million times. Always waiting across the street in the dark for foreigners to finish whatever took foreigners so long at the end of meals. Always sitting in the car for endless hours playing Snake, smok-ing, taking impatient calls from dispatch. Bracing himself and then calling the clients just across the wall, still inside the restaurant, to nudge them along.

Sir, I am your driver, I am arrive.

I told you I'll be out in a second!

Yes, sorry, sir.

While other foreigners, in other parts of the city, called too: *Where the hell is the car? I ordered it forty-five minutes ago!* As if the city wasn't full of traffic jams and security checkpoints. As if this wasn't *another* foreigner taking his damned time and causing the whole slowdown. In the new Afghanistan, amid all the other hazards, drivers had to manage the conflict that foreigners had with other foreigners.

But tonight was different. Tonight, he was parking on the street and leaving the car. Tonight, he was walking inside. Walking past the

HESCO barriers into the tunneled entryway. Past the lockers where guests carrying weapons left them for the evening.

Tonight, he was walking inside a foreigner restaurant for the very first time, and it was like a little universe opened up to him. Like seeing color for the first time. A perfect secret garden. Greens and pinks exploded around him, perfectly manicured flowers, plumes from hookahs, and the clean kind of cigarette smoke. The air felt calm, maybe a different kind of oxygen here. A soundtrack of low chatter and laughter, talking, no yelling, no waiters berating guests with today's offerings. Instead, here they had menus, and waiters were calm and polite. *Am I really this high class?* He'd never been anyplace so *clean*. Even the plants seemed relaxed. Where was all the dust?

Waiters smiled at him; he felt kindness in their eyes. He felt no stares. He didn't know restaurants could be like this. He felt like what the waiters showed him might actually be love. Guests made little heavens for themselves. He was just blocks from his house. Had this really been here the whole time? Behind blast walls, a perfect place.

He sat down at the long table reserved for the party, and only then did something change, a contaminant released in his bloodstream. Everyone was speaking English so fast. He couldn't follow.

He *didn't* belong here.

He should leave.

They knew he couldn't understand what they were saying. *These assholes are making fun of me.* Of course they were. Who did he think he was? What a fool! He was here only for their amusement; everyone could see how out of place he was. He'd been foolish to think anyone actually wanted him there. Maybe they'd invited him out of pity, thinking he'd know not to show up. Or maybe as sport. They thought he belonged outside, waiting in the mud with the rest of the drivers. He felt a flush of embarrassment and was about to push back from the table when a waiter came by, an Afghan saying something in English that Aimal missed, but he caught the gentle tone, and that was enough. The simmer in his mind settled; the heat turned down.

He looked across the table and saw me, looking like I'd only just noticed he'd arrived. My eyebrows were raised, like above all else, I was maybe just happy to see him.

The next day, I was gone.

CHAPTER 11

APRIL 2008

AIMAL POURED EVERYTHING HE HAD INTO ZUHAAK. HE HELPED his friends' new company for free. He let them use his mother's house for meetings. One of the first nights driving for them, he dropped a client off at a house he recognized. A woman he knew of lived there—a half-American who'd thrown parties he'd driven clients to before.

This time, he got out of the car. He was feeling bold. Now he'd been to a foreigner party. He went to the door, a trespass that would've been forbidden by Muqim, but Muqim had fired him, and now he worked for a company that couldn't afford to pay him yet, so *fuck it*— he had little to lose. He wanted to see what new paradise awaited him here, one of the thousand annexes foreigners had built inside his city.

The hostess answered the door. She seemed to recognize him, but he was focused on partiers over her shoulder. Thirty people, maybe fifty or a hundred. "Am I invited in?"

This one was more raucous. This wasn't people enjoying the quiet. It was the kind of booze-fueled affair that ripped headlong into the night until it ejected drunk foreigners leaking cash for the quickest drivers to catch. Aimal knew the outlines of it; he'd seen this party a hundred times from the outside. He stepped inside.

Foreigners swayed and leaned in close; aid workers and embassy staff shouted in each other's ears, passing full fifths of liquor. He moved through the party. The room pulsed. Around him, girls moved in new ways, like their limbs attached differently than they did in daylight. Dancing to a karaoke machine, all hips and joints, the mechanical parts of bodies he never saw outside. Were they trying to tempt him? *One of these girls could take me to America . . . maybe they're drunk enough to—*

He had another idea. He called the office.

Bring all the cars here. All of them. And wait outside. And so you know, I'm going to pretend I'm the general manager of Zuhaak.

He swam through the crowd to find the hostess again, leaned in to her. "Can I make an announcement?"

"What?"

"An *announcement!*"

"To say what?"

"I want to say, 'Allahu Akbar, God is great, I come to kill Americans!'" Hard in the mood lighting to tell if she rolled her eyes at this. He started again. "I want to say I'm from a new company, and since it's *your* party and we love you, we give free rides to all of your guests tonight."

She lit up. "But, sorry, Aimal—with your English, better let me do the talking." She dragged him up to the karaoke mic.

"Excuse me! Excuse me, everyone! Your attention for a second!" Groans creaked through the crowd. "This gentleman—this is Aimal. He's the general manager of Zuhaak Tours and Logistics. Zuhaak is a new company. When you're ready to leave"—a few boos—"*when* you go outside, the Zuhaak cars are red. Jump in a red car, get a free ride!" Boos morphed into cheers. "And remember to give a good tip!"

Aimal stayed and drank and even tried to sing with the foreigners, and when people finally started leaving, he watched them walk past Muqim's cars and go straight to the red ones.

All night on the radio, Aimal's colleagues were chatty with opportunity. What they lost in taxi fare they more than made up for in tips. In one night they poached a few dozen foreigners from the old company, and Aimal solidified his place as a key employee of the new one.

CHAPTER 12

MAY 2008

Soon after I left, as Zuhaak began to grow, a new foreigner slotted into Aimal's life, as if he was always supposed to have one to look out for.

Better this time: a woman, young and tall and beautiful. She was referred by a friend. They met in person for the first time at the airport, and she hugged him like there weren't benches full of scowling old men. Aimal was ashamed, excited, honored all at once. "You're like the hero of Kabul," she said.

Well, Western women know how to flatter. Or maybe he really did have a reputation now. Maybe foreigners talked to other foreigners and said nice things about him. He wondered, as he drove her to the guesthouse he'd arranged for her, if maybe, *maybe*, someone like her might take someone like him seriously. As a real romantic partner. He never said it; he tried to stop himself from even thinking it. She was there to work. Another freelance journalist coming to extract some value from the violence. He now knew how to serve people like her. He would keep his head down and help her the way he'd helped his first journalist, and try not to think about love.

She wanted to write about women. She wanted to see his country. He ached to show her the prettier things, that it wasn't all bombs. He tried to pull her attention from the violence, spent days with her on a tour of agreeable things. The city's women's garden, a walled complex where apricot trees blocked prying eyes and fountain water flowed, a place with changing rooms for women to leave their burkas and put on makeup. She tried to convince the guards to let Aimal come in. "He's my translator." But security at the Kabul Women's Garden was harder to sweet-talk than at the biggest bombings. They made him wait outside.

He took her to the world's first Mughal garden. Right there, in his city. Few knew his city had such wonders. Built by Babur, the first Mughal emperor. A tranquil garden running down a hill, flanked by cascading steps of water. A blooming chorus between man and nature that culminated, five generations after this one was built, in gardens guarding the Taj Mahal. She took it all in, and Aimal watched her. Maybe this one he could convince to report on the nicer things. She was funny, flirtatious, profane. She was beautiful. He saw some girls sitting by a tree and asked his new journalist to come with him while he introduced himself. He flirted, but the seated girls were uninterested, and as they walked away, she elbowed him. *How rude! You're flirting with them in front of me?* A show of faux jealousy.

Or was there any way it was real?

After each outing, he took her back to the guesthouse, wishing he could provide his own place for her to feel comfortable. He daydreamed. What if he had his own guesthouse? He wanted to smooth the war's rough edges and make her comfortable here. To show her the parts of the place he wasn't ashamed of. Each time he left his journalist, he counted down the time before he could be with her again.

But soon she'd seen enough of the city. Enough tourism—she wanted to get to work. "No problem," he said. He hid disappointment, as he'd always done, as he'd once hid hunger. His station here was to serve her, and he knew how to find stories the foreigners liked.

Back at the new company's headquarters, he tuned his ears to eavesdrop, looking to pluck stories for his guest. And at home, he spent less time with the dish on the faraway shows, more time scanning local news for horrifying things that were still contained in his language, that hadn't yet infected English-language channels. Things he knew would have interested me. It didn't take long. He heard about an inmate at the woman's prison who'd somehow become pregnant. It had all the ingredients for a story that would draw in a foreigner: injustice, misogyny, spectacle, sex. It was perfect.

At the prison, in a special room made available for the American journalist, Aimal translated questions. He managed well enough in the beginning.

What crime did you commit? Why are you here?

My husband said that I was seeing another man, and I was going to run off.

"She say her husband think she have the, how you say. She have the Affair."

"Aimal, ask her how she got pregnant." He squirmed. He apologized, tried to translate.

The guards sometimes ask me to dance; they give me cigarettes, then they ask me—

He tried to keep up. He translated back to English.

"But Aimal, ask her why they didn't use a condom."

He blushed. His mind slowed. He couldn't think of a polite way. Words tangled up in his skull. She saw him sputtering. "Aimal, stop being an *Afghan*," she said. "*You're* not the one fucking her!" He shifted his feet on the floor. He looked away from the inmate and scratched around for a gentle way to ask an impossible question.

Walking back to the car after the interview, he braced for a rebuke, and was ready when it came. "Aimal, I respect you, but I have to come back with a more professional translator." Relief nudged away shame. And still, she wanted him with her for everything else. She had him drive her all over the city, even out of it, tracking down the inmate's family. She had her teeth in the story. Mostly focused on getting this one report right, concerned with little else, but when a car bomb went off in Kampani, the same part of the city he'd taken me to cover a bombing a few months before, she said she wanted to write about that too.

As he drove her out toward the western edge of the city, she talked about a trip she wanted to take. She'd heard of the place called Bamyan, a day's drive. She wanted to go with Aimal to see the gaps in the sandstone where the giant Buddhas once stood. To see the country's highlands, where at least in photos there was so much emerald-green grass that it was hard to believe it was the same country they were driving through now. And if you went a little farther north from the Buddhas, there was Band-e-Amir, the Dams of the King, natural sulfur deposits that held impossibly clear turquoise water, where you could rent swan-shaped paddleboats and flutter out into the water. Side by side. "It sounds romantic," he said, and waited for her to reply. She looked at him sideways. A smile? Maybe an opening—but the main Kampani bridge came into view, and it was time to find someplace to park. So he wouldn't get an answer. He tried not to lose himself wondering what she was thinking. After a pause, she said, "Take me there, OK? Let's go. We'll spend a week. You can show me around."

Those fireworks in his chest again—would you spend a week with someone who was just an employee? He tried to block the images from the dish as a kid: the flesh, the white—*be respectful*. He snapped at himself for letting the idea in. *White girls are educated, professional; I'm just a driver. I should feel lucky to be spending time in a car with her, not get greedy hoping for romance.*

Up ahead, signs of the recent attack emerged as a thickening in the traffic. A soldier stepped out to block the car, resting his hands on a rifle strapped across his chest. Aimal was still trying not to smile.

He now had a quiver full of tricks he'd mastered with me. His journalist had an ISAF badge just like I'd had, and though it also said Media—!ESCORT REQUIRED! in bright-red letters, Aimal flashed it at the soldier, covering that part with a thumb just in case the soldier knew some English.

"She's from ISAF, brother. Let us through."

It took only a little haggling before they passed the first makeshift checkpoint. Beyond it they saw the cars. One flipped over from the force of a blast. A large bus that had suffered some fatal internal wound.

The two of them got out; she looked around; Aimal listened. A familiar current of grumbling. The "Fuck Karzais" and the "Fuck Americas." He glanced at her; he didn't translate.

He found a witness who said he'd seen the blast, and Aimal got to work trying to extract the details he knew I would have wanted. "Ten people died," the man said.

"Ten people are died," Aimal said to his journalist, now walking over, looking around, looking at him.

"The car came from that direction, and the explosion happened when it was on the bridge."

"He say the car come from over there—"

She was listening intently now. Using her eyes and the tilt of her forehead to pull the words from him like siphoning petrol, and there was a connection with her, for sure, a chemistry. He wasn't crazy. He tried to focus: "—and bomb blast happen right when car crossed to . . ." She was still looking right at him, almost *into* him, but then the focus seemed to leak from her eyes. A coin of red arose on her forehead. A whistle, an echo, and she flew back, like being pulled into a different dimension. On his face he felt warmth, liquid; she'd been looking at him, and now she wasn't. The desert froze. People were running. He couldn't move. A crackle of machine-gun fire sounded, a conversation between the mountains, but his feet bolted themselves to the ground, claws rising from below and grasping his ankles in place like the Earth was forcing him to look at her. He couldn't move. She didn't move. She was on the ground. She wasn't moving. Her blood was on his face, his shirt. His forearm pulsed. A stranger's hand clenched on tightly. "Boy, *run.*" And Aimal broke free. Running now, leaving the girl in the dried-out riverbed and finding a car to duck behind as tracer rounds zipped by and bullets crashed into panels. Tires spat out air, and glass erupted; people fell. Rifle barrels twisted toward the mountain as if they were all on an invisible wire yanked by a puppeteer somewhere up there. Now it was a firefight against unseen snipers, Talibs with better position, and Aimal had a hard time tracking how much time went by before it was quiet again and a huge American from the NATO coalition was standing in front of him asking too many questions.

Aimal understood that he had a dead American woman on his hands and that he was under suspicion. Guantanamo would come next, torture, the rumored prison at Bagram—he would be disappeared. The list of things going wrong grew too high and toppled over on him. His dead foreigner, their trip to the highlands, the swan-shaped paddleboat, the accusing soldier, the blasted vehicles, the firefight that happened while his mind whirled away to somewhere else. Aimal felt the heat rising up his neck to the back of his skull, his throat constricting. He screamed at the American: "What do you think? Do you think I shoot her?" His reservoir of English withdrew like it knew he needed it. "I don't care, I don't care, do what you want, just I try to translate, just I translate!" The American advanced on Aimal like he was about to throw a punch, and Aimal didn't care; he welcomed it. *Punch me! What do I have to lose? Break my jaw.* He didn't flinch, but he froze again when the American wrapped Aimal in a massive embrace, his biceps holding Aimal's neck in. They stood there, two strangers hugging. The soldier's head next to Aimal's, whispering, "We know, we know; you've done nothing wrong. Can you just explain? Just calm down and tell me what you saw." He couldn't even say her name. Scrubbed off his memory when she flew back and died. She was gone to him now.

But he remembered, like a diorama in his head, what had happened. She fused with the triangle of flesh at the morgue, her coin of red. She joined the ghosts who remained with him always. He remembered exactly where they were both standing. The scene, the landscape of that moment, carved into a corner of his memory where it could sit and haunt him. And if it was there, pulsing in the background, millimeters from imagining, it was also at least always available to serve him.

From then on, whenever he was with a foreigner and there was danger, that scene came back to him. He could scan the land like a battlefield map, finding where a shooter might be hiding.

From then on, he would cough, shuffle, make dirty jokes, and while everyone was distracted, he would slide his feet and shift his torso. Without anyone noticing, he'd use his own body to block bullets and protect people from threats they might not even see.

CHAPTER 13

JUNE 2008

ANOTHER FOREIGN GIRL FALLS INTO AIMAL'S LIFE. HE'S CALLED to Turkish Mountain to pick up a client and sees a perfect girl waiting for a ride. If she's riding with him, she must be foreign. But to him, she doesn't look white. When she speaks, it's in short, perfect sentences in his language. So she's Afghan, with citizenship somewhere else. "Dutch," she says, when he asks.

He gets to know her eyes first—only what he can see in a rearview mirror—so their relationship begins with the modesty their fathers might have wanted. She has the quality that people with friendly, open faces do, of looking familiar. She's one of those people you somehow feel you've always known. For him, she's the diaspora personified. Brought back to a country she no longer quite knows, even though she knows the language.

"It's your driver," Aimal says when he calls her. He's thrilled by the messages she sends him at night. He doesn't yet know she has a program on her laptop that can send text messages to cell phones and that she's holding conversations with a dozen friends at once. He lies in the drivers' barracks focused only on her. Other drivers asleep next to him, he stays up all night with his phone, trying to keep up with the messages he doesn't know she's typing with a full keyboard. His entire mind tunneled in on just her, imagining her in bed at Turkish Mountain with her phone hidden under the covers. He thinks he's in love. The drivers on mats beside him cough and fart and snore; he's a doughboy in the trenches writing by candlelight, trying not to disturb the other sleeping soldiers.

"If you ever do something bad," he tells her one day, "you come stand by me. I'm only Afghan, so I take blame." He's beginning to see his peers assigned cousins or family friends to marry, and he has no father to hold negotiations for him. He suffers for it, trying to find a wife all by himself in a city that's still good at keeping unrelated men and women from interacting. He should be good at it. Courtship is subversion here—as wrapped up in its own set of tactics and rules as espionage. Boys figure out the routes girls take home from school and follow them, write initials on fighting kites, lose them on purpose over her house and hope the wind cooperates. So he follows a code of courtship imported from places he's unfamiliar with and that he doesn't fully understand. Trends that loop around the world like chain letters and drop out of the ether onto his phone screen. He grabs on to them, deploys them at Fatima. "Choose one," he tells her in a text message: 1. Hug me 2. Hate me 3. Kiss me 4. Marry me 5. Kill me 6. Love me . . .

"OK," she writes back. "I'll tell you later."

He's excited. She's perfect. Pretty, smart, maybe best of all, a foreigner. Another person conjured from the dish. And then one night, hours into their nocturnal flirtation, the almost-perfect message he's working on is interrupted, the screen goes blank, then lights up again with the one American phone number he knows by heart: his first foreigner is coming back. Aimal thought he might never see me again, and after only a few months, I was on my way. Back to the university, for some job or another he doesn't fully understand, only he knows it has to do with women and that I'm working with that same kind boss who I still don't know offered him a job.

Aimal picks me up at the airport. "Yah, Jaff," he says, and winks, and begins to tell me about this new love interest. He thinks I'm listening; he knows I'm interested. The car is quiet for a moment.

"Does she have a sister?"

Gradually, Fatima becomes more playful with him. Aimal driving Fatima and her grandmother to the hospital for a checkup one day, and

Fatima sends him a message from the backseat: *Now would be a good time for that kiss.* Aimal takes his eyes off the road and replies immediately: *Drop her off and tell her you have to come back with me because you forgot something.*

Fatima doesn't.

But she does agree, later, to go on a kind-of date with him. He takes her to the only place in the city he can. The Safi Landmark Hotel. The place where a new breed of mallrats can act the way people do in movies from India and America. Where young, unrelated men and women can sit together at a café and commit what would otherwise be indiscretions. One of the few Kabul establishments that caters to foreigners but allows Afghans. A luxury glass-sheathed development with three floors of shopping, eight or nine floors of bedrooms, four restaurants, and glass elevators overlooking an atrium. One of the places people like Aimal go when they want to talk to girls because they don't have fathers willing to pick wives for them, or because they don't have fathers.

He takes her to the café on the ground floor, no one bothers them, and they sit surrounded by stores that sell clothing and kitsch, Chinese renditions of Japanese electronics, pirated DVDs that mostly don't work, and they talk. And there, at the café, he's certain. He likes her, she loves him, he has little doubt, and he's not worried by her better English. Her better education, her European upbringing. So what, she has foreign friends. He has a foreign friend. He wants to take her someplace special. She's only just getting to know this country, even though it's her country. And the more he thinks of it, he wants to take me someplace special too. A road trip, but without me paying.

It'd be a test, also. Because people can say "We're friends" like I did on my last trip, but that doesn't prove they really meant it. To know if it's real, you have to see if they show up when you ask them to do *friend* things. Even after what we'd seen together, even after dining together at his house, he still sometimes doubts that I really see us as equal. He's sure Fatima will accept. She loves him; he knows it. He's not sure I will. But maybe having Fatima along, a pretty girl who understands all my English, will convince me.

When I say I'll go, he decides it might be worth one additional test. Things are beginning to break in his favor. He's beginning to get his confidence back. He always had this belief that the people most special to you can bring good luck, and an object from someone who is good luck is also good luck. He wants me to have something of his, and he wants to take something of mine. He thinks I might get angry or uncomfortable if he tries to explain all that, so he doesn't; he just says it'd be funny to trade shirts. When I laugh and agree to that too, it's sealed. It must be that I really do see him as more than an employee. And when, at the beginning of the trip, I say, "You should put mine on now! You'll look better," he does because he doesn't want to insult me even though he knows that after the day is done, he'll never wear it again. He'll keep it near; he'll smell it when he needs good luck. Because he knows I'll leave again, sooner or later, and when that happens, it may be for longer. It may be forever. Because why would anyone come back here? Aimal wants something to remember his friend by.

THE DATE GOT OFF TO A ROCKY START. HE BORROWED A CAR, AND IT was all smiles as the little sedan chugged toward the outskirts of Kabul, but then once just outside of the city, a flat tire threatened to derail the entire trip. Aimal hunted down a street-side mechanic to fix it, then a place for a snack so we might still have a nice time, though when he wasn't looking, I paid for the fix, in front of Fatima. There was an ache of shame he tried to shoo away.

Back on the road, the weight thawed off him as he drove toward the mountain pass. Pride came back; who else had two guests to themselves, his to show the country to? Rocks climbed alongside slowly at first, then surged skyward until he was steering beneath sheer, near-vertical cliffs so steep they made his passengers quiet. Cheeks pressed to window glass, eyes skyward. The road wound into shadows. It darkened and cooled. The roar of a river casting up its own cold sealed us off from Kabul, the whole rest of the country, the world. Thoughts, restraint, decorum from the city. The war withdrew and was gone.

He looked for a safe spur of roadside and pulled off onto an oval of asphalt, a little cyst in the road where flat gravel leaked out from a turn. He turned off the car, and now here he was, a man, one day a lover, a host. From America, from the Netherlands, he was showing them something of his, something wonderful, he felt so filled up he could almost float up the rocks; it was like he'd stolen the most valuable treasure and gotten away with it.

He led the way, watching eyes for the thrill of a swinging rope bridge across the river, then blazed his own trail up the boulders, keeping an eye out for red-painted rocks, but it was like the wind lifted him. Halfway, he stopped to let the stragglers catch up. It felt unnatural not to just keep flying, but he needed to remember this. He wanted a photo with Fatima that they would show their kids, and he wanted a photo with me.

A little higher, and it was time to scout for a comfortable place to sit. He looked for boulders with the smoothest, flattest tops to lay out the picnic. Hard-boiled eggs and old Russian beer, and the company, and a view. He waited for us to reach him. He looked down at the tiny car and the country, a thousand miles below. The air was crisp, and life was OK. He'd seen things, he'd lost foreigners, but here he was, a weekend trip with people he loved. Things were good. Things were going to be good.

He heard a noise, the tumbling of pebbles. There was movement from the corner of his eye: two boys blipped into view from behind a boulder. A hundred yards away but as high up as he was. He sensed shrewdness in their movements, picking it up like a scent. He knew this kind of kid. He'd been one. These were cheetahs; they knew how to navigate this terrain. Boys this age could look harmless and have a killer instinct.

The two boys approached, eleven or twelve years old.

Aimal looked down at us. Fatima and I seemed relaxed, now sitting just below, giggling and playing a stupid battle game with our hard-boiled eggs to see whose cracked first.

In an instant, Aimal saw us the way the boys would see us. A young woman with two men, neither of them related to her.

Worse: a foreigner defiling an Afghan woman. He tried to whisper.

"Fatima, don't speak Dari." If she dropped her scarf, she could pretend she wasn't Afghan. She didn't hear; the boys were almost on us. He tried to signal to me, but I wasn't paying attention either. He tried to speak without moving his mouth. "Jaff, don't saying anything. Don't speak English. Stay quiet."

Then the boys were on us, and the moment we noticed them, Fatima greeted the boys cheerfully in Dari; I said "Hello!" in English, pulled a snack from my backpack and tossed it to them. Aimal ran through options. Now it was too late. It began to drizzle, and the air chilled. The boys stepped away; Aimal picked up bits of their arguing. Something about their conversation unnerved him more. There was entitlement. They returned from their little caucus and asked his foreigners for more. Trying to get us to talk, trying to gather detail. Now we were in danger.

"OK, go ahead, leave, guys." He shooed them away. He watched them, and the moment they were out of earshot, he turned to us.

"Let's finish the party; we should leave." Fatima and I frowned at each other and giggled.

He had to get us on the road, *now*. Before the boys could go tell their fathers and uncles about the indecency they'd stumbled across and send the cavalry. He knew it'd be worse if he scared us, so he used the beginning of a spitting rain as an excuse to leave so soon after we'd arrived.

He rushed to pack up, trying to make it look like he wasn't rushing. He moved down the rocks, this time reaching back to help Fatima down the slickened cliffside. When we reached the bottom, Fatima and I wanted to kick around in the river, and he took the bags across the rope bridge to the car to get everything ready to go, but before we'd put our shoes and socks back on, trucks started to arrive.

Aimal's heart sank. Men with submachine guns got out, and he knew the only move now was to go with them. There were too many moving parts here to talk his way out of it yet. The three of us forced into a car, part of a convoy heading farther from Kabul. Crammed in the backseat and pressed up against his friend, Aimal tried to get my attention. As we pulled into a remote police station, he tried speaking to me under his breath. "Don't say anything." They might not know I was American yet. Maybe. Maybe we could keep it that way.

We were ushered into a commandant's office, I immediately pulled out my American passport and started airing grievances in English. Aimal brushed a hand against my knee, trying to dial me down.

The men grumbled to one another. "Motherfucker with your fucking passport," one of them said. "Thinks he's God."

I kept going. Aimal saw I thought I was helping, even as I'd taken a bad situation and escalated it. Aimal needed me to calm it down. I was pulling out my ISAF badge. He ran a finger against my knee. Pulling rank was not working. The commandant said, "Tell him to put that shit away. I don't care about your badge."

I kept yelling things, Aimal knew he wasn't going to shut me up, so the next best option was to try and work with what I was doing. "Brother," he said to the commandant, "he's an important person. He's new in the country, but he has good connections. People will stand for him."

But he knew even as he said it, this wouldn't work. He could see the unseen game; he knew what was happening in their heads. What other reason could there be for three unrelated people to be alone, far from home, unless the woman was a prostitute serving the American? That had to be what they were thinking. And that made Aimal the pimp.

He knew that out here, we were unconnected to any other authority. Even if there were someone to call, he didn't know if he could get a cell signal. These men were essentially autonomous. These were real fighters. Not like the men in Kabul he knew, men who might be convinced to look away with some cajoling or a bribe. These were believers. He saw men who didn't care about rank or money. Only about honor, right and wrong, and these three trespassers had just come and spat in their faces. We were on our own. He needed something else. Aimal searched for a seam he could exploit. Fatima said something in Dari. "Fatima, stop speaking in Dari."

I was trying to pull rank. "Jaff." He squeezed my knee yet again, as if that might still staunch the flow of unhelpful words.

He was scrambling. He needed another tactic. It was his fault; he was responsible for this whole outing. Aimal, the poor kid from Kabul who'd reached too high and now had gotten an American and a high-class European woman in trouble, just a driver who had gone and ruined it for foreigners, and—he had an idea. "Look, she is Dutch. She is from Netherlands. Why would she come all the way to Afghanistan to be a prostitute? That's not what's happening. They are colleagues."

They seemed to be listening. He pressed on.

"I'm just a driver," he said. "How could I be a pimp? Look at this cheap old car of mine. Look at *me*. Look at these two foreign colleagues, way higher class than me, how could I be *their* pimp?"

The commandant moved his head; he didn't speak. Aimal kept going, letting his tongue take over, finding new ways to debase himself and elevate his guests, until he'd so thoroughly ensconced us in such different castes that the men appeared satisfied that at least he was who he said he was. One of them tried to get him to turn on us. "These foreigners are dishonoring you! This is a chance to punish them and teach a lesson about respecting your hosts."

Aimal saw his opening. "I'm with you guys, but I would not fuck with this guy because he's got power. Maybe if it was another foreigner, we could fuck him up and take everything from him. But with this one, he has power. I'm too scared to do that." He said I worked at the embassy and had big connections with people powerful enough and with enough time on their hands that they might come all the way up here to make life difficult. "I know with his size, he doesn't look American, but he is, and he works at the embassy. He has connections."

The commandant softened. This was no longer worth his trouble. Finally, he waved us off. "Get out of here," he said, "but be careful; there are others who are conservative and won't be so forgiving."

We left, but Aimal scrounged up some extra money from Fatima and me and told the men it was to cover the cost of tea they hadn't served us.

AFTERWARD, ON THE RIDE BACK TO KABUL, AIMAL TRIED TO JOKE IN the car, but he was angry. He idolized foreigners, but every once in a while the feeling changed. Why were foreigners always treated better? Even when they were detained, they got more respect than he did. He heard Muqim's advice again: "Don't call foreigners by their first name. To you, they're Sir and Ma'am." It had once made sense to him. Treating them better because they *were* better—made of more sacred matter. More and more, he felt they weren't better; they were just luckier and different by accident of birth. We'd all dropped down from the Almighty, pinballed down different celestial slides, looped around, and tumbled out of wombs on different landmasses. Foreigners weren't different; they just woke up in better places. They weren't better; they just had better documents. He did love these two people in his car. But he was feeling a needle of frustration with them, short of resentment, but tipping in that direction.

Just before entering Kabul, we were stopped again, and Aimal had to go through the motions one more time. These officers just needed money; they were easier to deal with. He could handle it almost by rote. *I'm no one; I'm just a driver, not even good enough to be a pimp. These are guests; they are high class; people like you and me don't want to bother them; here's some money for tea because you've taken your time keeping us safe and you must be thirsty.*

THE DATE HAD NOT GONE WELL, BUT HE RECOVERED. EMBARRASS-ment had given way to frustration, but he was still confident about Fatima. He knew she loved him. She called him soon after the trip to say her father was visiting from the Netherlands, and she wanted Aimal to meet him so they could discuss marriage. *To discuss marriage.* Had a woman just proposed to him? He gushed with excitement he hadn't felt since he saw the first dish images scrambling to life on the family television screen. He made sure Fatima's father knew his family would be honored to host him, but when he arrived, he asked that they meet at the City Center coffee shop.

Strange, a minor insult, but Aimal ignored it.

He ignored also that Fatima's father preferred a meeting with just the fathers first, without Fatima there. That was fine. Perhaps he was conservative, traditional; Aimal could handle it. But Aimal didn't have a father, so one of his brothers, Bashir, agreed to stand in.

On the appointed day, Aimal went to the barber to get a fresh haircut and shave, then put on his nicest clothes. Why wasn't he nervous? This was the day the rest of his life began. He walked into the coffee shop feeling lighter than air. He had no idea he and his brother were walking into an ambush.

"If my daughter marries you," her father said, dispensing quickly with pleasantries, "and says, 'Let's go on a honeymoon in Paris,' can you go with her?"

Well, no. He knew that was not possible. Even if Aimal could afford a trip like that, it'd be hard for him to travel on an Afghan passport.

"Or," her father said, "how would you feel if Fatima had a colleague, a male colleague, and *they* traveled to another country together? How would you feel then?"

"She could travel. I wouldn't mind."

"If my daughter goes out with friends and comes home at 2 a.m. drunk, what's your mom going to think?"

"I think"—what was this man getting at?—"I think she should be proud to drink, but when she wants to come see my mom, she has to respect my mom. I drink, we drink, we're not against drinking, but sometimes it's about respect. My mother's house is not a bar."

Where was this going? Aimal arguing his worthiness as a husband by talking about how much he and his friends sinned.

"You don't get it. If you want to marry, I won't stand in your way. It's her decision. But understand. We are up here," he said, and Aimal watched him lift one hand up high. "You are down here."

Aimal nearly exploded. He wanted to reach over the table and slap the man across the face. Stand up, throw the table over, kick him in the chest. *I grew up in a street fight.* He could murder this man with one strike. He'd once punched a kid so hard in a schoolyard brawl that his jaw slid sideways and Aimal fainted. He could rearrange this man's face too, if he wanted. Chemicals shot through him, powering up his body for combat, contracting muscles to launch him out of his seat, but he forced himself to stay down. He grasped for a thread and caught it, a link back to Fatima.

He stilled the violence inside him, though the man didn't deserve it. He was forcing it down for the girl because whatever the man said, she'd done nothing to Aimal. Forcing it down because whatever this man said, he was still technically a guest.

"And, son, how much do you make a year?" He kept goading. "What's your salary?" Aimal didn't want to answer. He didn't want to be here anymore. He didn't want to admit he made only $150 a month as a driver. "I make enough to be happy."

"Do you know that your salary for an entire year, I just spent on the ticket for this trip? On one plane ticket. How will you send my daughter on vacation? What if she wants to travel?"

Aimal needed to leave. He needed to escape before this got any worse, before he said something that might hurt Fatima, hurt his own family. But Fatima was already slipping away, disappearing behind those laddered hands: *You're down here; I'm up here.*

They left the meeting, his brother trailing an elaborate sequence of profanity, but Aimal had moved quickly, as he always did, from a spike of rage to dejection. It burned hot and then was gone. He checked his phone, and there was the text he knew would be waiting for him.

"What happened?"

He lit a cigarette. "Everything was good. Your dad's amazing." A little later: "I think we should take a break."

And in came a flood of warmth from Fatima: *I don't care; I'll never drink; it's not important; I won't travel; we'll make it work.* But it was too late. Her father was an asshole, how dare he say those things, but was he wrong? It took just a few hours for Aimal to look back and realize that the man had not said a single untrue thing. How would it ever work with Fatima? Would Aimal be a man living off his wife's better salary? He was nothing. He was a fatherless taxi driver. *You're down here.* He had never been to a European country before; he had never been to America. He was just a hungry street kid. He'd be an anchor on her life.

He turned his work phone on and saw I'd called for a pickup. Maybe seeing a friend would lift his spirits. But his face must've betrayed him because the questions came immediately and weren't comforting. What happened? How did it go? He tried to explain, but the feelings were too intense to translate; the things spinning in his head didn't fit into his passenger's language. He got frustrated, the anger spiked again, and he knew what came out wasn't making sense. "Her father said, 'If my daughter comes home at 3 a.m. from some wedding and is with drinking, falling around, you won't do anything.' And I am say to him, 'You are a fucking that I won't do anything; she will be my wife, and if she does that . . .'"

He could see I didn't understand. *I can barely speak English.* He was just a driver. Fatima's father was right; he wasn't good enough. He decided he had no choice but to push Fatima away, to keep from pulling her down.

But he would never forget those laddered hands. Her father was right, but one day, somehow, Aimal would be big enough to fuck him up.

CHAPTER 14

FALL 2008

THINGS GOT WORSE. I LEFT THE COUNTRY, AIMAL FIRST THOUGHT I'd come back, but he then learned I'd gotten a job in America and would be staying there for good. He'd known that day was coming. And the loss of Fatima. He knew he probably broke her heart, but what choice did he have? He was no one.

He started to get frustrated more easily. Little things triggered him. He still wasn't getting a salary at Zuhaak, even after all his marketing. It hurt more after Fatima's dad, and now his mother was in his ear too. "Why are you working 24/7 for them? At least at the old company they gave you salary."

"It will come," he said. "I just need patience."

But he wasn't sure. He didn't feel right. He'd all but single-handedly recruited the new company's customer base. Foreigners used Zuhaak because they liked *him*. The owners came to *him* every day for advice, Aimal was the one with all the ideas.

When the two Zuhaak owners had their first big argument, one of them wanted to break off into still another company. This time, he wanted *Aimal* as an official cofounder, and Aimal felt a heave of pride, but then the man said he wanted to bring his own brother into the new company too, and Aimal could see what would happen down the road. There would be some dispute or another, the two brothers sitting across the table from him, and he'd be outnumbered.

He liked the idea, though. Being a founder. And the offer reminded him of a conversation in the car outside the university, just after Muqim fired him. *Why don't you start your own company?* An American said he was capable. Afghans now seemed to think he was capable. Maybe he was. Maybe now it was time.

———

NO MONEY, NO CARS, A CITY FULL OF RIVALS. HIS MOTHER BACK IN his ear: "No one in your family has their own business. Your father, your grandfather didn't, your older brothers, why are you doing this? You'll only bring yourself trouble." She didn't get it. She wasn't changing with the times like he was. In the West, in the West's version of here, anyone could be anything if they worked hard enough or were a little more clever than the rest. He was both. He couldn't listen to her. Sometimes people who love you hold you back. Now, he was seeing a path no one else saw.

He needed another driver.

He needed cars. You can't have a taxi company without taxis.

He needed money to register the cars and the business with all the right authorities, he needed better English to make brochures and websites, he needed, perhaps more than anything else, a whole lot of luck. *I have balls, but I'm still just a street kid.* He'd burned the people who might have helped him along. He couldn't exactly go to Muqim and ask for seed money, or the vehicle registration department boss. He had no father or father-in-law to hear his pitch. And the longer the odds seemed, the more superstitious he felt. He would do this, but too many things had to fall in place. He needed money; he needed a charm. He sat in his room and thought: money, but perhaps even more, something to neutralize the worry and bring him good fortune. Not exactly a lot of small-business loans being offered in Kabul, especially for a kid who owned nothing of value, no collateral—no, that wasn't an option. Nothing of value—he thought now how little he had. No bank account, no savings, so few objects he could even say were *his*. The house that was his mom's, a few packs of cigarettes on standby, a shitty phone for each cell network and a few pairs of clothes. Clothes—he looked up at the blue shirt he'd traded for, still hanging in his room. His good-luck charm, still unused since the date with Fatima, and suddenly he knew what to do. He needed me involved. It didn't matter how, or how much; he just needed me to give his business my blessing. He thought, *That's right; that's all I need to launch*. He knew it was superstitious, irrational, but whatever, that was part of the way his mind worked, so why fight it. When someone in your life is lucky, you bring them into anything important you're doing. It had been Jaff's idea, hadn't it, sitting in the car outside the university? Aimal would call me and ask me to invest. He wouldn't tell me the reason he asked was for luck; that would be too much pressure. What if the business failed and I thought it was all my fault? He waited for night so it wouldn't be too early in America, and when I picked up the phone, it sounded loud where I was, maybe not a good time, but he asked anyway.

"How much do you need?" I sounded hesitant, or maybe just distracted. There were cars where I was.

"Yah, Jaff. Anything, you should not to trouble yourself. Any amount." And he was being polite, but he meant it. Any amount did help. If he had his friend's investment, he'd have his friend's luck, and that's what he needed most.

And when I wired him $700, he felt first flecks of gold were winking up at him. The business had a chance. It didn't matter that it was a strange amount, hardly enough to purchase anything of value. It was exactly what he needed. Just enough to cover the fees he needed to pay in order to get the business registered and get all the right licenses. Just enough to turn Aimal, street kid from Kabul, into, officially, the owner of his own business. And just enough, even more, to bring his business luck.

Now, name registered and business blessed by his luckiest friend, he felt unstoppable. He was something. He was confident, invigorated, caffeinated. *Qaf, Yeh, Ghani*. He was ready to solve the puzzle no one else saw. He needed cars, and they couldn't be shitty ones. He called the same neighbor who'd gotten him that first meeting with Muqim, and he signed on to Aimal's venture without haggling. Then, even better. He came through with a chunk of money from a relative in England, a loan to buy one vehicle. A start. A car to compete with the eight cars from Zu-haak and the twelve or fifteen that Afghan Logistics had all around the city. Aimal needed at least one more to start so at least he and his neigh-bor could drive at the same time. He thought of using his brother's old sedan, but it was too run-down; he wanted nicer cars for his foreigners.

He had an idea. He went to his brother. "How much do you think your car's worth?"

Naheb thought for a moment. "Four thousand," he said, "maybe five thousand."

"I'll give you $7,000 for it," Aimal said. "But: you have to give me six months to pay." Big, kind Naheb, helpless to refuse his younger brother, bouncing with ambition.

Aimal took the old sedan up to the nearest dealership. "That silver Corolla out there," he said to the attendant, "how much more valuable do you think that car is than this one I have here?"

The attendant looked at the beater Aimal had chugged up in. "That Corolla you're looking at has to be worth at least a few thousand more than yours."

"OK. I'll trade you my old sedan here for that new Corolla," Aimal said, "and I'll give you *more* than a few thousand extra for it." He thought of a number. "I'll give you *seven thousand* extra for it, and the only condi-tion is, you have to give me six months to pay it."

Now Aimal was in business. Fourteen thousand dollars in debt, two cars, two drivers. Still competing with fleets of vehicles and barracks full of drivers at the other companies, but he had momentum. He and the neighbor began sleeping in the cars because they had no barracks and because Aimal wanted them ready to go at a moment's notice. They still couldn't afford to hire any support staff, so Aimal taught himself to be a dispatcher and a driver at the same time. For the first time, he had to be economical with words. He fielded requests for new rides from the driv-er's seat, packing sunshine and manners into clipped sentences so as not to disturb the foreign passenger already riding with him. He taught him-self little adjustments—"Hi, thanks for calling!" instead of "Welcome to Golden Tours!"—because foreigners in the backseat wanted to feel like they were his only friend. Speaking to other customers was adulterous, so he pretended he wasn't.

He targeted highly visible clients with connections. He was a businessman now, still just a kid in debt but hustling, coiled, and poised to leap into the ranks of real human beings, of people who Fatima's father would be ashamed to have wronged. He learned from the first few fares, people speaking more freely with him now that it was his own company, that there was an American, the chief for a big USAID contractor, who liked to hang at Da Red Rose, one of the safest nightspots for foreigners. Red Rose benefited from security for a couple of nearby embassies, and had its own series of checkpoints too. Even in the high tides of violence that swept through the city, the seasons of carnage, security directors at foreign companies often kept Red Rose on their green lists. Aimal heard the chief was there almost every night, and the chief was a man he aimed to befriend. If Aimal could get some time with him, he could prove *I'm a nice guy, I can help you*, and the chief could be a channel to all sorts of other blessings. His job, as far as Aimal could tell, was handing out millions of dollars to companies building things in the country. He was a valve controlling the flow of largesse the West was trying to take credit for. Aimal needed to find a way to get close, and the obvious answer was to drive him, but the chief had his own private driver. Aimal needed to get between them. So one night, he drove out to Red Rose, pretended to be waiting for a client, sidled up to the chief's private driver, and suggested they pass the time playing cards.

Aimal tried to time the next steps just right. As the night wore on, he started losing hands on purpose. When it was close to closing time, Aimal said, "Shit, well, I'm out." He handed the pot of cash over to the private driver. "I guess snack time is on me. Why don't you go ahead and get some food."

The driver hesitated. Aimal encouraged him. "Go ahead; it's OK."

The chief came out to find his driver gone, and Aimal went in for the kill. Standing by his just-washed car, smile tuned to friendly and confident but not cocky, promising a comfortable ride, pushy but not too pushy. *It's late. It's no problem. I'll get you home safely.*

Once in the car, Aimal chattered but throttled his talk just so, showing he wasn't a threat, showing approachability, careful not to annoy his passenger. Mostly he listened. The chief had been drinking; he mumbled something about hashish.

"You want hashish?" Aimal had his opening. He could take the chief through back alleys and find a dealer; he knew where to look. But it was late, that'd be dangerous, a hoodlum would see a kidnapping opportunity, and those places were unlit. Too risky.

He thought through the options, remembered something from his first few days driving for Afghan Logistics—how he'd come to see everyone in this city as needing a drug, no matter their position. Even police, though their salary wasn't enough to afford liquor or anything special. A few hits of hashish lasted hours and cost a few dollars, the economical way to ingest some forgetting. The better bet, he figured, if not the expected move, was to see if police officers at one of the checkpoints had some of the drug tucked into their pocket, and at this hour it'd be safer to try and make a deal with a police officer. He was dressed well, his car was clean, the passenger in back was impressive looking. They wouldn't look like addicts or criminals.

He pulled aside at the traffic circle, threw a hand up at a police officer, spoke quietly, and made a deal.

In the back, the chief was impressed. Aimal dropped him off, passed him a card, and said, "Call me for anything—see you next time."

He began waiting outside Red Rose most nights, and on nights when the chief wanted to make a pit stop, he started dismissing his other driver. He took to Aimal, as Aimal knew he would. Word spread. Aimal got calls from the chief, and soon from the chief's colleagues and friends, asking for rides and sometimes asking for other things too, various kinds of contraband. His customer base expanded. He was discreet. More foreigners learned to trust him as someone who could procure them any kind of forbidden thing. Hashish, hotel rooms under false names, brief freedoms and sin when they needed it. It was Aimal who could pry apart the hidden city and pull from the dark whatever the foreigners might covet, bound and caged and rich. All for just five dollars a ride, but Aimal wasn't thinking of the taxis as the point. The taxis didn't need to turn a profit. Not for a while, at least, not until his loans were due. He needed the company name, *his name*, diffusing through the city so all the right people would hear it. The cars were just a fleet of sleek, silver billboards on wheels, and he wanted *Aimal* associated with quality, Western excess, class, quiet, trust. He thought of the taxis not as the product he offered but as advertising. He knew there was more opportunity here, in the space between his people and the foreigners. He knew he couldn't see its exact shape, he just knew it was there, money to be made, his share of the incoming cash, and that if he covered enough space, and if enough people heard about him, eventually he'd find it.

CHAPTER 15

WINTER 2008

He made more friends. The higher-class kind, the made men or at least men on the make, who drew to him more easily now, and he knew why: in their eyes he was becoming more civilized. A sheen from the foreigners he mingled with rubbed off on him. He could feel himself starting to sparkle. He could see it in the people across the carpet, drinking tea or liquor with him. He began to spend time with the giant colonel from the NATO base just to drink and gossip, the one nicknamed by drivers at the old company "Buffer" for his thundering voice. Aimal's nighttime drives with the USAID chief helped Colonel Buffer feel more comfortable around him too, and being with Colonel Buffer helped him attract others. New friends helped him make newer friends. He met another hustling Afghan, a little older, impressed with Aimal's access to foreigners. Staying at a hotel Aimal drove by often because it was near his mother's house, living there, really, because he was from out of town and determined to stay in Kabul as long as it took to get what he wanted. A new friend who said he was a candidate. He'd once been a fighter of medium rank and good repute from the Panjshir Valley, but Aimal didn't hold that against him because this candidate was trying to do what Aimal was trying to do. Defying a script built into the condition of his birth, lowering a shoulder and forcing a route through to his own story. The candidate didn't want to be a fighter anymore. He was trying to go straight and serve the people; he said he'd meet every power broker it took to get himself a position in government. He liked to drink too. The candidate was someone Aimal could see himself someday doing some kind of business with. Aimal was building the network he needed, and now it was time to activate the next part of his plan.

He needed more control. He needed his name in the minds of even more foreigners to make sure he heard about big opportunities first. He needed to skim more customers away from other companies, more reasons they'd prefer his service to others. He was already offering something extra, a driver doing concierge duty for the foreigners, and that was good, but it was not enough, and he had an idea for how to carve out an edge.

He'd picked up on how impatient foreigners tended to be. In the West, schedules must be shrunken, unrelenting; Americans didn't know how to sit. If he could make rides *quicker*, he'd have a bigger advantage. He couldn't drive any faster than he already did. Traffic was traffic, and he'd maxed out the shortcuts he'd picked up first as a vehicle agent and then by plying the city streets with other companies.

But everyone knew the slowest parts of driving in the city were the times when you weren't moving at all: security checkpoints. When you had to stop, cops and sergeants ran wheeled mirrors under cars to check undercarriages for bombs, rifled through trunks, and foreigners had to sit there and wait. Aimal could almost feel how the foreigners hated that. Checkpoints made them nervous, they hated waiting, and he could tell they didn't revel in having Afghans show authority over them either.

That was where the margin was. If he could find a way of evading security, he'd be not just the best servant to the foreigners, but the fastest. That was where no one thought to look. He would.

He called up Colonel Buffer because Colonel Buffer had access to the liquor at his base's PX but also a weakness for hashish. That was ideal. Out in the city it was the opposite: liquor special and expensive, hashish cheap on the street if you knew where to look. He invited Colonel Buffer over to relax. *I'll provide the hashish, although to be honest, I don't have much booze,* and the colonel said no problem.

After a night smoking and drinking, Aimal easing the colonel into a sense of comfort so it didn't feel too transactional, Colonel Buffer went home with a pocket full of drugs and left Aimal a case of beer and a few cases of liquor.

Now, having arbitraged cheap hashish for expensive liquor, Aimal took a drive to visit the highest-security checkpoints. He invited police to take a break with him, ladled them glasses of whiskey from his stash in the back of the car, shared lewd jokes, made sure to keep his face in the light.

Three nights into his delivery runs, he'd worked his way into the good graces of all the officers manning the slowest checkpoints. The change was almost immediate. His passengers started to marvel: Aimal's cars weaved around the lines of vehicles waiting to be searched, allowed through without so much as a second glance. Passengers laughed and poked his shoulder. They called him "Superhero" and asked how he'd become so professional that his cars never got searched. Who did he know; how had he done it? They called him their guardian angel. Word spread even more. Aimal got more calls than he could field from his driver's-seat office. He was becoming known.

—

NOW THAT HE'D LIBERATED HIS FOREIGNERS FROM THE TYRANNY OF security searches, he looked to fill the concierge role more fully. What other ways might there be to keep them comfortable?

He knew the highest-ranking foreigners were always trying to stage escapes from their own security directors. From backseat chatter he knew that foreigners tended to see the people tasked with protecting them as prison wardens. Aimal's growing roster of VIP clients complained endlessly about the rules they had to follow. An epidemic of cabin fever had begun, and the temperature rose every time a new bombing set overexcited security personnel off on their showy power trips, crossing things off and hacking up the lists of locations that their charges were allowed to visit. Aimal saw another need, and he set about finding a way to meet it.

One of the places almost always deemed safe for foreign VIPs, even when security tightened, was Boccaccio, an Italian bistro behind blast walls where Russian-speaking waiters served pasta to suited embassy workers slipping flak jackets off at the door. Aimal came up with a plan. He found an alley near the restaurant where he could hide his car and wait, stakeout style. VIPs got out of their cars, walked into the restaurant, waited for their own vehicles to leave—then walked right back out to get in Aimal's car.

And then they were off. They were free. Aimal took them wherever they wanted to go, spending hours touring the city and then delivering them back to Boccaccio just in time to meet the vehicles from their own organizations, arriving to pick them up from the restaurant, never knowing they'd been anywhere else. Aimal showed the highest-ranking aid workers, embassy employees, and contractors parts of the city they wouldn't otherwise see, the parts that weren't performed for them. He showed them Afghans who weren't expecting guests, who hadn't vacuumed, hadn't piled the detritus of lives as messy as anyone's into a back closet, hadn't yet pushed their infirm or injured, their feebleminded, into back bedrooms and hushed them up. The ones who drank in their homes, who had the good hashish, who elbowed each other about girls.

He learned to let the foreign VIPs think they were in just a little danger, even when he had full control, and he always had full control because even now, though the hustle helped distract his ghosts, they always caught up. The morgue after a bombing, the open-eyed journalist and the blood flung onto his clothes—Aimal smiled at his clients and spoke his endearing shitty English, he behaved like he carried nothing on him but confidence, even as he saw the foreigners in front of him mutilated by high-velocity rounds, limbs torn off by explosions that hadn't happened. He'd never let it happen. He delivered his clients back to the bistro enlivened, intact, in his debt, in possession of some essential sense of the country that they were otherwise only partway in.

He hustled harder.

It was all beginning to work. The company had been blessed by his lucky charm, and his faith in it was as solid as any heavy alloy. *It will work.* He had a growing Rolodex of Western VIPs in his head. The rest would come. It had to. He knew it would. His mother was in his ear again; he never slept, he worked nonstop, and after gas he was still making hardly any money. She worried about him: he was going to get himself in trouble, and how would he ever pay back the debt he'd taken on? Where's your brother's car? But he had even less doubt this time; she was uneducated, his blessed mom, widowed young, and somehow, with no income and no husband, she'd kept her dozen sons and daughters alive, but among the prices she'd paid was missing the chance to lift her head up and look around. The country had changed. The world had changed. The West was here. Aimal had changed. She needed only a little patience now, he was certain.

———

WHEN THE BUSINESS WAS STILL ONLY A FEW MONTHS OLD, AIMAL GOT the call he'd been waiting for. The one that would turn his company from a taxi service into something else entirely.

A man who handled logistics for an organization Aimal had heard of, a for-profit company that had received hundreds of millions of dollars in American aid money. Saying he'd heard about Aimal from the USAID chief; he'd asked around and found that a lot of people knew of Aimal already, that he could be trusted, and that he was good at getting foreigners whatever they needed, however large or small. He needed something large. "You have those sedans," the American said, "but what about arms? Do you have armored vehicles?"

Aimal did not. "Of course, sir. How many you need?"

"Three or four."

Aimal thought quickly: if this American was asking for armored vehicles, then he must be worried about security. If he was worried about security, he was under pressure. And if he was asking Aimal rather than some established business partner, that meant he'd tested the market already and hadn't found what he needed yet.

"It's $14,000 a month for each one of my vehicles." Aimal started high and readied himself for the bargaining, but the man on the phone didn't even counter. *Yes, fine, deal, here's where to deliver them*, and now Aimal needed to find the vehicles he'd just said he had.

Who might have an armored car to lend him? What kind of person bought an armored car but didn't actually need it? What kind of person had four?

He had an idea. His new friend from the Panjshir Valley, the candidate staying at the nearby hotel and trying to give up his past. Since the candidate had been a fighter before, Aimal figured he must have weapons. He might have an armored vehicle or two. And since the candidate said he didn't want to be a fighter anymore, he might not need them. Plus, if he wanted to be a politician, he'd have all sorts of campaign expenses, wouldn't he? He might need a little extra money. Aimal paid him a visit. "You have access to any armored vehicles you could rent?"

"I might have a few . . ."

"Want to make some money on them?"

"How much?"

Again, Aimal thought quickly. The candidate would be happy with any profit; this was money for nothing. He didn't need to know that Aimal had struck a deal to rent the vehicles out for $14,000 each.

"I can rent the vehicles out for $9,000 each."

The candidate considered it. "OK. If you give me $8,000 for each, $1,000 in profit is yours to keep."

But it wasn't a thousand in profit for each, it was five thousand, and altogether, three vehicles, for four months, cash to be paid up front—Aimal had just made $60,000 on a single deal. He could hardly believe it. How long ago was it that he was making a $150 a month? He'd just made more than four hundred times that with the stroke of a pen, more money than he'd ever seen. A kid so hungry that his cuts didn't heal, a suitor so lowly that even a factory worker knew his daughter was too good for Aimal. *Now look at me.*

Before something could happen to the cash, he drove to the car dealership to pay off the Corolla, plus the premium, then he bought another Corolla, then he brought his brother's old sedan back and gave Naheb his premium too. With so much cash on hand, he called Barialay and hired him away from Zuhaak, promising no drunk soldiers shooting through the roof because this new company had only high-class customers, the kind with the authority to approve big contracts. And Aimal started looking for more opportunity in what had just clearly revealed itself to be the far more lucrative trade. His small company, seeded from a $700 investment and an injection of luck, was no longer a taxi company. Aimal was becoming more like an arms dealer.

CHAPTER 16

SPRING 2009

MONEY BEGAN TO FLOW. HE WAS EARNING IN THE BREACH, THE connective tissue between Afghans who had things and foreigners who needed things. The gap in knowledge is where he thrived. He brought two sides together; he learned to keep two sides apart. He wouldn't show Afghans what his deals with the foreigners looked like, and the foreigners didn't need to know how much he was paying Afghans.

Still leery of keeping cash on hand, he put some of the money in property, one thing his father taught him before his mysterious death. *You'll never lose your money in gold, bricks, or land.* Aimal bought property out in the provinces, getting acres in Mazar near a planned railway spur. He bought a parcel in Kabul and started building an office. His was more luxurious than the other car companies because it *wasn't* just another car company. He wanted foreigners in his space to feel safe, and warlords to feel safe, and foreigners to feel safe around warlords. He wanted people to feel feted; he wanted them comfortable walking in unarmed because he'd known since my going-away party at the old Lebanese restaurant that when people sat without their weapons, everyone was calm, smiling, laughing, in their own little heavens, brightly lighted to burn the city's storm clouds from their minds. The weight of a weapon anchored you to this place. He wanted people unarmed when talking about dealing arms; that was the catch-22 behind successful arms deals. He learned. He started hanging out with a young man whose family ran one of the fancier hotels in town. He became a friend to the heir, the Paris Hilton to Kabul's premier brand, which was just one hotel but boasted a top-floor restaurant and a shiny, gold-looking facade that somehow wasn't always covered in dust, somehow wasn't ever bombed. The heir was as ostentatious as the real Paris Hilton but in a different way. Aimal liked hanging with him; there weren't many people who knew more than Aimal had picked up about hospitality, but also because the heir was always awash in contraband. Driving around with a sniper rifle riding around in the backseat like a mascot, always a joint in his mouth, a fifth of vodka in the cup holder, a few hundred thousand in cash on hand just because, and always a stack of passports from different countries. He traveled whenever he wanted. "How'd you get US citizenship?" Aimal asked. The heir took a hit and didn't answer. "How'd you get Canadian citizenship?" Maybe just a smirk.

There was a story about the heir: he'd been attacked once, an operation to snag him while he was moving some of the family's cash around. But his father, the hotelier, was so well connected, got to the criminals so quickly, and frightened them so thoroughly that they came back an hour later, returned the heir and the money, and apologized for their mistake.

That was connections. Driving around with the heir taught Aimal just how much you had to be able to operate backstage. You had to make the connections to manipulate the rigging in the shadows, even though what you showed, to anyone, was a smiling face, ease, calmness, a shiny gold facade.

He hired two attractive young women with good English to sit at a desk and call themselves office managers, a term he'd heard on the dish, though he didn't really know what "office manager" meant. They were there to make the whole thing seem more professional in the way he felt only professional-looking women can. Once finished, once furnished, he called the candidate—*I have a place for you*—and invited him to stay as long as he wanted for free. Having the candidate around made finding armor when requests came in easier.

More foreigners heard of his company as the safe purveyor of whatever you need, especially armored vehicles. Cash poured in. Two armored cars for one foreign company, four for another, and the candidate called his friends in the valley to wrangle up what Aimal needed to serve his growing client base. He learned to see the armor market as a lagging indicator for violence in the country. He learned that big bombings boosted security budgets, armored cars became scarce, so Aimal charged more. He learned supply and demand. Now he was making close to $100,000 every few months. He made the office more opulent; now it had a long royal table, gold-rimmed chairs with overstuffed velvet cushions, and tea service out of a pharaoh's house. The money became harder to hide.

A request from another American came in for six armored vehicles, but this time, the candidate couldn't help: "Sorry, brother. I don't have any to spare." He couldn't find any from his friends back in the valley. The candidate thought for a moment. "But I know someone who will have what you need." He said he was willing to make a special introduction to a man who'd likely have arms of all kinds to spare. "But if you fuck this up," the candidate said, "you make sure you bought your one-way ticket from Afghanistan because he's going to chase you down."

"Who is this guy?"

"Don't worry. You'll know him. Everyone knows him. Let me set it up. I'll call you."

Two days later, the candidate called. "We're going. Just try to stay calm."

They met up and together drove south. The candidate still wouldn't tell Aimal who they were going to see, as if he might have doubts about bringing Aimal into the fold like this, but as soon as they crossed into the northwestern neighborhood of Khair Khana, Aimal knew: this was the ophthalmologist's domain. It all made sense. The eye-doctor-turned-militia-member-turned-aspiring-politician. The biggest man Aimal could think of, and his Kabul headquarters was there, in a neighborhood peopled mostly by Panjshiris, the same group the candidate belonged to. Just like the candidate, he had belonged to a militia lauded for fighting the Taliban and also cursed for destroying swaths of Kabul. Probably responsible for some of the rockets Aimal dodged as a child, but Aimal wasn't thinking about that now. This was the new Afghanistan, where dreams were possible, a street kid meeting the most famous person he knew to discuss business. *Am I seeing all of this right?* His mind cycled through a kaleidoscope of emotions. Disbelief to excitement, then hopelessly nervous, then energy—he felt consecrated. *What's happening to me?* He was being rewarded faster even than he'd imagined.

The guards recognized the candidate and ushered them in. He and Aimal moved through an anteroom full of extravagances. Aimal tried not to stare, it looked to him like walls filled with ancient volumes of poetry, lush paintings, it felt more like a museum than a receiving room. Through one building, then out, the candidate led Aimal to a second room, a kind of inner sanctum. It was obvious this was not a place many visitors got to see.

And there sat the ophthalmologist, watching over his domain like an emperor of some forgotten kingdom. Trademark clipped beard announcing a jaw line, holding court before a gauntlet of monitors flickering with every part of the compound. Aimal recognized a chair from television addresses. Was it a chair? Less a chair than a throne.

Aimal had *arrived*. If he could sit with the ophthalmologist, he was *somebody*. His nerves eased. He knew these types had tempers, but the man was welcoming. He smiled. *Be cool.* He was calm. So Aimal became calm.

The ophthalmologist looked on with what seemed to be kindness as the candidate introduced Aimal. "A partner in business. He has a good connection with the foreigners. He sometimes gets the biggest contracts, but he doesn't have the equipment to supply them. I trust him. He's smart. He knows how to get the job done. . . ." On and on the candidate went, the ophthalmologist's eyebrows dancing along in approval. The candidate unfurled a whole exaggerated résumé for Aimal, an aria of compliments Aimal knew was just the candidate protecting himself before this important man, but still, it felt good to be spoken of like this. Had anyone ever spoken like this about him? He thought of those hands: "I'm up here; you're down here," *and now I'm here; where are you? I'm getting my ass kissed in front of a man who could buy you a thousand times over.*

The ophthalmologist listened and looked at Aimal. "You're so young." Back to the candidate. "He looks so young. I thought you brought him for chores." A joke? "OK, so tell me, son, what do you need?"

Aimal pulled the brake and launched headlong into his pitch: "I have a company, but I'm always in need of armored vehicles to rent."

"And how much do you rent armored vehicles for?"

"Ten thousand a month." Did he say it too quickly? "Sometimes twelve thousand." The ophthalmologist tilted his head.

"OK. And now"—was that a smile? It wasn't anger, Aimal didn't think—"and now why don't you tell me the real price."

Aimal fought back a smile. What was happening? He was sitting with a famous warlord, negotiating. He'd ridden a rocket to the moon. "OK, I'll tell you. With all respect, it ranges from fourteen or fifteen to maybe sixteen or seventeen—it depends on the client."

Now the ophthalmologist seemed satisfied. "How about this. Any vehicle you need from me, I'll rent it to you for $13,000. After that, I don't care what you rent it out for; that's your profit."

He turned to an aide. "Take his signature, and get this young man the vehicles he needs."

———

AND THAT WAS IT. WITH THE OPHTHALMOLOGIST'S BLESSING, AIMAL had access to an entire fleet. The aide took Aimal to a giant warehouse on the property and opened the door to at least sixty brand-new, gleaming vehicles, maybe a hundred, maybe two hundred. Here was a museum of Land Cruisers, soft-skin vehicles, armored vehicles—everything. Trucks with gun turrets, wall-to-wall bulletproof paneling. It was like an entire car dealership right on the property. He couldn't imagine why one man would need so many vehicles, and though he would later, he wasn't in that moment thinking about the implications—that he'd just sat with a man anointed by foreign countries as a vessel for their influence in this country. That foreign powers here tended to buy influence with money and gifts, and that the money for this particular kind of influence had to be hidden. Once Aimal actually thought about the ophthalmologist's ideas—who his relationships were with, who his policies were likely to benefit—it began to seem that most likely all this armor came from Iran. Part of an effort to win influence with the ophthalmologist and help him win influence in this country. The aide spoke: "You have access to anything in here."

Holy shit. "Can I take six?"

"I'll get the papers."

IT ALL WENT SO SEAMLESSLY.

Aimal went back to the client who'd asked for the vehicles, signed a deal, and made the ophthalmologist $78,000 a month.

Soon, another American security contractor called with an even bigger request.

Then a British security company Aimal understood was working with MI6, then another American company, and now he had clients all over Kabul.

A call came in with a request for *thirty* armored vehicles, and the client wanted them for half a year. Aimal said "No problem," and for the first time, he knew it actually wasn't a problem. So much cash was coming in that storing it became an issue. Everyone dealt in cash because sending big sums of money through banks drew the wrong kind of government attention, and for all his planning, Aimal hadn't yet thought to open a bank account. He didn't want so much cash on hand, he especially didn't want cash that wasn't rightfully his, so his first order of business after taking payment for each deal was driving the ophthalmologist's cut over to his compound. He didn't expect to see the ophthalmologist there, Aimal figured he'd be off doing important things, but when Aimal arrived with cash from a thirty-vehicle deal, his new business partner was there waiting to receive him.

"I heard you're *killing* it. See, I knew you were a nice guy. You could've taken the money and run."

Aimal spoke without thinking. "Guess I could've made everyone look real stupid and run away, but not you, Doctor. I wouldn't do that to my godfather."

It slipped out, as things sometimes did, before he had the chance to turn it over in his mind. The ophthalmologist looked at him. Something changed.

When he spoke, it wasn't the same. "Ah, you know how to talk, don't you?"

Aimal kept his smile. This time he let the ophthalmologist fill the silence.

"You know what? I have three daughters . . ." His eyes drifted away, as if scanning for the point he wanted to make, then landed on the security monitors. "So that's your car?" Aimal's sedan was centered by a camera pointed out at the parking lot. "Come on. You just made so much money, you should drive high class!"

Aimal jagged toward modesty. "I can't afford it."

"You know what? Jump in my car. We're going for a ride."

The ophthalmologist had business in the provinces, but said he had an idea, and together they rode out toward the Panjshir Valley, where his power base was. Before arriving, he had his driver stop at his favorite car dealership.

"This is my buddy Aimal," he told the dealer. "Let him have any car he chooses. Send the invoice to me."

Aimal thought he heard wrong. "Are you sure?"

"Don't come to my house with that old car of yours again."

———

THEY LAUGHED—AIMAL AND THE OPHTHALMOLOGIST LAUGHED AT the American and British security contractors who showed up for meetings with the ophthalmologist, all proud of the gleaming armored vehicles they traveled in, unaware that those vehicles had come from the very man sitting before them. Or that as far as Aimal knew had come from Iran. Hadn't American leaders called Iran the "Axis of Evil"? Didn't American presidents consider Iran some kind of ominous threat?

And here were American spies driving around in armor provided by their rival.

Business grew.

The ophthalmologist found more ways to look after the young entrepreneur he clearly saw promise in. He arranged weapons licenses. Aimal had permission for only two, and now with the snap of a finger he had permits for seven. He went to Colonel Buffer for help upgrading his personal weapon, and Colonel Buffer managed to get him a US Air Force–issued Beretta with an extra-round feed system.

He got a special allowance for machine guns. He had AK-47s for a growing posse of security guards, among them a malnourished man who looked like a boy because his mother hadn't fed him, but Aimal hired him half out of charity and half because he was small and wiry and could follow Aimal down the street mostly unnoticed. He got permission for more signs of status—special permission for tinted windows and removing license plates from his cars. The best way to be seen these days was to show you didn't need to be seen. Aimal spent months trying to get the telecommunications ministry to make his phone number appear as hidden.

Business grew more. The ophthalmologist was busier than ever. He was popular in an important part of the country. Aimal wondered if he'd run for president, and then he announced he was going to run for president. Again, Aimal couldn't believe his luck. Friends, partners, brothers with maybe the next president of the country. He was twenty-five, but it wasn't out of the question that he'd be named minister of something. Transportation? The ophthalmologist even said, in a moment of private optimism, that if he won, Aimal would get a rocket launcher for his car. *Then we'll see who stops you.*

That was for tomorrow, though.

Today, it was beginning to feel there was limitless money to be made. Now that there were national elections coming up here, America and the rest of the Western countries were pouring even more cash into Afghanistan. Humanitarian aid, construction contracts, defense contracts, piles and piles of new programs and funding. Someone had to receive it all, and Aimal was learning how. All the new foreigners arriving in the country needed security. Foreigners landing in Afghanistan in more force, having decided collectively, or perhaps having just followed the Americans, that these elections would decide *the* future of the country. They would potentially represent the first peaceful transfer of power. It wasn't just Afghan politicians on the ballot; it was America.

A hundred thousand troops were already here, and now democracy-building organizations were staffing up, election monitors were descending on the country, more grants were going to aid organizations, more aid money was being given to for-profit contractors. Defense contractors staffed up to help secure polling places, and a parade of Western observers arrived to unofficially observe the first election to officially be observed by Afghan observers.

Things heated up. Insurgents would try to intimidate people, they would kill people, they would bomb polling places. The Taliban would try to keep turnout so low that the elections would be irrelevant and democracy would be revealed as a failed experiment. The West appeared to have no spending limits in trying to prevent that from happening.

On top of all the aid money already coming into the country, a new $200 million allocated for the elections came just from the US, and NATO effectively paused the rest of its war to focus on securing polling stations. But legions of soldiers in combat gear staring down voters wouldn't look like the peaceful transfer of power, so ten thousand tribesmen were hired for security, and instead of tanks next to lines of voters, the better visual was exactly the kind of armored car Aimal now had a reputation for providing. Demand soared. Aimal hustled.

All day every day working the phones, signing deals with foreigners, calling the ophthalmologist's aide to line up more armored cars. He could lease them for $25,000 a month and get away with it. The ophthalmologist needed to be a silent partner; he wouldn't want to be seen making money on an election he was running in, so Aimal was free to operate as he saw fit. And it was during the run-up to America's big election that Aimal became a millionaire. He earned more than $5 million in just the few months before voting. He leased so many vehicles that he nearly emptied the ophthalmologist's garage.

The country grew even more violent as the date of elections approached. More than thirty attacks a day at one point, and then the government blacked out coverage in the hopes that people wouldn't be too frightened to vote, but Aimal was flying his highest.

———

THE ONLY PROBLEM WAS THAT HE KEPT PROMISING VEHICLES BUT soon began to run out of them. The key to his business was his reputation. He didn't actually own anything of value. It was his personality and the ability to find what people needed. When someone asked for something, he had to be able to get it or they'd stop calling him, but there was more demand for vehicles than he could meet.

When an American intelligence agency heard that Aimal could provide armor, Aimal got a call with a request to meet. They needed twenty-nine armored cars. There was no way, but he couldn't admit that there was no way. He wanted these spies to call on him again, for whatever hardware they needed in the future. Instead of saying no, he quoted a ludicrous price he knew they'd laugh off. Better they think him unreasonable than incapable. "There's no vehicles on the market," he said, "but I can get for you."

"How much?"

"Forty-five thousand dollars." He braced for the *get the fuck out of here*. "Per month."

"Yeah, OK. When can you deliver?"

Fuck.

Where to turn now? The ophthalmologist's garage was empty, over 120 vehicles already out to Aimal's clients.

The only armor not leased to customers was the armor the ophthalmologist was actually using for himself. Aimal called him, somewhere out in the provinces, wearing himself thin on the campaign trail.

"Can you spare any vehicles from your convoy? It's a good customer . . ."

"I can give you one or two."

"Give me more!"

"It's an election! You want to get me killed?" But for Aimal, he said he'd find a way to shift things around. He was moving around with a security detail of a dozen armored vehicles. Maybe they could make do with seven or eight. He was willing to expose his own security detail for this deal his protégé was all excited about.

Now Aimal could at least put a dent in the order, but he needed more. He sat in the office and thought. What was he missing? Who hadn't he yet thought to ask? *Think, Aimal.* He was trying to force himself to focus when his phone rang, a nuisance call from an old client. No time for this now. The voice on the phone saying headquarters in Washington or London or something—*Who cared? Why were they telling him this?*—was recalling them from the country to wait out the elections elsewhere. Too dangerous, security unstable, more attacks against foreign civilians, Aimal wasn't paying any attention.

Then, suddenly, he was. He saw the solution: "OK, brother, yes, be safe and have a good trip. And you know what? Extra service for special client. Let me to send drivers. We should take the vehicles for you for oil change so they should be like new when you return."

He hung up and called the ophthalmologist: "I figured it out. One of the clients on a long-term lease is leaving the country; I can double lease those cars to the spies. We'll earn *twice* on each of those vehicles!"

The ophthalmologist was pleased. "How much are the spies paying?"

And it just slipped out: "25K a car."

He was lying. Why had he lied? It didn't occur to him to worry. He was earning his partner millions of dollars, even more than his partner had expected. If Aimal was making more per vehicle than he said he was making, why should anyone care? It didn't occur to him to worry because he didn't think anyone was getting hurt. Three letters for the price of two. Everyone got what they wanted. This was just

Aimal thriving in his habitat, that space, that breach in understanding between the people from this country and the ones pouring money into it.

He called the American spies. "I have your vehicles. Let us we should sign the deal."

Tension!!!.

CHAPTER 17

EARLY SUMMER 2009

Aimal stands inside a compound. It's 9 p.m., maybe a little later.

He's a mile or so east of Tapa-e Scud: "Scud Hill." It's habit here to call foreign things by their foreign names. A way of using without assimilating, so language sometimes seems as shaped by invasion as the buildings are. Scud Hill, for its part, comes from missiles the Red Army kept here; it's the reason the Mujahideen paid special attention to this place in the worst years of the country's war against the Russians, and then the war against itself. Aimal always thought his mother's house saw the harshest glare of falling rockets, but here nearly every building is hunched over from ordnance. Floors collapsed in on each other, buildings all in defeated bows. A part of the city all the dollars missed, or caught up to lately and strangely: near the old Scud base is a development a politician's brother is overseeing. A suburban development called Omid-e Sabz, or "Green Hope." A place where repatriating Afghans are landing and becoming landed elite, where people like Fatima might live, or her father, if he ever stooped low enough to come back to his own country. A place for the people who've learned life in Germany, or Holland, or London, and somewhere along the way got to thinking their daughters were worth more than Aimal could offer, just because no one ever brought him far enough to earn citizenship anyplace worth being from.

Now, he's built himself into a big man. Now he's here, meeting with the most powerful spies in the world. *I'm here.*

181

Now, with all the armor rented out, he's driven to meet the spies in a soft-skin sedan. His old neighbor and a new employee named Umbron come along for backup, though Aimal isn't really worried. Aimal is now the kind of person people know not to fuck with.

He walks to the compound and leaves his friends outside with the car. Bored, ambling. Umbron on the phone with a girlfriend to pass the time. The neighbor paces, gentle and smiling always, though he's a young man with a fierceness in him. With Aimal inside, he wanders from the car. Parked a full fifty yards from the gate because the compound's guards don't like Afghans getting close. Always different rules for the natives, even when what the natives are selling is safety.

A fierceness in him, but it's usually subdued. These little insults slide off him, usually. Making money off the conquerors can make the little apartheids go down a little easier, though there's something odd about tonight.

INSIDE, AIMAL SIGNS A CONTRACT THAT SAYS HE'S RECEIVED PAYMENT. The spy says, "Follow me," and they move toward a flight of stairs. "You want to take it all now? It's dark out."

"No problem, brother, don't worry. I'll take it now."

Another breath. "Are you sure you want to walk with this much money? How many people are with you?"

Some substance in Aimal is jostled. He senses something. The membrane of a threat he can't see clearly yet. "Me and two guys."

"Are you driving armored vehicles?"

"No, soft-skin." *The American is going to take advantage of me. Somehow.* The man is trying to swindle him, *somehow,* he's not sure how, how . . . *somehow . . . somehow . . .*

He figures it out. The man is trying to convince Aimal it's safer to come back tomorrow, and when he comes back tomorrow, the American will say, *What? You already have the money. Look: here is your signature saying you took it.* Then it will be an American's word against an Afghan's, and Aimal doesn't like those odds.

The spy asks a third time. "Are you sure you want to take the money?"

Aimal needs to show strength. "Don't worry, brother. It's my money. I have a good connection."

"Mm-hmm. OK. Then can you turn around, please?"

For just a moment he accedes, showing his back to the American. There's a *whoosh*, and when he turns back a door he didn't know was a door has opened, a wall has vanished, revealing a hidden room with perhaps a hundred shelves of neatly stacked currency. Aimal is stunned. He steps in. Here, in the middle of this un-rebuilt part of the city, is a fortune hiding in a vault. He can actually smell the money. The light catches it; the money shines.

The American counts, $800,000 in cash while Aimal tries to keep his composure. There doesn't seem to be anything to put it in. He wraps the cash in a piece of brown paper and gives it to Aimal. "Go, then," he says. "*Go.*"

Aimal hurries out of the compound and through the gate. He looks around. No one is following him. The fifty yards to the car is endless, but now he's home free. He nearly laughs. He throws the cash in the backseat and flips the courtesy light on so his two friends can see just how much it is, but only for a moment because then he jumps into the cash like a rapper in an American music video. He props his jaw on his fist like a centerfold model. *I'm the king!* "Fucking drive, brother!"

The neighbor laughs, turns the car on, and they drive—three friends and almost a million dollars. Aimal resting on the money, *look what I have done; look how far I have come.* Two years ago, stretching $150 across a month. Tonight, a million in one meeting. He hasn't just figured out how to make money on cars he doesn't own; he's figured out how to make money from two clients at the same time. The ophthalmologist will get a kick out of this, that the deal went smoothly, whenever he takes a break from the campaign. His garage empty, every one of his vehicles earning money—some earning twice. Aimal reclines with the money, and even in his reverie he's aware of tires whining on pavement somewhere. There's a *boom*, and at the same time, in the front seat, the neighbor's body does a little shimmy. Aimal feels blood splatter on his face; he feels liquid warmth and then a blast of heat because one of the windows has shattered.

Now Aimal can see a sedan coming toward them, still listing forward, and he sees the neighbor jerk for his weapon.

Aimal is disoriented, unsure what's just happened, what's still happening. He hears more shots, and then he's sitting half in and half out of the car, still clutching money and watching Umbron raise his arm with smoke leaking from the muzzle of a gun. And now Aimal is thinking, *I have a gun too*.

Aimal leaps fully out of the car, holding his pistol sideways, the extended-mag Beretta that Colonel Buffer gave him. Squeezing two, five, eight times, then ten, and twelve . . . how many? The neighbor fires too, then drops from view. Fifteen shots, sixteen, and then Aimal knows he's been trying to fire from an empty magazine, so he drops the gun and slides around the door to the neighbor. He stumbles and gropes through the blood until he has the neighbor's weapon, and then there are tires whining again, the other car taking off. The neighbor is still down, losing blood from his arm, and Aimal is standing up next to Umbron as they walk out after the attackers, two young men firing at night.

Tires screeching again, but this time it's Aimal driving, he's taken over without thinking, his body has taken over so he doesn't have to, the neighbor lying in the backseat now, bleeding on money. Racing through the streets. Running to the hospital, running from attackers who could come back at any moment. Who must've been some kind of vultures, opportunists, who figured out the compound had cash and waited around for people dumb enough to walk out with it. Or maybe something more sinister. The spy and his strange questions . . . Aimal has the pedal on the floor. He was a driver two years ago, delivering his journalist to the sites of violence before competitors could get there; he can still work the shortcuts at lightning speed, electricity dancing across a circuit board. Two turns, a third. Time warps ahead.

They're pulling up in front of the EMERGENCY sign at the hospital. They're lugging the neighbor's limp body through the entranceway. Aimal pacing furiously as the neighbor goes into surgery.

How long has he been in surgery? Minutes, hours? Time is not working right. Aimal is locked in this hallway; he feels a bodily need to stay close, like something worse will happen if he's not there to take care of his neighbor, his business partner. That feeling again, the need to protect like he felt with me and with his whole starving household back when he was a kid being trained as a tailor, the only brother young enough to make money for his family.

Money. Fuck.

Downstairs, there's a soft-skin car with a million in cash. *It's just money.*

He stays, pacing the hall.

But it's not all my money. A lot of that cash belongs to the ophthalmologist. *It's not mine to ignore.*

He's not sure what to do. *Someone was willing to kill for it.*

Shit.

He takes off running. He leaves the neighbor and runs outside the hospital, straight to a car with a backseat full of blood-stained cash. It's still there, but he can't guard it on his own. He's flustered; he calls the ophthalmologist. The aide is in the city and promises to come help. Aimal blinks, and the aide is there, barreling up in a small convoy, scolding Aimal for taking a soft-skinned car to pick up so much money. The aide gets in the shot-up car himself and drives away in his convoy, leaving a clean SUV for Aimal, and in the chaos, as Aimal heads back into the hospital to be close to the neighbor, he doesn't yet realize the key strategic mistake he's made. He never corrected the lie he told, how much he actually charged for the double-leased vehicles.

He doesn't yet remember that the bullet-ridden car the ophthalmologist's men just drove away in has more money in it than it's supposed to.

CHAPTER 18

AUGUST 17, 2009

AIMAL IS EXHAUSTED. THE NEIGHBOR IS ALIVE. THE OPHTHALMOL-ogist's men are taking care of the money. Who knows how. Cleaning it? Everything's happening at once. The elections are days away.

And there's one other thing he's forgotten: I'm coming back to the country for the vote. Why did I have to choose now to come? There are crises all around him to contend with; he doesn't have time. Over the phone I say I have an assignment to write about a long-shot candidate, a sixty-year-old academic with an American passport. His name is Ashraf Ghani. A member of an ethnic group Aimal doesn't belong to, but also a PhD from an American university. *Why are the Americans always interested in other Americans?* Aimal's business partner has a real chance to win; this man has none.

He knows he should send one of his drivers to pick me up from the airport. He has a million things to do. He has 130 armored cars in play; his neighbor is recovering from a nearly fatal shooting; his other business partner is growing impatient on his final campaign sprint. Aimal has no time for the American's visit, but then maybe he could use a break from all of his other troubles. It's irresponsible to skip town a few days before the elections, in the midst of the biggest business deals of his life. He decides he will anyway.

He decides he'll pick me up at the airport, take me wherever I want. Maybe it'll be healthy to be with someone who knew him before all this. All the way down to Jalalabad to translate for me if that's what I need. He has no armored vehicles left, so he picks me up in an old sedan. It's not the safest, and he's just learned the risk you take traveling in a soft-skinned car. If I ask, he'll say it's better to be incognito than make a display of your armor. He half believes it, anyway.

Straight from the airport, we head down toward the desert. Past Camp Phoenix, with all the damaged Humvees and armored vehicles sitting on flatbeds. Even though they were damaged, he could probably lease those for, what, $15,000 a month each? Probably more.

He begins to see how exhausted he is. He knows he's not present. So many things on his mind; he says he was at a wedding last night and scored some liquor. He tells me he's hungover, to avoid causing offense. We stop for cold drinks sold from storefronts fashioned out of shipping containers. The chirpy little salesmen are so young, dusty, and hustling that Aimal sees some lost, first version of himself.

He tries not to think of the shooting. The spy, the look, the safe. That hidden room and the questions. *Why not come tomorrow?* The sedan emerging from nowhere. What reason would the American spies have to work with a bunch of thugs? It wasn't some kind of setup. He'd have known if it was a setup; he'd have sensed it. The American spies couldn't be involved. He's sure. He's almost sure. Was there anything in it for them?

An American convoy comes into view, soldiers manning turrets. He doesn't slow down. He doesn't leave responsible space between them, but gains on them, then stays close, as if he might extract some answer from their faces. A soldier in a roof-mounted turret keeps looking away and looking back. Aimal tries to read his eyes. He feels himself pushing the pedal a little more. He wants to get closer.

The convoy pulls off the road. An unanswered question. Aimal continues.

He pulls the car over at a checkpoint. He knows why this checkpoint is here. This is the route toward the Black Cave, where bin Laden was almost caught in 2001. This is how you get to Tora Bora. An officer says, "Do you have a weapon?"

Aimal says, "No, no weapon."

They search him and find his weapon. "Why did you lie?"

"I didn't think you'd actually search me."

An hour later we're on our way again, and Aimal finds his way to the wedding hall where Ashraf Ghani is speaking. He watches me get out and start taking pictures, and then the speech begins. Aimal tries to listen, but he hates the way this man speaks. Sweeping and stabbing, screeching about power. Aimal doesn't want to be here. His head starts to throb. A hall full of Pashtuns in tribal clothing. It's not a good time for Aimal to feel outnumbered. He can hardly stand to listen. *This guy is speaking bullshit.* He has to force himself to pay attention so he can remember and translate for me later.

Finally, the event is over and we can head back to Kabul. He sees the river and asks if I want to stop; maybe wading in will wash off some of the sweat and vitriol from the day, the smell of a thousand turbaned bodies in poorly ventilated space. A riverside chef stands over a grill and offers fish cooked in hashish, but the last thing he needs is to cloud up his mind any more. He needs to get me home and sleep for a year.

———

A FEW DAYS LATER IS ELECTION DAY. IT ALL LEADS UP TO THIS. FOR Aimal, for the ophthalmologist, for their country, for America's experiment, for the West. For the 120-odd vehicles he's sent all over the country.

I'm still in Afghanistan for some reason he doesn't fully understand. I'm making reports, still building a name for myself, but there's something else. Some other project with that school I seem to love out in the Hazara slum his drivers never want to go to.

I call to say I want to write about Election Day. "Can you take me to some polling places?"

Aimal's already spent a day he shouldn't have spent driving me around. His neighbor still recuperating, today he's being summoned all over the city. He's attending meetings and fielding calls about problems with vehicles all over the country. He can't be with me too, but he's worried. He knows it's going to be a violent day. He knows not just from the news reports or the fact that the reports are now blacked out. He knows by the price of armored cars. Forty-five thousand dollars meant the market expected carnage. He's torn. What if something happens to me? But he has millions of dollars of the ophthalmologist's property in play. He can't just send any driver to look after me. He sends his older brother, but implores him, "You better not let anything happen to him. And if anything happens with him, you call me, not the cops."

He checked in constantly with his brother to make sure I made it through the day unscathed, but not everyone did. He kept a tally. The Taliban launched more than 130 attacks, seventeen Afghans were killed, also two Americans and a British soldier. The whole country wobbled and threatened to tear apart. He heard reports of votes being sold in southern provinces, and that was sure to anger the ophthalmologist; reports from monitors watching boxes dumped out with ballots still attached to ballot books; and reports of some ballot boxes that, when emptied, didn't have any ballots, just pieces of paper with a final tally written down. Ashraf Ghani barely registered, but Aimal's business partner did. The ophthalmologist secured over 30 percent of the vote, more than anyone else in the race besides the incumbent, Hamid Karzai.

In the crowded field, no candidate won over 50 percent, which meant a runoff election between the top two vote getters. A stipulation meant to give some ballast against conflict, since it guaranteed that whoever won had the support of at least half the voters.

The ophthalmologist still had a good chance of becoming president. Aimal still had a good chance of becoming a minister.

The ophthalmologist was exhausted after all the campaigning, though, and Aimal found him bitter. He was certain all the fraud had favored Karzai, even though Karzai was claiming to be the *victim* of malicious schemes. Conspiracy theories circulated about America rigging the runoff so Karzai would lose, America rigging the runoff so Karzai would win, but to the ophthalmologist and his followers, it was clear the election and the country were being stolen from them.

As the country teetered in the aftermath of the election, Aimal's silent business partner seemed to keep growing more irritable. Aimal arrived for a meeting at the ophthalmologist's compound and found him already at top speed. He seemed exhausted, hyper, overtired, and stretched thin from months of talking nicely on the campaign trail, now facing the prospect of even more campaigning. Aimal walked in and thought he heard cursing: "Hey, motherfucker, you scamming me?"

Aimal looked behind him, saw no one was there, and realized, *He's yelling at me.* "What the fuck you talking about?" Aimal was confused, so he responded in the same tone. The aide stood to the side, impassive, concern on his face.

"You charged $45,000 for the car, and you give me $13,000?"

"It's none of your business. We agreed your cut is $13,000."

"I don't care how much you made for me—how much did *you* rent it for? Answer me! I know you rented it for more than $25,000. Give me the rest."

"No, no, it's too much now. I gave you $20,000 for those vehicles!"

"You think you're me now? You're taking a bigger cut than me? On my cars? You're a sneaky motherfucker, you know that?" Now he seemed exasperated. He turned to the aide and grumbled something. Aimal thought he heard *Will you please just shoot this motherfucker?*

The aide moved toward Aimal. "Just be calm, OK? Can you shut up? You're young; he's old. Just show some respect."

"No. Fuck him and his respect. He's talking shit to me. Get the fuck out of here. He can't touch me." He turned to the ophthalmologist. "Your husbands are outside," Aimal said. "There are Americans out there; just try to touch me." The aide stepped closer, trying to back the two away from each other. Aimal barely registered his presence. Aimal was seeing red. He felt his voice rising louder and louder, something in him snapped, and he couldn't stop the rage. Flung spit and fists pounding the air moved in front of him until the ophthalmologist's posture softened, as if he'd had enough and was ready for the argument to be over. He seemed to have the same ability Aimal had, to heat up but cool down just as fast. He sighed. He was taking the high road. He'd been cheated. Aimal knew he'd cheated a man he'd once called his god-father, and now his godfather was trying to make peace.

"You're like a son to me," he said. "You know I love you. You're like a son. That's why I yell at you."

But Aimal wasn't ready for an olive branch. "Go fuck yourself. You're not my father. I was here for business, and that's it."

He showed the ophthalmologist his back and stormed out.

CHAPTER 19

LATE AUGUST 2009

HE KNOWS HE'S BROKEN SOMETHING VALUABLE, AND HE DOESN'T yet know what horror he's released to deal with later. Why couldn't he shut up? Why'd he lie about the price?

His head spins. He can forget for a moment, but the stabs of regret viper out of the day and strike; he can't escape it for long. He'd made something of himself; now he's done something rash and maybe unmade it all. There is some coiled possibility he doesn't want to see. Dark and waiting, and he gets a call. I'm still in the country but leaving today and want to see him before leaving. He goes to pick me up and brings me to the office so we can sit together, and he wants to be a good host, but his mind is lit up and aimed elsewhere. He's just broken an important relationship, and he needs to figure out what to do. Go back and make amends? Does he have it in him? How is he going to keep the business running without his biggest supplier? And the ophthalmologist has *reach*. Not just vehicles. A network, security, more connections than Aimal has. He wonders whether he needs to rethink his own protection. Is he safe? In front of him I recross my legs, and Aimal falls out of orbit. Are his friends safe?

"Yah, Jaff," he says. "I think maybe you should to carry gun now."

He knows I have no idea what he's been up to. He can see a poorly hidden confusion. Aimal is rich and powerful, he has gunmen protecting him, and surely I must know taxis alone don't get you this rich and at risk. But how to explain, where to start? With a few minutes left before he has to get me to my flight, he can't think of how to begin. *It's not really a taxi business.* Or it's not *just* that. Mostly, it's not that. I have to know, don't I, that $700 couldn't launch all this? How to explain he's taken the money and the luck and made himself into . . . an arms dealer? The money and the luck, and maybe turned friends into enemies?

He has an idea. He takes the Makarov 9 mm from his waist, looks at it, leans forward, and presses it into my palm. He knows it's a strange thing to gift a weapon, but if I'm going to keep coming back to this country . . . if I'm going to keep being around *him* . . .

He sees my face; he understands my pause. Of course, why didn't he think of this. He's forgotten this is a friend who perhaps does love him for real, Aimal thinks, and who doesn't want to leave him exposed. Aimal knows what to do.

"Don't worry," he says. He goes to get the Beretta from Colonel Buffer. "I like this one better anyway." He watches me, he sees I'm unconvinced, so he waves the Beretta to show how comfortable he is with it. "With this one, the recoil is *little, little,* and it never go off by itself." But I'm leaning forward with the Makarov, extending the weapon grip-first back at him. He worries he's made a guest uncomfortable. He needs to end this losing streak.

"Yah, Jaff, probably we should get you to the airport so not you should miss your flight."

We ride mostly in silence. It's too hot for small talk. At the airport, a guard lowers his head to the window, and Aimal watches him watching me.

"Are you carrying any weapons?" the guard asks.

Aimal looks to the passenger seat and winks. "He ask if we have weapon."

"Oh. Well, no."

Aimal aims his smile back at the guard. "No, brother," he says. "No weapons today." The guard keeps an eye on him for a moment, as though checking to see if he's lying.

"OK. Go ahead."

Aimal turns to me. "He ask to me, 'Why not?'"

CHAPTER 20

2010

MAYBE ALL LIVES HAVE INFLECTION POINTS. MOMENTS OF UN-
folding, when the railcar of a moving life hits a switching yard and
starts to curve away. Sometimes we don't see the turn as we're taking it;
sometimes never at all, sometimes we do but not until years later. You
wake in middle age, a town or two away from where you planned to be.

And then sometimes those moments call out as they happen. A
sudden loss, an illness or affair, sometimes extraordinary violence. A
moment of narrated change as bright and clear as a direct revelation.

Aimal had spurned another halfway father figure and walked out
with a sense of mounting pressure that still hadn't abated. Soon after
their argument, the ophthalmologist makes a strange public statement.
He gathers a crowd and says he's dropping out of the runoff election
because there will be too much fraud anyway. "This decision," he says,
"has not been made in exchange for anything from anybody." Aimal
thinks the Americans paid him off. Whatever the reason, it means
there's more time available to settle scores if the ophthalmologist is
inclined to do so.

A month passes, then two months; the pressure in Aimal's head
hardly eases. Trying to keep the business growing as the surge of cash
that came with the elections thins out, after he's frayed a relationship
with his biggest supplier and maybe invited the wrath of a man who has
all the tools to take his revenge whenever he wants.

It all just keeps building, squeezing in from the temples, until one
night Aimal decides he needs a release. He calls his neighbor, healed

now, an impressive scar but no worse for the wear. Invites him out, calls some girls to see who's free. What do you do when you've achieved everything you wanted and then risked it all in one moment of spite? Aimal needs to think, so for one night he needs to not think at all. He needs an evening drenching the pressure in liquor, in feminine energy and acceleration. A party on the move, passing a bottle back and forth. The city blurs by and bursts in the mirrors, not quite real. This is what he needs. For a while, it works. He can feel the worry pulling back, slipping from his chest, dragged out and pinned down in the slipstream. His moving party noses ahead, losing the worry in the straightaways, until it's just a flicker disappearing in the rearview.

Then there's something else flickering in the rearview—a car riding so low on its suspension that even his leadened senses register it as heavy, it's armored, it rocks on its chassis as it swoops down from nowhere. He could swear he knows who sent it, or it could have just been thugs because by now he is known, and people have come with guns for his money before. A window lowers; a few jagged moments of violence sear open the night. Aimal is clawing the fog from his own mind and trying to focus on escape. Finally, the other car slips away, closed up and gone. All is quiet in Aimal's car except the sound he's heard while touring bomb sites with his first foreign client, that sound of people discovering their own wounds.

Afterward, he goes to see the parents of the girl shot and killed in his car. He stays with them, drinks their tea. The words of sympathy come to him easily enough, shrouding the handover of cash to make it feel more graceful, but he walks outside after understanding what's happened. There will be no justice for the girl, not really. None besides a little stack he's just nudged across a carpet to her father. He thinks, *No one will suffer the consequences.* Not the attackers, not any warlord, not any henchman. No one will pay. She will be forgotten, all this suffering for the sin of letting him take her out for a night. He is a protector. He's been his own family's father from the age of eight. He's provided for his older siblings, he has in his blood this need to protect the people near him, but the people near him keep getting hurt.

Driving away, he begins to wonder whether if you spend enough time around gangsters, you just become one. He's lost himself. He sits in his loudly anonymous car with its show of tinted windows and no license plate. What is he trying to prove? That he's a warlord? Is he different from the American contractors rumbling over a country like they've forgotten it has people in it? What happened? His intentions had been pure. He wishes he'd never worked with Americans, never met me and the ophthalmologist, gotten into the racket, never made all this money. Foreigners mean death. The man in the morgue. That gray half-body, the journalist shot to death in front of him, warm spray on his face, the neighbor's blood on money. He wishes he'd just been a taxi driver. He's seen people killed without reason; he's seen people bleed out in the streets. They'd been the obstacles he had to skip over as a child. They also had no justice. Warlords in the mountains weren't punished for all this dying down in the streets. American pilots weren't punished for the wedding guests they bombed. He feels soiled. There's no atonement. How to cleanse himself? He goes home and says all the duas and vows the foreign NGO taught him as a kid. *By Allah, by the power of Muhammad, if you let me pass this test, I will pray a hundred Ra'akats under the name of the prophet; I will donate to charity.*

He repeats them each three times, pursing his lips and whistling them into the city. He's talked himself out of trouble, but he can't talk the stain off himself. He needs another way to wedge himself away from greed and death, some other way to process in justice, to atone for what he's done, and it's just then that he gets his first call from the Taliban.

CHAPTER 21

JULY 2011

AT FIRST, JUST A GETTING-TO-KNOW-YOU CONVERSATION. LETTING him know they already knew him. He didn't believe the caller at first. The first time the Taliban tried to recruit him, he hung up. He wasn't in the mood for games.

Two days later, another call, more menacing this time. A hidden number, a different voice, and Aimal was hearing his life narrated back to him. "You drive a Land Cruiser, 2009, no plates, with Hamid Karzai pictures in the back. Your business operates with silver Corolla. Your office is on Street 3 in Taimani. You love to drink whiskey, to be like the Americans, and if you hang up on me, I will pay you a visit."

Now Aimal was nervous. "How can I help you?"

"In the name of the prophet Muhammad. We're Muslim, join us; shouldn't we help each other? The way Christians help each other? The way the Christians and Jews help each other under NATO?"

"What would that mean, 'join you'?"

"You drive Americans around. You'll just deliver some of them to us. We'll tell you the location and the timing. That's all you have to do."

"I don't know who you are. Maybe you're just trying to scare me. I'm a businessman; I have rivals. Maybe you're trying to intimidate me. Anyway, I'm not here for all the terrorist bullshit."

"No, no, brother. I'm not a terrorist. Who gave you that idea? You've got the American mentality. This is self-defense. We're defending our country. I know the bigger picture," he said, as if he could see some future Aimal couldn't. "In the end, the foreigners won't be here to be your friends."

Aimal tried to make it sound like he was considering the idea and wiggled off the phone call.

The next night, one of the guards came into the office with a letter left at the door. Official stationery from the Ghazni Central District office of the Islamic Emirate of Afghanistan. The Taliban.

"As-salamu Alaikum wa Rahmatullah. This is the final warning letter to you," it said. "This is in relation to the issue between us. You are not fulfilling your commitment."

Aimal tried to keep calm.

"You did not even take a lesson from your father's death. Therefore, this is the final warning to you, and if you do not cooperate with us, all your family members are under death threat."

How did they know about his father? The day after that, another call, again a hidden number. "This is not working for us."

It was not the same voice. Heavier, gravelly, grave, the pressure on, like Aimal's case had been escalated to senior management. "We've been polite with you. You're trying to convince us we're wrong, but this is not the time for debate. You don't know me, so I'll be clear. Take this as a warning. I know about your family. If I were you, I would cooperate with us because these Americans are not going to be around to help you with your family, and we can. Or"—Aimal knew what was coming—"we can *not*."

The threat hung out there. Aimal didn't know what to say. Speechless—an exotic feeling. He tried to steer out of another call without hitting a trip wire, hoping to quiet the vibrating part of him triggered whenever someone presumed authority.

Then it was Ramadan, the holy month of fasting, and Aimal could hope the Talibs had more holy things to worry about than bothering him. He planned to spend the month the way he'd learned wealthy people did. You were supposed to fast from sunup to sundown, but since he'd come into money, he saw that people who could afford not to work just switched their schedules. They become nocturnal, eating big meals in the middle of the night, and rather than enduring hunger during the day, they just slept. Now that Aimal was like them, had drivers to handle parts of the business that needed constant attention and staff to keep track of all the armor dispersed throughout the country, he'd do it that way too. And just hope that the Talibs would be too distracted, too anemic, or too holy to continue their planning. Maybe they'd forget about him.

Early in the holy month, he was nodding off at the office with his head of security when he remembered he'd promised his mother he'd be home for a big midnight meal. The guard rose to come with him, but since it was the middle of the night, and the guard couldn't skip out to sleep during the day like Aimal could, Aimal told him to stay behind and rest.

He drove out into an empty night, turning out of the office like he'd done a million times now, thinking he was running late, his mother would've been cooking all day and night for him. *I know you're busy, but please don't skip this time*. By now, she probably thought he'd forgotten. A twinge of shame about how he'd missed so many meals she'd prepared for him over the past few years. He turned off Street 3, and the night tore open. A car swerved into the street and lurched in front of him, brake lights screaming red. Aimal jammed the brakes. Gravel crunched, tires scrambled for purchase, and he nearly slammed into the car now blocking his path. It had to be the ophthalmologist. *His fucking henchmen again*.

He threw the gearshift into reverse, swung his arm over the passenger seat, and turned to gun it backward, but another car veered in from behind, blocking his escape. *Fuck*. The men had him trapped this time. There was no way out, just death in a haze of dust rising off the tires.

In front of him, car doors swung open. The voice in his head banged too loud and fast to make sense of. *Fuck, Aimal, you're done now*. No life flashing before his eyes, just solid black, sludge filling his mind, his thinking clumping to a halt. *Think, Aimal, think*. No clever path presented itself, no route others couldn't see, just a scroll of violence. He reached down and rubbed a thumb across the barrel of the pistol to make sure the hammer was back. The men on foot drew closer. Time shifted so that it seemed to take them longer: things moved slow; things moved fast. The men slipped through vibrating halos of light from generators guttering somewhere, and he saw Kalashnikovs poking under their robes. His pistol useless against all that firepower, but also, a breath of confusion, the men wore turbans, and the ophthalmologist's men would never do that. A beat of relief. *It's not them.*

Then brand-new terror: *Talibs.*

———

BREATHING HEAVIER, BOWELS LOOSENING, BRAIN DOWNSHIFTING further. The walls of his chest pulsed with big thumping heartbeats. He could hear his own blood flowing. His own door was opening. A Talib climbing into the front next to him, their leader then, their mullah, two climbing into the back.

"Follow them."

So they wanted to execute him somewhere else. He drove in a trance. The three men surround-sound breathing, their used air filling the car. He could smell them; he could hear the functioning of their bodies. Breathing and shifting, the structure of them filling the space. Taking him to whatever dusty, deserted patch they had in mind for his end.

Farther and farther from the city center, driving in silence, until they reached a lot near a strip of tire stores. The mullah finally pointed and said, "Park here."

That's all he said for a while, like he was savoring the moment. Then: "Brother, relax. We're not here to kill you. My boss was in touch with you."

That was a lie. Aimal recognized the voice. He keyed in on the heavier consonants. It had not been any boss on the phone; it had been *him*, now trying to save face because Aimal had ignored him before.

But now, having recognized a deceit, Aimal's mind was pilot-lit: frozen with fear but coming back online.

"You're our brother," the mullah was saying. "We have love for you. We just want to talk with you. And you should start respecting my boss."

Aimal felt the men shifting behind him. He saw scenes from the movies in his childhood rental store, images from the dish. Assassins in backseats rising to garrot a driver, gun barrels to the back of the skull. He said, "Can we go to your car?"

"What's wrong with *your* car?"

Think.

"Can I tell you something?" He made his voice low, like he was taking the mullah into his confidence, and nodded outside. The mullah hesitated, then complied.

Aimal had the mullah outside the car now. "You know I'm working with ISAF, NATO. The foreigners. They may have put a listening device in my car. If we're going to discuss these things, we should do it in your vehicle."

The mullah squinted, seemed to consider, then approved.

Now Aimal had some momentum. As they approached the Talib's truck, Aimal made a second ask: "Can we sit in the back? It's better; there's no console between us." No objection this time either.

Once in the back, with the courtesy light on and the two other Talibs climbing in the front, Aimal tried a new tack, his ability to see the unseen puzzle returning to him.

He had a sense that the mullah might respond to radical candor, so he took a flier. "Brother, to be honest, during the Taliban time, before the Americans came, you guys were in power, but you didn't do anything for me. I studied Islamic religion, but it was the foreigners who taught me. The foreigners taught me how to be a Muslim. They taught me funeral rites. In my thinking, these people came to help us. Now I have a car. During the Taliban, I didn't have a car. And you're telling me to go against the people who gave me money. Why? To be a better person? Because they're Christian and Jews? But I don't care if they're Christian or Jews; they helped me. I'm not God. They have to answer to God, not me."

"Yes, brother! But God sent us to punish them. Do you wonder why you're here, why you're breathing? It's God. You go against God because you own a car? How much money do you need to go with God? You tell me. How much money? We'll give it you. You've been brainwashed by them . . ." And off he went, the mullah launched on a sermon, trying to convince Aimal about enemies of Islam, about Americans faking their commitment to regular people, Aimal peppering in the occasional "yes" and "mmhm" and "maybe you're right." And then finally, when the mullah was done, Aimal acted half-convinced.

"So what do you want? You want me to put on a suicide vest? I'm not going to do that. Better just shoot me now if I'm going to die either way."

"No, no, not that. We have different soldiers for that. You are our highest level of soldier. We just want you to give us a few foreigners. We'll tell you where to drop them. When they go to party, when they're drunk, so it's easier, you bring them to a quiet place, and we'll take it from there."

Now a pause. Aimal sensed this wasn't it.

"Or . . ." and Aimal didn't even need him to finish, could almost feel what was coming next. "We know your cars don't get checked when you go through checkpoints." Now he realized the critical mistake he'd made. Finding a way to save his foreigners from security searches hadn't saved them at all; it had exposed them. "Hire our men as drivers."

So they were thinking of a Trojan horse–style operation. The mullah explained that the plan was a spectacular attack for the tenth anniversary of 9/11. Using Aimal's cars, and Aimal's access, the way he'd manipulated security checkpoints to deliver attackers, unsearched, right onto bases where foreign soldiers and civilians worked. With no one checking whatever cargo they carried, bombs or guns or probably both, they'd kill dozens, maybe hundreds of Americans, Canadians, Europeans.

"OK. I need time to think about it."

"What do you need to think about? Are you taking their side? Should we just kill you after all?" He was playing mind games now. "We'll send our drivers tomorrow."

Think. *Tomorrow?* He needed time. "No. I need some time." He had a narrow lane in which to lie; he needed these men to think he was cooperating. He scanned his memory across the last few months, trying to picture when the Talibs would have been monitoring him, how they knew what they knew about him.

They knew where his home was, that was clear. His family, his patterns, they knew his cars passed through checkpoints unsearched.

But they hadn't been *inside* the cars. Maybe they didn't know *how* he managed to get through checkpoints. That's where he could gamble.

"Once you send me their information, I have to put in a request for them to get their badges from the NATO coalition. They will have to go through a screening."

This wasn't true; he was vamping now. "Then if the Americans approve, they'll make the badge for your men to get past checkpoints, but that takes two or three months." He thought of another wrench he could throw in the attack plan. "Your drivers, do they speak English? They'll need to speak English."

Was it worry that flashed across the mullah's face? He leaned to his gunman in front and began speaking low. *No,* Aimal thought, *you won't find an English speaker to do this, will you. English speakers are smart, watch porn, use Google—they don't want to go blow themselves up.* He interrupted the private conference between the Talibs. "So when you find them, send me their CVs, and I will take care of the rest."

"I'll get back to you."

"I'm ready," he said.

And how to make them think he was really planning to cooperate in their attack? "And what are you going to do if there's damage to my cars?"

"Don't worry about the cars. We'll stack bills until they're as tall as your cars, and all that will be yours." As if to prove he was good for it, the mullah reached inside his robe and handed Aimal a stack of bills.

"I can't accept this." Money changing hands would be a seal. Once that happened, there was no going back.

The mullah patted his hand. "I know you do pick-up and drop-off to make money. This is for your time because tonight we kept you from your business."

He got out of the car and summoned Aimal. In the wash from the headlights, he wrapped Aimal in a hug.

"Welcome to our group."

———

HE'D KEPT IT TOGETHER, BUT NOW HE WAS NEARLY SPASTIC. HE pulled over for an energy drink. *Should I go tell my foreign friends? Should I call Jaff? Should I go to the American military or someone in ISAF?*

He played it out in his head. *As soon as you open your mouth about this, no one is going to use your company again.* His head was going crazy. He drank another energy drink. He was wired. The sun was coming up. He wasn't going to fast tomorrow. He needed to think. *Think.* There were obstacles everywhere he looked. The ophthalmologist's men. His ruse with the Talibs wouldn't last forever. If they were planning an attack on 9/11, they'd begin to get pushy again soon.

By the time it was bright and the muezzin sounded the call to prayer, things had settled into place, and he knew what he had to do.

CHAPTER 22

MID-AUGUST 2011

On the way to the airport with hardly more than the clothes on his back. Aimal had gone as fast as he could, but he couldn't leave without telling his neighbor, his brothers, his drivers. He couldn't leave without saying good-bye to his mother.

The Taliban knew his movements. They knew his habits, they knew about his family, they could be following him to the airport right now. Would they kill his mother, or his brothers? He figured without him there, maybe they wouldn't know who to approach. Maybe his own persona was so soundly glued to the company that with him gone, the company would fade from the Taliban's attention. He'd put the business in his youngest brother's name; Omar was only eleven, so maybe the Talibs didn't know about him yet. Whatever they were thinking, with Aimal gone they'd have no way to get past checkpoints unsearched, at least for a while.

He had no good options. He could stay and help the Taliban kill foreigners in a massive 9/11 anniversary attack. Or he could leave his family, perhaps forever.

The ophthalmologist's men were after him too, or maybe they'd cooled off. Or maybe it had been someone else who'd attacked him; he couldn't be sure. How many enemies did he have now? And the ophthalmologist had dropped out of the election. He'd have more time to settle scores if that's what he wanted to do. The walls were closing in. Aimal had no visas to other countries, no viable way out, but he had money now and an idea of someone who could help. He'd called his friend "the heir," the country's Paris Hilton, who always drove with his handful of passports, his glut of underworld connections, his trunk full of contraband. Aimal asked for a meeting. With the heir and the hotelier up in that rooftop restaurant, he couldn't admit why exactly he was leaving—the hotelier knew the ophthalmologist, for one thing—so instead he playacted the libertine, saying he just wanted to go West for a taste of white women. "You're sick," the hotelier laughed. "Man, because now you're rich, Dubai's not good enough for you? You want to go for real game."

But these were the kinds of things the heir and the hotelier could arrange. They gave Aimal a phone number and a code word to give to the smuggler. When the smuggler picked up, they agreed on a price of $35,000 in cash, which Aimal would give to the hotelier, to hold in trust and give the smuggler only if the operation was successful.

The smuggler showed up at Aimal's office, took his picture and his Afghan passport, and just before leaving, said, "Don't call me. But when I call you, you need to be ready to go."

Aimal spent the next days looking over his shoulder. Eternal days because it was still Ramadan. Hot, slow, hungry. Days wondering if his escape plan could actually work. And even if it could, would it happen soon enough? He'd bought himself just a little breathing room with the Taliban. If he wasn't gone by the time they came back for him, that'd be it. He'd be killed or forced to help.

It was four days before the smuggler called. It was 4 p.m. "Be at the airport at seven tonight. Someone will meet you there." He had only minutes to say good-bye, probably forever, to his mother. He willed her not to cry because if she cried, he knew he might not be able to leave. He walked in the door and came right out with it, *I'm leaving, and I might not ever come back, but I have no choice,* and she didn't believe him. She thought he was joking, hoped he was joking, then started to weep in great heartbreaking heaves. He saw what he was doing to her. He'd never seen this before. All he had to offer, his quick tongue stilled by mistakes, was a quiet "Don't cry." And then "Mom, I need some cash."

"If you take from an animal her kids, she attacks." What was she talking about now? He didn't know what to say. He watched the clock; he'd forgotten to get money from the office, and it was too late to go back there now.

"Mom, I have to leave. Please just hug me and let me go. Hug me. And Mom? The cash."

<hr/>

THE REST, IN FLASHES.

In the car, leaving his stunned mother, his youngest brother riding behind and asking from the back, "Can I have some pocket money?"

The airport parking lot, a stranger approaching, just like the smuggler said. "You're going to Dubai," the stranger told him, handing Aimal's own passport back to him with a new Dubai visa and a plane ticket. "When you get to Dubai, go toward Arrivals. Just before you get there, make a right turn toward Connections. Don't go all the way."

The stranger reaching into his pocket and handing over a small envelope. "Take this SIM card. Turn it on when you get there. Someone will call you." And he was gone.

Aimal hugged his brothers and left without looking back, to keep them strong. The flight to Dubai was smooth, a well-worn route. A rising flow of people and money beginning to move from Afghanistan into Dubai, a neon city where half-built towers rose up on tax dollars and tax dodges and rerouted aid money bouncing around the region's rebuilding countries. Several flights a day now from Kabul to Dubai, businessman and thieves riding a giant exhale of value. The first leg was easy, Aimal a speck in the current.

Once in the Dubai airport, he found the borderland between Arrivals and Connections and stayed there. *Wear comfortable clothes*, the smuggler had said, *nothing flashy.*

Should I wear a suit? To look professional?

No, Westerners like to be comfortable when they travel.

Aimal put the SIM card in the phone, turned it on, and waited an hour, then two. No one called.

He remembered: *Once you've been in the Dubai airport for a while, change your clothes. That way the security cameras don't see the same person hanging around for too long.*

He went into the restroom, changed his pants, put on a hoodie, stuffed his jacket into the trash. He put on a pair of oversized headphones and emerged a stranger to the ceiling-mounted security cameras. Another hour, still no call.

Four hours passed. Five.

Now nervous again, he started to spend money. He bought a beer. He bought KFC. He bought another beer; he bought his way into an executive lounge and ate everything he could get his hands on.

He went out and spent more money; he didn't even know what he was buying. Somehow $1,000 disappeared. Where would he go if the smuggler didn't come through? He'd have to buy a ticket and go back to Kabul. The Talibs would take his mother or kill a brother to get him to cooperate. Or the ophthalmologist would come back around, and this time he would mean it. Or he could try his luck here. Wander out in Dubai, overstay his visa, get deported back to Afghanistan or maybe join the ranks of Tamils and Bangladeshis working themselves to death building buildings no one ever seemed to occupy.

Six hours into his stay at the airport, the little Nokia chirped to life. A hidden number. A voice told him a gate to sit by, said that a man with further instructions had just landed. *He'll give you a hand signal. Follow him. After that, he's in charge. I'm done. Don't try to reach me.*

Aimal found the gate. A man entered his peripheral vision, angling toward him. Somehow he knew. The subtlest of head nods, a scooping motion with a hand at beltline.

Aimal got up. He stayed twenty steps behind, and followed the man into the restroom.

They nodded into the mirror, heads angled a degree inward. The man said nothing. He waited for the stalls to empty, double-checked them, then stood facing the mirror again. He didn't look at Aimal. Aimal understood. *We don't know each other.* The man gave a wink. Aimal gave a nod. The man slid a passport across the sink. Aimal took it, opened it, and had the strangest of feelings. *It's me. My face, my birthday, every-thing*, only transformed. The passport was British. In a bathroom at the Dubai airport, Aimal became a foreigner.

Can I keep the old one too?

Why do you need the old one? The man held out his hand for the old passport. The real one. Aimal handed it over. He was no longer Afghan. He no longer had a legal passport. He was now stateless.

The man handed Aimal two more plane tickets.

———

THE FIRST TICKET WAS FOR A CITY IN EUROPE, BUT THE FLIGHT WAS delayed, which seemed to scramble whatever was supposed to happen next.

He landed, missed the connecting flight, tried to take a taxi to a hotel, didn't know any hotels. The taxi driver finally found one with vacancies and an English-speaking receptionist, a moment of relief, but the receptionist needed a credit card for the deposit. Aimal didn't have a credit card. He'd never used one in his life. He took out a bundle of cash. "What about this?"

The receptionist looked confused. "US dollars?"

Shit. "Because my friend sent to me at Western Union, but now I can't reach him."

"Western Union gave you US dollars?"

"Sorry, I mean my friend *met* me at Western Union. *He* gave me US dollars, and he took out . . . your currency."

"And now he's gone."

"Yes, unfortunately."

Eventually the hotel took pity. Aimal went outside to pay the taxi driver, who also took pity and accepted his US dollars.

He had a room. He had no flight. He tried the smuggler he wasn't supposed to call, got no answer, left a message.

He went out into the streets to find a bar, drank enough to lose time, and wound up at a strip club. For a moment, he wasn't worried. The night colored, darkened, swirled. He liked this city, its foreign colors.

He liked himself. He had something better than money in his pocket. He had a taste of the power a Western passport gives you. And he also had money. He thought of Fatima's dad. *We're up here; you're down here.* At the strip club, the women touched him like a human. *So much power in a passport.* Backs of hands up and down his leg. Women not afraid to touch him, and not just the imported girls at Crazy Eight in Kabul who had to drink their weight in bathtub vodka to get all handsy and forgetful. White girls touching him. *I'm powerful, I'm white, I'm someone now.* In the morning, back at his hotel, he found himself $3,000 lighter. *Need to get smarter.* He needed someone to show him where to go next. He needed to pray. What prayer for a situation like this?

He tried to summon the lessons from the foreign NGO during the Taliban times. The duas and the vows they taught him for the test they said he'd surely have one day. *Oh, Allah, by the power of Muhammad, if you let me pass this test, I will pray a hundred Ra'akats under the name of the prophet; I will donate to charity.* He repeated it three times. He blew, to spread the prayer out so whatever angel assigned to this strange city might hear. He felt better. Uncertainty turned to freedom. They would call; someone would. The smuggler still needed his money, Aimal would get to where he was going, but for now halfway was good enough. He was officially British. He was as good as white, he was rich, and he was just beginning.

OUT AT A BAR THE NEXT NIGHT, HE GOT THE CALL. THE SMUGGLER had his tickets for the next morning. The rest of his life awaited him, a drawbridge lowering and light blasting through. Aimal was so happy he bought rounds for all the strangers and too many for himself, and woke up thirty minutes before the flight. How had he fucked this up? He'd pray more duas and make more vows and race to the airport anyway; maybe God would keep other cars off the street.

The streets were packed. He inched through traffic and arrived two minutes before the scheduled departure time—there was no chance.

But he scanned the departures board for his flight anyway and saw a blinking red notice: Delayed.

Now he was coasting. With a British passport that no one questioned the next flights went smoothly. The big test would be once he landed in Canada. He recited the smuggler's instructions to himself.

Destroy the passport when you land. But not in the plane lavatory. They can recover it there. Whatever you do, make sure they can't find your fake documents.

The plane landed in Edmonton. *I'm actually in Canada.* Aimal got off the plane and slipped into the airport bathroom. He went into a stall, slid the bolt, took out his new passport, and shoved it in his mouth. He started chewing.

Here, he had time. He chewed until it was unrecognizable. He took part of it, balled it up, and dropped it in the toilet.

He went to another stall and dropped another wad in that one. Then another. He distributed pieces of the fake passport into six different toilets and flushed them. Before realizing they would probably all end up in the same place anyway.

He waited. *Don't go to Immigration right way. Stay in the restroom for at least five hours. Let planes from different countries land and people get off. That will mix up the Immigration people.*

He remembered: *And destroy the SIM card too. They can track it.* He chewed the SIM card and sat there playing Snake on his SIM-less Nokia. Each time the bathroom emptied, he got up, went to another stall, and closed himself in that one so no janitor would see the same shoes in the same stall for hours and get suspicious.

After five hours in the restroom, he broke the phone, walked out into the hall, and followed chattering passengers from the latest flight down to the Immigration line. He winked at the attendant pointing him to the line, and then when an officer waved him up, he presented himself at the booth. A dark-skinned twenty-five-year-old who might as well have materialized out of thin air. The border services agent reached his hand out.

"Passport."

"I don't have anything."

"Passport."

"I don't have one."

"Where'd you come from?"

"Afghanistan."

"*Where'd* you came from?"

"I don't know."

"There's no direct flight from Afghanistan."

"The guy I paid, he brought me here."

The agent retracted his hand. "A guy—can you describe the guy?"

If they ask about me, throw them off the scent. "Sure, brother: big nose, big mouth, long tongue, big hair. Do you have a cigarette?"

CHAPTER 23

LATE AUGUST 2011

Edmonton International Airport, Alberta

THE QUESTIONING CONTINUED IN THE INTERROGATION ROOM AF-
ter a thorough search revealed that this strange specimen had indeed
arrived in the middle of the Edmonton airport without any identifying
documents.

"Do you have a contact number?"

"No. My friend, no. I'm hungry."

"Didn't you get food on the plane?" *A trap! If they know what plane
you were on, they can send you back.* "No, no food on the plane."

"OK, how about this: the plane you came on—what color was it?

He'd flown KLM, blue and white. "Black and orange."

The agent shook his head.

"What was your route?"

"From Afghanistan to . . . another country."

"What country was that?"

Aimal stammered, "Ah, sorry, I don't know."

"Was it Muslim?"

"Mixed."

"Did you see mostly white people, black, brown?"

"Mixed. Both. All of them, brother." *If they can't send you back right
away, then after a while they'll have no choice but to give you a court
hearing.*

Another officer: "Were people driving on the left side of the street
or the right side?"

"Ma'am, I didn't went outside. I was in the airport. So how I should know?"

The officers looked at each other.

"Ma'am, I'm very tired and hungry. Can I please rest?"

"What's your name?"

"I have to eat; I have to sleep." *Keep repeating your needs. In Canada, they have human rights; they can't push you too hard.*

"You want me to lie? I need to eat and sleep. I'm just about to explode. My head is going crazy."

———

He woke up in the interrogation room, the officers more bemused than angry. *They'll try to make you scared. They'll tell you they can send you back, but if they don't know where you came from, they can't. And the longer you stay, the more complicated it is for them to try. Don't cooperate. Don't give any information.*

There were two officers now. One was beautiful: blonde and tall. He tried not to stare.

"I know you know English," she said. "What uniforms did the air hostesses wear when they fed you?"

"I was so tired."

"What movie did you see on the flight?"

"I just fell asleep."

"You're a smart guy. Come on. What language were people speaking on the plane?"

"The smuggler guy gave me headphones, so I didn't hear."

A knock on the door, a man entered, whispered something into the pretty officer's ear. She turned to Aimal. "There are no fingerprints on your cash." *Any cash you have left, wipe it down. They can use prints to trace you.* "Come on. At least give us a little. Give us something. Do you know anyone in Canada?"

———

Now Aimal began calculating: he had a distant relative he'd planned to call once he landed. The last part of the plan. But only after he landed, so the uncle couldn't say no, and wouldn't be able to alert other authorities while the plan was in progress. His uncle's phone number was one of the few he'd memorized. He recited the number to the officers. They left to call it, then came back in shaking their heads. They couldn't release Aimal to his uncle. They didn't say why. *Did he refuse to take me in?*

After stalling for what felt like a day, Aimal decided to give them something. Maybe enough time had passed, per the smuggler's guidance, that they couldn't just kick him out of the country. He let on just a little—his name, the fact that he had a business in Afghanistan, that his documents were with a friend there. He gave the officers the second phone number he'd memorized: the number for his own company. *Make sure someone is waiting, ready to send documents to you. Make sure they don't tell anyone on the phone what your route was. Make sure whoever is waiting with the documents acts surprised that you're in Canada. Even if you speak in Dari, be careful; they may have interpreters listening in.*

The neighbor back in Kabul picked up. Aimal didn't know what time it was back home. He didn't know what time it was here. He heard his old friend's voice, a few thousand miles away, through the polycom at the center of the interrogation room.

You motherfucker, the neighbor said, hamming it up. *You're not in Canada. Where are you really?*

"I need you to send me my ID card and all the documents. Send it through DHL. And after you've sent it, call this number and give the tracking number."

With nothing else to do about this strange specimen who showed up without documents in their airport, the officers had to take him to a jail. To wait in detention for his chance to go before an immigration judge. Aimal didn't mind. He was confident now. One way or another, he'd get to stay here.

His cellmate was an Indian man Aimal could speak to because he knew some Hindi from the dish and all the Bollywood movies he'd rented out as a kid.

Out in the yard, Aimal lay on the bench and tried lifting weights. He met a kind-faced Black man who seemed interested in the genial Afghan with the bad English and offered to spot him—hadn't Aimal seen friendships bloom like this in movies? They spent the rec period together, and afterward, when the detainees had their phone time, Aimal saw just about every inmate line up to make calls. His new friend asked, "Anyone put money in your account?"

Aimal didn't know anything about an account.

"You have anyone to call? A sweetheart? Someone out there waiting to hear from you?"

Aimal sensed it was important to blend in, not to be seen as a loner. He knew from movies that in jail, belonging was important. He thought of his mom.

"Can I call Afghanistan?"

The Black man laughed. "Don't know about that. Cheap calls to America, free calls to Canada, but I'm not paying for whatever Afghanistan costs."

"America call works?"

"Give me the number."

Aimal read off the third number he'd memorized, his new jail friend dialed, and once it started to ring, handed Aimal the receiver. The phone made its weird clicking, buzzing; it didn't sound like Afghan lines. The line connected. "Hello?"

"Yah, Jaff," he said. "It's me, Aimal. Here I am in Canada now."

PART III

The Road and the Inn

Our Story: 2011–2022

CHAPTER 1

OCTOBER 2018

Sana'a, Yemen

ONCE, YEARS LATER, WHILE COVERING WAR IN YEMEN, I STOOD inside a delicate house whose face had been sheared off by a thousand-pound bomb. A gulping skull of a structure. We climbed through it, an interpreter and I, like carrion beetles. I could see the blanket where a family had been sitting for dinner when a bomb invented in Texas peeled the ceiling back and entered. The interpreter saw me seeing it and gave a shrunken little smile. He said something dark and funny, and he and I became bonded in a covenant. Unspoken but clear: *so this is how we'll cope, being inside a sudden tomb.* He tried to chew his smile away, though, and his face shifted. His chin pushed down like he'd tasted something rotten, his eyebrows arched up a hair, a flicker of self-amusement rippled down his face.

In that moment, standing inside the naked half-house like actors on a set, a strange thing happened. I saw my mother's features slide onto this new friend's face, then my grandfather's. I did a double take: I thought maybe it was some aspect of the eyes they all happened to share, or something in the expression. The shape, a ratio of tendon stretched over bone, the ridgepoles of sinew that pull flesh over cartilage underwire to make up a face. Or it was something in my own brain.

There was a girl I'd been with briefly who had lost a sibling to suicide. For a year afterward, she saw this sibling everywhere, all the time. "How strange," I'd said, but she said no, it actually wasn't strange at all. That when the lives of loved ones vault away too fast, they often return. You see them, your own holograms of them. You see them full of life. Blowing on a cup of coffee across a café, standing by a store window you're hurrying past. A corner of them turning away in a crowd. Shamans say it's the departed coming back down, borrowing a body to check on you. Scientists and psychiatrists and the more ardent explainers call it a trick of the mind, a projection. You yourself bring your loved one back so you can add something to your good-bye. The mind is sometimes a lonely inventor, they say, building a robot companion. The mind has ways of massaging itself.

So in faraway places, on strangers' faces, I'd begun seeing my mother before I knew she was leaving. I must have already noticed things by then, symptoms that mostly camouflaged themselves against a history of messy desks and misplaced keys. She fought it. She could fake it, for a while. Before we knew that the front two lobes of her brain had decayed so severely that when a doctor finally saw it, scans marked in troubling colors, he would just shake his head. "Devastating" was all he could say, and that would turn out to be as good a diagnosis as any.

At that exact same time her father, a picture of health and a lock to reach ninety, gave in. He fell one night alone in his apartment and decided not to get back up. Dying of we're still not sure what. Of having decided life was fine but he didn't really need any more of it.

These things were in process, and I suppose I must have known. I stood in a war zone staring at a Yemeni man in traditional Yemeni garb, a young man in a turban whose face had, for an instant, turned into my mother's, my grandfather's. Already, both of them were sending me messages from the other side of the world. Or I was sending them to myself.

It was the last time I saw that phenomenon, departing family flickering across the face of someone else, until one of my trips up to see Aimal in Canada.

By then, I had what some were beginning to call but still didn't feel like a successful career. After grad school came a book deal built on the foundation Aimal had helped me build in Afghanistan. Then magazine stories, a series of awards, adventure reporting on wars and outbreaks, from Iraq to West Africa. Investigative stories on Russian assassinations, Guantanamo Bay, death row in Oklahoma, and more books, including one adapted into a Clint Eastwood movie that's pretty funny if you're drunk. All of it building on those first adventures with a skinny kid who made it his mission to keep me alive and who was now, as his face did that thing, driving me around a new habitat he had already adapted to.

I watched him work the wider, cleaner Canadian roads in his over-sized GMC pickup, a bigger vehicle than I'd ridden in with him in Afghanistan. So much more space and time here, and still he insisted on being my driver. Even now, when we had nowhere to go, even when we just wanted to sit and talk, a living room wouldn't do. Always driving, driving back and forth down his favorite stretch of highway. East then west, east then west, in a souped-up truck that jiggled your ass when you got too close to the guy in front of you.

And I saw that thing. He gave this look, a glint of mischief across his face. A face hiding a smile, there and gone in a moment. I thought, *Mom.* I thought, *Pops!* Just in profile, seeing it from the passenger seat, but the same thing. Them, my blood, my family, in him. Maybe everyone looks the same when they smile at something they know they shouldn't. Maybe mischief is a universal language. Or maybe there were some impalpable forces at play. Some ancient, Joni Mitchell "we are stardust" kind of thing, a buried genetic relic. A falling grain a few billion years ago sucked up into gene sequences, banging against code and beaconing some silent chain reaction in roving generations of cavemen, expressing now as matching muscle choreography on faces, continents apart.

Or maybe, as it had been in Yemen, it was a warning.

CHAPTER 2

AUGUST 2011

Riverside Park, Guelph, Ontario

AIMAL WAKES UP ON A PARK BENCH TO AN EXPLOSION OF LIGHT IN his face. Breaching a murky surface from sleep, for a beat he's home again with an American soldier firing a Humvee-mounted spotlight back at his car, igniting his windshield. Aimal, blind with anger and glare, slamming the brakes, flinging a forearm up to bat the light away. *This is MY country. These aren't YOUR fucking roads!*

"What are you doing?" He crashes back into himself, a cold hard park bench, beached in this new country. He's seeing the silhouette of a police officer, dark and faceless behind a flashlight beam.

He'd been given a chance, and he's fucked it up already. A few days in jail and then he was brought before a judge like the smuggler said, a judge who, like the smuggler said, didn't seem inclined or maybe wasn't allowed to send Aimal back home after he'd been on Canadian soil for a few days. The judge had him released from jail, said some things that seemed to be in Aimal's favor: "refugee protection claimant," "record of landing." All good things.

The judge gave him permission to stay in Canada for five years, and gave little else.

The officer stares down at him, wiggling the flashlight.

"I'm sleeping here."

How did it come to this? The only grace was that Guelph, sixty miles from Toronto, had real rivers, not the dried-out trickling shit-filled scar through Kabul he was used to. It was different here. Green and fluid, a place with so much clean moving water that it ignited an embarrassment of growth, and there were public parks all over. He'd found one, found a bench because he needed to sleep, needed to think, needed to start over. He had a few bills in his pocket, bought a pack of cigarettes; now he had nothing.

"Where do you live?"

Where does he live? He lives nowhere. He lives here. He lives on this bench. Was he homeless now? "Do you have any alcohol in your system?"

"No, officer. I'm not drunk." For good measure, "Or on drugs."

"Let me have your ID."

ID. He's unidentified here; he's no one. He has nothing to show. Not *nothing*—he has the papers given to him by the judge. "Landing papers." He pulls them from his pocket, uncrinkles them, and the officer joins the ranks of Canadian official types who can't quite believe what they're seeing.

"You've only been here two weeks? What are you doing here? Are you lost?"

"I'm not lost."

"Then what's your plan?"

"I don't have a plan. I haven't figured out a plan."

"Do you know anything about Canada? You'll die out here if I leave you. It's getting cold."

The officer hands the landing papers back. "Do you know about homeless shelters?"

———

IN A HOMELESS SHELTER NOW, WITH NOTHING TO HIS NAME BUT three cigarettes and the clothes on his back. He could call Kabul, have one of his brothers send him some cash. He has a fortune there, but he made that fortune in Afghanistan; it belongs there, for now. It's tainted. Or asking for it now would be admitting failure. Or both. He can't do it. He's halfway aware that pride conspired to land him in a homeless shelter in two ways. He'd been on a park bench because he'd argued with his uncle. The judge released him, his uncle finally stepped up and let Aimal stay with them in this town Aimal never heard of, Guelph, but Aimal didn't last a week. All the questions, the belittling. The advice Aimal couldn't stand to hear. Over dinner: "What's your plan?"

"I'm going to start a business."

"No, boy, you can't think like that. Don't try to be a businessman; you'll mess up your life. You know what you should do? Get a factory job. They pay well. And down the road, maybe you'll find a girl; you'll get married. Then you two work hard, you can afford to buy a house. Pay your mortgage. And we'll come to your house; you're going to cook for *us*!"

"I didn't come to Canada for that."

His uncle shook his head. "Look what I've done for my family. My son is a police officer; my other son is going to be a pharmacist."

"I had a business in Afghanistan."

The uncle shook his head again. "You need to let go of those dreams. You'll only get yourself a cruel life. Better to keep your head down and work." So his uncle was another professor of the lungs, everyone a scholar of their own voices. How many more of them did he need to tell him he wasn't good enough? Why did people feel superior just for standing on Western dirt a little longer than he had? Fuck this guy. Fuck his one cop son and one pharmacist son, fuck them all. If his uncle didn't think Aimal was good enough to be more than a factory worker, he could go fuck himself and his precious sons and their careers.

Aimal dropped his silverware, said he was going out for a smoke, and never came back. He'd make it on his own, he'd show them, he'd start from scratch once he got home. *Home.* He didn't have a home. He had a home once. He walked; he counted his money. He'd left Afghanistan with plenty of cash, but a round-the-world trip, a vice-filled layover in Copenhagen, and the endless hedgerows of bottled duty-free temptation—in the West, money was like water. You didn't have to spend it; you just had to ignore it for it to evaporate. Wherever it had gone, he had less than $20 remaining from the almost $10,000 taken from his weeping mother's house only a few days ago. Ten dollars wasn't enough for a hotel, so might as well use it for a hit. The nicotine would fire his brain, and he'd figure it out. He used the last of his money to buy a pack of cigarettes and would live life one decision at a time. The plan would unfold before him like it always did.

And now he's in a homeless shelter.

Reeking, smelling the stink of others around him.

Now he has only crazy old men for company. But fuck it, he'll charm them too. If he's going to be living with them, they'll be his friends. He'll soon leave them behind, but for now, his station is no better than theirs.

He needs money.

He can't get a factory job because his work permit hasn't come yet, and he doesn't have the special form everyone say he needs, with a Social Insurance number. A number that would make him a real person here, as far as the government is concerned. He can't get money from Afghanistan because his pride is a wrought-iron door. So in the mornings he leaves the shelter and roams the streets of Guelph, passing factories and looking for the smaller family-sized enterprises that might operate in cash, and it doesn't strike him as coincidence, but rather as this new country finally warming to him a little, that one of his first stops is a convenience store with a help-wanted sign, and the old man behind the counter recognizes his accent the moment he opens his mouth.

"You're Afghan?" The old man looses a fusillade of Afghan greetings. *How are you? How is your health? How is your life? How is your family? Tell them I said hi!* before settling into the usual inquisition. The old man takes a shine to the young emissary from his motherland, tells Aimal that he hasn't been back in ages—what is it now, thirty years? And by the way, who *is* your family?

"No, no," Aimal says. "No family. I am here alone."

The man cocks his head. That seemed to offend him. He offers Aimal a job off the books for seven dollars an hour, and Aimal knows he's in no position to haggle. Stocking shelves, mopping the floors, tending to the register, he'd do whatever, and in no time, the old man—Uncle, as Aimal takes to calling him, out of respect—blesses him with the responsibility of closing up at night.

A promotion that presents a problem. Uncle wants the store open until midnight. He doesn't know that the last bus Aimal can catch leaves at 11:45 p.m. If he misses it, the walk back to the shelter is brutal. Summer is giving way to fall, Aimal facing down his first Canada winter, and the windchill keeps creeping lower.

So he locks the store every night at the last possible moment. Not midnight, but 11:42 p.m. He sprints to the bus and figures the eighteen minutes of lost commerce won't kill anyone if no one finds out.

Uncle finds out. It doesn't take long for a customer to come by the store just before midnight and find it closed, mention it a few days later to Uncle, who checks the security camera footage Aimal figured no one ever checked. "It doesn't work that way here! This is not Afghanistan! If I say 12, it means *12*. This is a warning," he says. "Next time I'll have to let you go."

Aimal adjusts. He tries staying to midnight and walking to the shelter, but he has just the one pair of clothes, nothing appropriate for the season. The cold stabs at his ungloved fingertips, and the wind slices through his shirt and braces his skin like he's naked. How do people survive these winters? Why did he come here?

He has another idea.

He asks Uncle to schedule him not just for closing but to open in the morning too, and then he starts sleeping in the back of the store. It works for a week until Uncle finds him one morning and Aimal has no choice but to admit he's homeless.

Uncle's face reddens. "You're living in a homeless shelter this whole time?"

"So what? They give me food."

"You're Afghan; you've been sleeping at the shelter while I have a house?" He looks like Aimal had slapped him. "From now on, you stay with me in my house."

"No," Aimal says. "No way. I'm not coming to your house; I can't."

"I'm not going to let you go to a shelter, and I'm not going to let you sleep in the back of a store."

An impasse. They stare each other down. Uncle won't let it lie. Aimal can't accept charity. Aimal can't pay rent. Uncle finally comes up with the kind of work-around that Aimal used to think of easily.

"How about this? Every week when I pay you, I'll cut $50 from your paycheck. And you'll stay with me."

He can live with that, so for weeks, Aimal lives with Uncle and his wife and two daughters while he saves up and waits for his work permit to come.

His wardrobe grows. This strange thing—Uncle keeps showing up with clothes that don't fit anyone in the family. Strange, Aimal thinks, that the sweatshirts and shoes Uncle is getting rid of are often brand new. That they always seem to be around Aimal's size. "These idiots sent me the wrong size again. Aimal, could you use it?"

"How much does it cost?"

"No, no, if you don't take it, I'm giving it to someone else anyway."

And strange how at work, at lunchtime, Uncle always seems to have extra food. Aimal refuses it. He's starved before; he can skip lunch. "Sit with me," Uncle says. "I don't like eating alone." Then, a few minutes later, "Ah, shoot. You know what? I forgot something back at the house." And he leaves, a feast still laid out for Aimal.

He settles into a rhythm. For weeks, he helpfully prevents Uncle's leftover food and mistaken clothing from going to waste. He comes to feel comfortable in the home, the whole close family padding in around him to soften his fall. But even then, he knows he's using Uncle as a stepping-stone, and the moment he receives his work permit, he thanks him and gives notice.

CHAPTER 3

OCTOBER 2011

Canada

HE TAKES A JOB HE'D SWORN HE WOULDN'T. ALSO JUST A STEPPING-stone. Working the line at the Linamar automotive plant for fifteen dollars an hour. Making camshafts and gearbox housings, machined components shipped to Ford and General Motors and the world's other automakers. Just a few weeks since he was a high-flying merchant of gleaming armored cars; now he dirties his hands on their oily innards. Still, just a step. He's graduated from a park bench to a shelter to a mat in the back of a store, and now he can afford a small apartment.

The factory isn't for long either. He's come from a country that had hardly any factories. Markets back home were mostly outside; commerce was mostly outside, stalls and carts in the open air. It isn't his natural habitat to be slotted into precise corners of a room, the particular carrels of minutes and seconds burrowed into a day. It felt like violence done to time. Time passes. Wild ideas occur to him. Maybe money was his problem. Business was the problem; he'll do something for the government. Back in Afghanistan, he'd never known a clean cop, so maybe he'll be a one-man corrective. And if he's going to be a cop, might as well be the best kind. Not some provincial bullshit like his cousin. He'll be a *Royal Canadian Mounted Policeman*. He'll be a fucking Mountie. He takes a year of community college, but the college loses its charter, and the plan fails.

He falls back to his old ways, trying to build something of his own. What to sell? He looks around and sees people toking from strange little metal phalluses. Metal cigarettes—this could be a growth opportunity. But it's like starting the first business back in Afghanistan. No credit, no collateral, so no way to get a loan. Maybe it's time to swallow his pride and use his cash stashed back home. He looks for a way to get hold of it, finds a butcher in the unlit, off-limits part of a Toronto grocery store who serves as a human node in the ancient South Asian money-transfer system. A man who has a friend of a contact of a cousin of a friend who works out of an office in Afghanistan down the street from Aimal's brothers. He takes a small taste of his fortune. Repurposed American tax dollars streamed around the globe and back to almost where they'd come from, to help him sell vape pens to Canadians. He's close to closing on a strip-mall storefront, a wide-eyed lessor looking at a few months in cash, before a new friend says to stay away because the market for robot smoke is saturated. So he starts a rice business that goes nowhere. Emeralds from the Panjshir Valley that go nowhere. He opens a pizza restaurant. He puts so much time and energy into the store, and his partner is such a headache, that he decides the whole enterprise is bad for his health and sells his share for almost nothing. He loses a mountain of money and tries not to think about it.

He goes to restaurants, goes to bars, a thing he can do here, happy hour without strip searches. He steps outside to smoke one night and sees a tall white woman sitting on the curb, lighting a cigarette. It's like seeing the maple leaf, the kind of person he came to Canada for.

"Such a bad woman," he says. "You're gonna kill yourself with those."

She shakes her head. "You're an idiot," but he hears no malice.

"No, I'm not idiot. I'm stupid." *What the hell does that mean? Doesn't matter.* He lights his own cigarette, thinking, *And that's the beautiful thing about this country. You go somewhere and don't know what's gonna happen.*

They become partners. She's a school-bus driver, of all things. She isn't pushy, but for a time he becomes a vegetarian for her. She takes him on double dates, usually with her sister and her sister's boyfriend, Frank, and when Frank hears the size of the haircut Aimal took on the pizza shop, he takes pity. Frank makes his pitch: you could make ten dollars an hour minimum wage at Tim Hortons. Or you could make twenty-five with me.

"Doing what?"

Frank says he's in the roofing business.

"Let me to think about," Aimal says. But he already knows he's in.

He shows up at the jobsite and learns, quickly, what the angle was. It's never been more obvious. The angle is the *angle*: you're never standing on a flat surface. Roofing is hard; it isn't for everyone. But he's comfortable up here. It's like he's up above the family's yard under the Taliban again, cutting away dried-out grapevines for the dish signal to pass through. Even after he breaks up with the school-bus driver, he sees her all the time and likes being around her. He keeps working with Frank. He dates a Vietnamese masseuse with a business mind and a grade-school son, and he dresses up as a father figure. He spends his money on violent PlayStation games for the kid, buys a house with the new girlfriend, then splits with her too, but she doesn't mind him being around either, and he can't bring himself to stop seeing her son. He loves the boy. Or he has something to prove about fatherhood, or both. He comes by the house to abscond with his ex's kid, takes the boy to movies, delivers him high-calorie food, spoils him. He does what he thinks a dad should do, though he can't really know.

He meets a cousin at a wedding, visits her in Amsterdam, and when her father talks a big game, he begins to think about marriage. Her father knew his father, he says, calls him a hero. Aimal allows it. The girl is young, Muslim, educated: what more does he want? She says she's willing to move to Canada. Why not marry her? Dating in the West hasn't worked out yet. It bagged him a job and a kid that wasn't his to spoil but not a spouse, and maybe an Afghan just needs to be with an Afghan. She's about his age, a similar vigor, and he decides maybe this was a part of his heritage he didn't have to run from.

CHAPTER 4

MARCH 17, 2016

Amsterdam Airport Schiphol

I'D JUST TURNED IN THE FIRST PASS AT A MANUSCRIPT FOR A BOOK I wrote with three young American men who had stopped a terrorist on a train to Paris, when I got a call from an old friend inviting me to a wedding. In Amsterdam, of all places.

I didn't know much about this fiancée. On earlier trips to see him in Canada, I'd met the Vietnamese woman with the cautious gaze and the bus driver with the wide-open face, but this one I knew nothing of. Except that she grew up in the Netherlands and hadn't spent time in her motherland. She sounded like Fatima to me. Only this time, Aimal was paying for an extravagant wedding, and I understood that made for a key difference. There was no place for an arrogant father to remind him of caste.

I felt this was going to be a milestone, an apparent one and a hidden one. Like the moment would be important in some way, beyond the obvious. So even though I'd never met her, and even though it was a transcontinental flight away, I decided, why not. I could combine it with a research trip. The manuscript I'd just turned in was missing something, and I thought maybe it was that I hadn't actually seen what the terrorist saw, or what the young men who stopped him saw. They'd begun their trip in Amsterdam, so I could go to Aimal's wedding, get on a train, retrace the steps of my young hero friends, and retrace the steps of the terrorist too. I could add details to the book in a later draft. Even in where he planned his wedding, Aimal was helping my career.

But I landed in Amsterdam and sent Aimal a text message, then another, and got no response. I called him, and he didn't pick up. I called him again and began to get annoyed. I'd flown across the Atlantic to watch him marry a woman I didn't even know, and I didn't *ask* him to pick me up; I would've made arrangements. He hadn't even let me know where I was supposed to be staying because he wanted to make all the arrangements himself. So I needed to find a car service now, and I needed to find what hotel I was supposed to stay at from someone else in the wedding, but I didn't know anyone else in the wedding. I wasn't sure there were any other guests from my country, or even my continent for that matter. I rode the escalator down into the arrivals hall thinking, *thanks, Aimal,* when I saw a sprawl of gangling limbs I somehow recognized splayed across four chairs, unmoving. I felt a little jolt of excitement. *Why am I so happy to see this asshole?* It was like my body sensed adventure, or maybe protection. Or humor, or love. A little opiate flow of calm hit me, and I was happy.

But it was important I teach this motherfucker a lesson, out of principle.

"Hey asshole," I said. "What the fuck? I've been texting you."

CHAPTER 5

MARCH 11, 2016

It's a week prior, and Aimal is scrambling to get ready for the wedding.

There are arrangements to make ahead of a few hundred people traveling to a country he himself has only even been to a couple of times, and also a blow: his mother and younger brother have been denied visas. His one surviving parent will not be there to see her son marry. He knows why. Every Afghan is a threat to overstay. No one trusts them. Some consular officer probably thought the wedding was a ruse to get out of the country. His wife's whole extended family will be there, hundreds of them. He won't even have a parent.

Then it gets worse. Aimal has just arrived in the Netherlands for the last few days of planning, has just learned that at the last minute I've decided to come, when he gets a panicked call from his mother. His kid brother, Omar, still young, cocky, and invulnerable, reacted to the visa rejection the way Aimal might have, by trying to find a work-around. He tried to get himself smuggled from Afghanistan into the Netherlands for the wedding. He'd managed to get to Turkey and then into Greece and was on his way to the smuggler's next lily pad when the wheels came off. He'd walked into a hemisphere-sized refugee crisis at the worst possible time. The Arab Spring was now five years old, the civil wars that spun from it now fracturing a dozen countries. Continents were ejecting refugees by the bargeful, fleeing dictators, American bombs, terrorist bombs, and crises of food, water, and sanitation. Receiving countries were closing doors and enforcing quotas, and Omar was caught on an over-trafficked route somewhere in the Balkans.

Aimal, in the Netherlands meeting with his in-laws, has no idea where. Omar has gone dark and hasn't been in touch for days now. Finally, Aimal gets a call from a strange number and knows it's Omar—his brother comes on in tears, saying his passport's been taken and he's been injured, a serious leg wound. "They've rounded a bunch of us up and forced us back to Athens." He's gotten himself into a situation he can't get out of, and Aimal can't get him to shut up long enough to extract his exact location before whatever phone he's on cuts out.

It doesn't occur to Aimal to stay put. His wedding is in three days. But if he doesn't go help his brother, who will? He leaves his fiancée, and as guests begin arriving, he flies out of the country.

He lands in Athens and begins searching. He thinks he knows where to start. His brother must be in Victoria Square. He just knows. The "warehouse of souls," where the unwanted from all the broken countries are deposited. He walks among Syrians, Pakistanis, Kurds, Afghans. Young boys are negotiating. Ten or fifteen euros, a shower and a bed for a night in exchange for sex. Two migrants are hanging from a tree, maybe Pakistanis. A green electrical box is ripped open—teenagers braving high voltage to wire phone chargers—and other young boys from some country or another whisper which nearby cafés let you use the bathroom as long as you buy a coffee—if you can buy a coffee.

It takes Aimal most of a day, but, somehow, miraculously, he finally finds his little brother. Omar's leg wound is hardly serious; he's exaggerated out of shock or because he's desperate for Aimal's help. But he's been beaten; he's terrified. Aimal is able to talk him down, get him calm, and promises things will be OK. He comforts Omar in the way only an older brother who always comes to the rescue can. He knows in Omar's eyes, he's capable of almost anything.

Aimal works the crowd. There has to be someone here who can help him get Omar proper documents. He checks his watch constantly because he's now a day from his wedding, just hours from when I'm due to arrive. Omar seems to think Aimal can get him on a plane to Amsterdam with him, and maybe he can, or could; with more time he could've found his way around the warehouse of souls to the right kind of smuggler.

He talks to someone in the square, who introduces him to someone else, who introduces him to someone else, who seems like a reliable kind of fixer and promises to look after the boy for a price. Aimal gets a read on him, makes sure the man knows there's more in it for him if Omar gets to safety, makes sure he actually has a way to get documents and get him out of Athens. Omar is big, but he's pretty, and Aimal doesn't say it but knows that it's not safe for Omar here. Greece seems worse than Afghanistan. At least this sad, crowded part of it.

He gives Omar a wad of cash, tells him he'll be OK, listen to the man and with a little luck they'll see each other somewhere safe, sometime soon.

And with Omar taken care of for the moment, Aimal rushes back to the airport, checking the time compulsively, so he can make it back to Amsterdam for his wedding.

There are no flights.

There's not a single flight, no matter the connection, that gets him back in time to pick me up. There's no route that gets him back in time for his wedding. The closest one lands two hours after his ceremony is supposed to start. Already hundreds of guests are wondering where he is. My flight's due in tomorrow. No, wait, *today*. Aimal hasn't slept in, what? Forty-eight hours?

His mind starts working again. He finds a flight that touches down in Hamburg a few hours before my flight lands in Amsterdam. Close, sort of, but there are no flights from Hamburg to Amsterdam in time. He stares at a map, and thinks. No flights, but there's something else: the Autobahn. Of course. *I'll drive*.

He books the flight and lands in Hamburg four hours before I'm due to land in Amsterdam.

He rents a car, hurrying the agent through the paperwork. He has three hundred miles to cover. He finds the highway and mashes the gas pedal to the floor. He pries his eyes open to keep from sleeping and hauls ass down the Autobahn. He checks the clock. Halfway to Amsterdam, my flight's arriving in two hours. He's catching up, making time. He's barely awake. He negotiates the math of stopping for coffee. He's not supposed to smoke in a rental car.

An hour from my flight landing, blessing him with my presence at a wedding, and he's going to bring shame by not even being there to pick me up.

Thirty minutes.

He zooms into the airport, tires screeching. His vision is foggy. He has to summon all his concentration to avoid rimming a curb on the way into the garage. The plane's probably touching down. He finds short-term parking—deplaning now—and he runs out to find the terminal, then an empty row of bolted seats in the arrivals hall. He sits down, looks up the escalator at the sprinkle of passengers beginning to descend, and immediately passes out.

He wakes to a phone full of messages and an impatient-looking American standing in front of him. Aimal has teased his body with 130 seconds of sleep; it's still in rebellion and won't let him move just yet. So he just smiles up into the morning light like a groggy lover the morning after.

"Where the hell have you been?"

"Nowhere. Just I'm tired, little, little." He stretches. "Yah, Jaff. You must be tired. Let us to get you to hotel."

CHAPTER 6

MARCH 18, 2016

Amsterdam

THE WEDDING WAS A GAUDY AFFAIR. I ARRIVED EARLY AT THE VENUE
because the hotel Aimal put me at was nearly two hours from the wedding hall, and that one time, he let me handle my own logistics. His
older brothers trickled in next and were an ocean of kindness. They
treated me like the angel investor I only technically was in the company that was still running in Afghanistan without Aimal. I still didn't
know any of them that well, but they were like extensions of his hospitality, gentle planets in a solar system that moved around him. I didn't
really know anyone besides Aimal, and he was busy. He showed up and
then kept disappearing to handle religious duties I didn't understand.

There was a cake with sparklers in the wedding hall, and there
were disco lights to help set off the dance numbers choreographed by
the bride's young cousins, all of them in fiery makeup that made them
look twenty years older. There was a fog machine.

There was Aimal, disappearing and reappearing, looking hand-
some, but for some reason looking, to me, a little thuggish. Maybe it
was the suit. The nicest thing I'd ever seen him wear before was my
secondhand blue shirt. Something about it all made me a little sad,
and at first I thought it was because I had no friends and this event
felt like middle school again, but then I thought it might be just that
Aimal wasn't smiling. I started watching his face closely. I began to
sense the weight he was carrying. Without a parent there to help, he'd
arranged an entire international operation. It felt like every country

was represented, not a wedding really but a summit, and one he had to choreograph alone. I left him alone and tried to mingle.

I found some young men slugging vodka from teacups in the parking lot. My tribe, at last. We tried to understand one another's accents, then blasted ourselves with Binaca before returning to the dance floor. I wandered around some more. Mostly I was a free radical, bouncing among all the welcoming people, not entirely belonging, and wondering, finally, what happened to Aimal to make him want to grow up when I still didn't. I knew in his family he was late to marry by about nineteen, but now we were at an age when even my friends were beginning to pair off in epidemic numbers, and I hadn't yet come close. I did a quick accounting, passing the time: I'd dated a kind young woman whose sister lived in my building. The Vietnamese friend of a Vietnamese friend. A yoga teacher and masseuse I considered a healer and had met in Barcelona. My father had taken to suggesting the daughter of this or that friend, but I was never into it. I was afraid; I continued to see paired-off friends as boring and conventional right up until I ran out of unconventional people to drink beer with. I blamed a career, said self-important things like "It wouldn't be fair, with me taking all these risks." My mother never suggested anyone. Sometimes, I later learned, she whispered disapproval of the women others tried to set me up with. So here I was, at another destination wedding without a partner. Or where the only "partner" I had was the one getting married. And when the night wound down and people filed out, it was again Aimal I found a new way of depending on.

I'd tried to find my own way back to the hotel. I tried calling a taxi. The wedding hall was in the middle of nowhere, I kept losing cell signal, and when I caught a furtive bar of service, it vanished before I could find a car. By the time I resolved that I was stuck, all the guests who lived in the Netherlands had already gone home, and I couldn't get a ride with any out-of-towners because they were all staying at a different, closer hotel. I realized, only then, that I was the only guest staying at the same hotel the bride and groom were. Aimal had wanted me near him. As if he needed to look out for me, even on his own wedding night, even though we weren't in a war zone; we were just in Europe.

But what it meant now was that I would have to sleep at the wedding hall. Perhaps get a ride back in the morning when taxis were back out. As the band packed up and militant caterers attacked leftovers with plastic wrap, I skirted the walls looking for a place to hide for the night, some hidden closet. Aimal wrangled the lingering dozen or so with a convincing display of patience, saw me facing a wall like a glitchy video-game character, pretending to be occupied on my phone, and somehow he seemed to know. "Yah, Jaff. You'll come with me."

I wanted to protest but couldn't think of how. So when Aimal and his new bride set off in the Just Married car, I was in the back with them. Riding along like a child. One more time, even on his wedding night, he insisted on being my driver.

After that, we went our separate ways. I lost track of him a little. He was growing up, and I still needed to. He tried being a husband, and I went on my next adventure alone. I continued my trip, that trip, but something strange happened.

I left the wedding for Brussels, to retrace the steps of the terrorist who tried to attack a train to Paris the year before. I left alone, I'd lost Aimal, I thought maybe for this, reporting in Europe, I no longer needed him or some copy of him. He was married, and maybe I was moving on.

I got to Brussels and found my way out to the Molenbeek neighborhood easily enough, the mostly immigrant district the terrorist had nestled in and then left on the day of the attack. I found his sister's house easily enough. I found his subway entrance easily enough, to the line he took to the train station, though it was closed. Also I was beginning to notice how quiet it was. It wasn't early, but there was no one out, as if I'd stumbled into not a neighborhood but an imitation of one, a Hollywood lot before extras arrived to give it life.

I walked to the next subway entrance, but that was closed too, then the next, and the next one too. Every single subway entrance was closed after that, leading all the way to the major Brussels-South station, a hub that flung high-speed travelers all over Europe. The station was a hive of activity by the time I arrived, sweaty and footsore and confused. The whole thing wreathed and taut with yellow caution tape, sirens blaring, and ardent little military vehicles hurtling past me toward the entrance. The odd oblivious civilian driver bumbled along toward the entrance anyway, was forced by pistol tip to stop, then yanked out and thrown to the pavement while security guards in aggressive squats kept guns trained on them. A row of heavyset civilians laid out on the sidewalk, round and pale and dumb, the police pacing above them like pleased fishermen. I took out a cell phone and filmed like I felt I was supposed to.

It wasn't until I made it back to the hotel that I understood what was happening. In trying to retrace a thwarted terrorist attack, I'd walked into a successful one. Terrorists had attacked two subway stations that I tried to enter and had set off bombs at the airport, so everyone figured Brussels-South was next. Thirty-two civilians had been killed, but the meaningful thing for me was that the targets were all clearly transportation related, so I was stuck in Brussels with no Aimal to find me a way out. The book's editor—also this book's editor—wrote to see if I was OK. The trip had come together last minute, I hadn't even told him I was going to be in Brussels; he just somehow sensed I might be. My mother called to get involved, she wanted to help me get home, or at least help me get a little farther west, but she seemed a little confused and I didn't have time to explain. I let her gesture at helping for a while; then I got frustrated and hurled some impatient insult over the phone so she'd leave me alone. And later, when things calmed down and Aimal called to tell me about his first week of marriage, I told him I'd had some fireworks too. I said I was in Brussels during the Brussels attack, and didn't know if I had good or bad luck, and he said, "No, Jaff. What it is, you have a lot of people praying for you."

CHAPTER 7

SUMMER 2016

Canada

AIMAL TRIES TO SETTLE INTO MARRIED LIFE. HE TAKES HIS WIFE on drives down a boulevard that reminds him of a city back home. Victoria Boulevard, with trees arching over the road. They drive; they like the smell of cows, the smell of the villages—do villages have smells? Together, he and his bride try to squeeze themselves deeper into Canadian life. They want to buy a house, but at first she's uncomfortable with the idea of a mortgage. Interest is usury, and usury is *haram*, and he remembers that his father once told him nothing is as expensive as when someone gives you something for free. He pretends to convert to Christianity, for the neighbors. A smart, attractive young couple who patiently debate with him for seven months until he has a dream he swears isn't a dream in which the young neighbor is there in front of his bed, in the middle of the night, with Jesus. Why does he always dream about white people?

Then, after the election of Donald Trump, when he sees a wave of anti-Muslim sentiment, he switches back. He thinks they believe all Muslims are terrorists, so he starts introducing himself by the most Muslim-sounding of his names, Ahmad. "I'm ambassador to religion," he says. "So I show I'm Muslim, I do sex before marriage, I drink, I work hard: I'm not a crappy guy." He keeps his other names handy. "Then when I do stupid thing. I say my name is Alex."

He works hard, maybe too hard. Roofing is hard work, hell on ankles because you're always on a slant. But he's found something like happiness. At least purpose. He's on the roofs all day, and when I come next to visit, he gets the day wrong and has to call his wife, whatever she's doing interrupted because her husband didn't tell her his friend was coming until he's already sitting at the airport bar.

CHAPTER 8

SPRING 2017

Toronto Pearson International Airport

I COULDN'T TELL IF IT WAS PROGRESS, OR THE OPPOSITE, OR NOT a sign of anything at all that for the first time, Aimal didn't pick me up. I sat at an airport bar talking to a Canadian who was nice I think because Canadians are nice. When Aimal's wife arrived, she was the picture of sweetness, gentle and strong, but riding in the car with her I felt like I was in the presence of a celebrity. The last time I'd seen her she was a painted enchantress at the center of a thousand people swirling her like dervishes, dying and reanimating from smoke-machine clouds. Riding home in the back of a Just Married car, with only enough light to think, again and again, that they're still in their complicated clothes.

At their apartment she entertained me, her unexpected guest, for hours before Aimal got home and put on a show of not being exhausted. When he mustered a real second wind, he took me to drop a meal off for his younger brother, working the night shift. Omar, now in Canada too, just settling in. Reaching Canada through a series of maneuvers more ludicrous even than the ones Aimal had used for himself. Now, Omar worked at a factory, and Aimal pushed the notion on him that he needed to give back to the country that was taking him in. So even though Aimal had to drop food off for him, and even though Omar was becoming a bit of a playboy, a good-looking kid who took up air in the room and always had something edgy going on with his hair, he still volunteered twice a week. At a food bank and an

243

assisted-living center. Not with any school group or club, he'd just walk in and ask to help.

Back at the apartment with the attractive couple he'd converted for before converting back, Aimal knelt on the ground so there were enough chairs for his guests, and we talked. We talked about dinner, about our adventures together, we shared war stories, and Aimal brought up the morgue. He asked me whether I thought he should start his own roofing business. I suppose I thought he could do anything. I said, "Why not?" And he turned to me with that glint in his eye. We were in one of those strange moments where he didn't seem to know what to say. He said "Do you feel like ice cream cake?"

And then he was up on his feet with the keys in his hands, springing out of the apartment and leaving his wife to entertain the guests. We drove nearly an hour to his favorite place, a chain where girls beneath buzzing halogen lights crouched over a counter and tended to frosting designs with a dedication verging on worship.

"Are you celebrating anything special? Do you want it to say anything?"

"No thanks."

"Yes," Aimal said, maybe first and definitely louder. "How about 'Welcome to Canada, Jaff.'"

My face reddened. *It's OK*, I thought. *They'll think Jaff is some nine-year-old having a birthday.*

"This is Jaff," Aimal said. "By the way."

The girl gave a pouty little fake smile, and I turned to pretend I was interested in unicorn-themed party platters. Aimal paid, and then came a version of a race we'd done a hundred times before. Me holding the *oh shit* handle and Aimal ashing a cigarette out of his window, knowing by feel where the problems were. The cracks and seams in the pavement already uploaded to the mental map he had, and I began to feel that same thing I felt a decade before. Urgency and purpose, danger, freedom, except we weren't at war now, dodging bomb craters and trying to skirt checkpoints to get to some horror before anyone else; we were speeding through the suburbs to get an ice cream cake back to his fridge before it melted, and to get his wife some backup before the neighbors reconverted her. Things had changed. It seemed, then, that everything was going to be OK.

———

WHEN IT WAS TIME FOR ME TO LEAVE CANADA THAT TRIP, I HUGGED Aimal but avoided his wife. Her head hadn't been covered once since I saw her, she wore tights and showed no judgment, and still I thought I'd seen a look of stretched patience when we opened the liquor I brought. I knew then that she didn't love Aimal's habits. It seemed she was trying hard to tolerate things. That she was succeeding, but that it took effort. It didn't strike me as a bad sign. It struck me as marriage.

CHAPTER 9

2018–2020

Canada

AIMAL'S BEEN MAKING GOOD MONEY ROOFING. LONG HARD DAYS, but he's paid in cash, and he's saving. Frank starts to trust him. Frank lets him run off-roof errands for the company. He sends Aimal to take an invoice to a client, and when the client hands him payment, Aimal has an epiphany. By now he knows the cost of products; he can ball-park the profit. After materials and labor, he figures Frank just cleared something like $18,000, on a single payday.

Aimal has found his business.

He thinks through what his edge will be.

First: he'll do it without scaffolding. It's illegal to have workers higher than ten feet without protection, but he looks into it: it doesn't have to be scaffolding; they can use harnesses instead. He'll find real men to work for him and pay them double the going rate. It seems like a waste; it's not. It's just a puzzle not everyone sees. He'll end up with better workers, but the kicker is, he won't lose the day it takes to put scaffolding up before a job and the day it takes to take it down after. He'll complete more jobs, make more money, so long as he can get some clients.

He starts thinking about how to get clients. He starts coming up with marketing schemes. He outfits his basement with six monitors, fifty inches or bigger, one monitor each for Instagram, Twitter, Facebook, Google ads: a 2,000-square-foot tech hub. He sits down there trying to get the company trending on social media.

He uses a strategy the Taliban used on him—he pretends he's not the boss. Once he can afford to buy a pickup truck, he introduces himself to potential clients as just a supervisor. *You think my Denali is nice, you should see what the owner drives. This company is high class.*

The business begins to take off. Soon there are too many clients for him to keep track of who owes what, so he invents a hack. He enters names into his phone as "Amir $7,500" and "Bill 10,000." Each person identified by the money they represent, and names change as people pay.

He takes on a business partner. Samie, another whip-smart young Afghan, raised in a refugee camp, now a Canadian citizen. They see growth potential in religion. Every Muslim in the city should use their company. Aimal goes to a print shop and makes a Ramadan calendar with time of sunrise, sundown, prayer times, mealtimes for each day of the holy month, plus his company's logo. Muslims in Guelph think of Aimal's company whenever they look at their fridge to plan their fasts, their *iftars*, all their closenesses with the Almighty. He goes to mosque on the twenty-seventh day of Ramadan, a holy day among holy days. When the imam asks for donations, the most generous members offer $3,000, $4,000. Aimal raises his hand. "I'll give $50,000."

The imam thinks he's heard wrong. "You'll give fifty dollars?"

This was strategic too. After a splashy donation, his name will be launched in the community. And he doesn't have to give cash; the mosque needs a new roof, Aimal can make a donation worth $50,000 that will cost him only $7,000 in materials, maybe $10,000. A generous donation that looks even more generous than it is. People gather to thank him, to hug this young man blessing the mosque with such generosity. An old man lingers after the rest have received him and withdrawn, and Aimal sees the man has tears in his eyes.

"Aimal. You gave $50,000?"

There's a familiarity to him. Aimal squints, and the face resolves into familiar angles. The shopkeeper. *Uncle.* How many meals had this man given him? Had anyone ever navigated Aimal's pride so skillfully?

"Because God gave it to me," Aimal says, "and I have to return it."

WITHIN A FEW YEARS OF STARTING BACK FROM SCRATCH, STARTING his own business, Aimal is employing forty-eight Canadians. He brings in millions a year in revenue.

He wants to give back, really give back, and not just in a way where there's something in it for him. He thinks of his mother, widowed young with a brood to care for and no marketable skills. He has this wild idea of a business and a charity fused together. He's seen organizations wither and die because they depend on donations; what if they didn't? He and Samie will buy a factory in Afghanistan where widows can work and have comfortable places to stay with their children. He'll put his money into it, his and Samie's at first, but then one day it will make its own money and last forever.

They buy property back in Afghanistan.

Aimal casts about for the right business, and it doesn't take him long: oil.

He calls me to see what I think. I say it was only a matter of time before Aimal got into oil, but he says, "No, not *that* kind of oil. *Vegetable* oil. Corn oil." The low-quality cooking oil Afghans use makes them sick. Nobody knows this about Afghanistan, he says, but it has so much diabetes. It also has lots of corn. He'll empower women while improving health while using a plentiful, cheap resource. He thinks about what his new organization needs and decides that besides a factory, it needs a protected space for women, and the best equipment to make the purest oil. Paperwork filled out, and, of course, office managers. He still doesn't really know what those are, just that Westerners with successful businesses always seem to have pretty girls at desks. Important for legitimacy. Somehow. He finds two sisters back in Kabul, hires one as vice president, and puts the other on the board so they have real jobs in addition to managing the office. And as he spends time looking back to Afghanistan, he has stayed in Canada long enough to becomes a citizen. Now, officially, he's home. Now, things are good; things are finally OK.

And then, things begin to change.

CHAPTER 10

MARCH 2021

Philadelphia

WE TOLD MY MOTHER SHE WAS GOING TO A SPA. A NICE PLACE TO eat well and get her weight back up. We didn't tell her she would probably never leave.

My two sisters drove her the first time. A cover story of getting their nails done. The kind of thing I'd never known my mother to like, but now a treat for her. All of them singing Simon and Garfunkel in the car, my two sisters taking breaks, pretending to forget the lyrics because if they cried, they'd give it away.

We'd gone through storage units and the basement and garage to find furniture for her new room at the memory-care unit, but then we were told not to use furniture she might recognize. It was going to be strange for her to be in a foreign place, but it would be stranger if there were flecks of remembered life. So we collected family photos for her to remember us by, and then we didn't give her any of them. A spa wouldn't have photos of her family. We weren't supposed to give her pictures of us until later, until she'd absorbed a sense of routine, comfort, only when she'd resigned herself to the fact that this was home could we bring fragments of her old home to her.

That day, my sisters went inside the memory unit with her, the decor at first contact cooperating with the ruse. A fake French café, an empty movie theater, a boozeless bar, all clean and casino-chic. A salon. And when it was time to leave, my two sisters, advised by staff to calibrate their good-byes more for a long weekend than forever, remained stoic. "Mom," my younger sister Jenna said, "isn't this place kind of like a lodge in Montana?"

My mother brought her in for a hug and said something destabilizing. "I'm really open to this," like she might know more than we thought she did. Or like maybe, with whatever fog she was staring through, she was trying to comfort us. "I'm open to the experience."

But then she hugged Margot, and when Margot was right by her ear, said, "I'm really scared."

Margot was knocked off-center. "It's going to be OK," she said. "These people are going to help you get better." But this was a thing you don't get better from.

My sisters stepped back across the threshold, smiled, cocked their heads, and waved as the doors swung closed, an electric lock hummed, a bolt slid into place. My mother must have wondered what kind of spa had locking doors. Or maybe she knew.

——

AGAIN AND AGAIN, WE LOCKED HER IN. EVERY TIME WE VISITED. TAKing her out on walks, locking her back in. Taking her to the mall, which she used to despise but was now ecstatic for, locking her back in. Browsing the aisles of Michaels, marveling at the fake plants. We expected, each visit, that *this* would be the time she refused to go back without a fight. A prisoner on furlough refusing to just submit. *This* time would be the scene with a pulsing alarm, her body thrashing on a gurney, hustling orderlies with syringes and wrist restraints.

But each time she just hovered on the other side of the threshold, waving while the doors closed and sealed her in. So peaceful, so resigned, we found ourselves wishing she would detonate. Put her shoulder down, charge through, pull a runner so we'd at least recognize her. The center had a word for that, "eloping," and I guess that was because "escaping" sounded too much like prison.

But she never tried. She let her family seal themselves off from her again and again. She let the curtain drop on her life, fade to black, without fighting it.

There would be crises. Spitting, yelling at attendants. She spent hours in front of the TV without knowing that she was watching the same episode of the same show on loop. So much time sitting that her hips inflamed and ratcheted her body down into a hardened arc. Two years after hiking ten-mile loops at eight thousand feet, reruns bent her over a walker. She used it as a jousting lance, lifting and pronging attendants who had the nerve to claim authority over her. She threw things. She beat her chest. She spat at people, and we found bruises on her arms. Meds were adjusted. Doubled, tripled, halved. She calmed down. She became her sweetest self, which wasn't entirely herself, or hadn't been for a while. Each time we visited, each time we said good-bye, she looked into our eyes and smiled, as the swinging doors closed her in on the other side, the electric lock hummed, a bolt slid into place. We went outside and wept.

———

ALL OF US DID, EXCEPT FOR ME. GRIEF CAME IN STRANGE WAYS, waves, and didn't identify itself at the door. It came first as weaponized memory. Sharpened nostalgia, weighted slate arrowheads flung from nowhere and striking my diaphragm. A catch in my breath, a sense of loss unrelated to her, to anything. There was a sense of pain around gone moments that seemed like islands in my memory, images connected by no landmass to anything relevant. A sun-dappled afternoon on the college quad with a casual friend. A shower after a freezing soccer practice. Not good memories, not bad memories, often not memories in which my mother was even onscreen. Memories I believed to be unrelated to anything at all until a journalist friend told me they all had one thing in common, something so obvious it had never occurred to me: they were all memories of things that had happened before she got sick.

But other than that, I was protected from grief. By resentment for the mother I may have wanted and didn't have. She'd been a complicated person; we'd had a pained relationship. I didn't forgive her for her shortcomings, but I'd settled into blaming her for most of mine. So I was protected by her flaws, which had for a time risen to the level of caricature because of what was going on in her brain. By the gravel of her past, deposited in our laps like sediment from a receding flood, as we went through her emails and shelves of letters, and her secrets stopped being secrets.

And protected by the demands of a task at hand. She had turned into a crisis to deal with, and I was at home there. An illness was just a dangerous and exciting thing to navigate. The scene of a bus bombing, an air strike in rebel-held territory. I needed to assemble the right personnel, put them in the right positions. Find the Aimal, find my stand-in for Aimal in Yemen, Iraq, Guantanamo, Kashmir, or some other far-flung ground zero where the people being hurt weren't me. I needed to assemble a team to build water filters in some hidden island republic, assemble a team to build a business school for unemancipated Afghan women, assemble a team to handle the violence occurring in the medial portion of my mother's temporal lobe. There was work to do. I equated action with help; I mistook distraction for strength. The last thing my mother gave me, as we moved her closer to that locked ward, was purpose.

CHAPTER 11

MARCH 2021

Canada

FOR A TIME, AIMAL'S LIFE IN CANADA HAS THE GLEAM OF AN IDEAL. The American dream. A refracted version, set in Canada. The North American dream, seed-funded by rerouted American taxpayer dollars. He has an apartment packed with new electronics. His wife seems to be settling in, even though she's far from her family. He works too hard and exhausts himself, but his new business grows. They have a child and are happy; they have two more, and the whole structure of their life collapses.

Aimal is never home. He is running a cash business. Driving around Guelph all day or else up on roofs with a nail gun, or going out with his employees on payday to drink down their wages. His wife, in his extended absence, allowed to wonder, he's now sure of it, what a young father with a successful business and fistfuls of cash is up to. He makes them money to spend, he gives her things, but only later, when it's too late, does he decide that women don't want money or things, not really; they just want time.

And why, he jabs at his forehead with his fingers like he's just remembered something, *why didn't I give her that?*

He throws money at everything. Money for day care, money for travel, money for her. Cash to be left alone. When Yusuf was born, Aimal's first child, it was a gift almost too large to comprehend. Yusuf made Aimal a father. Aimal looked at him and felt a dart of pain through his gut, a terror. *What if his childhood is like mine?* The room wobbled; Aimal felt unsteady. Yusuf's oblong little head pitched in the crease of his arm. What if he doesn't *have* a childhood?

Yusuf looks like Aimal. The same shock of black hair, the same sliver of mischief in his grin, even as a baby. And later, in the way he tumbles around the room with his toys, watching how people react. He has a gift for winning adults over with body language, and he has a pattern-less tendency for rage at authority. The three of them go to the doctor once, and when the doctor starts touching his mother, a not-yet-two-year-old Yusuf starts to shriek. He gives Aimal a conspiratorial look that's all commandment: *You're gonna kill this guy for touching her, right?* Aimal nearly laughs in the exam room. *Who is this ISIS son of mine?!* But that's not what Aimal is really worried about. He is being eaten away by fear for Yusuf's future, which he keeps confusing with his own past. Yusuf is a pitch pipe tuned to the key of Aimal's youth. Aimal remembers hunger, the Taliban, death, learning to cheat, a dead journalist springing away from him and her blood on his shirt. A triangle of flesh in a morgue. That's where Yusuf is going. It's in his poisoned blood, ready to come out unless Aimal stops it. He has to protect his son from that. From not having a childhood. From never getting to be a child. Already, Yusuf has this tendency around babies; like he dislikes them. He isn't gentle.

Aimal has to work harder, make more, build a fortress of cash around his children. They need to know what it's like to have clothes as nice as anyone else's. To be as good as anyone else. They need to not worry about passports. They have to take travel for granted, to have enough food to make them chubby, and to own as many objects as any playmate has. No TV show about foreigners will make them feel unworthy. They will know vacations and go all the time on the camping trips white people always seem to be talking about, though how pretending to be homeless was fun still mystifies Aimal. He will work as hard as he has to. And yes, as he and Samie sometimes admit to each other, at least some of this ceaseless drive is for themselves. Samie is Afghan but grew up in a Pakistan refugee camp, so his, too, was a youth infused with inadequacy. They agreed on this. Success proves that even though we're just refugees, even though you see us as a second- or third-class species, you don't admit but you do, we have arrived and we are too large to overlook. We come from camps in poor countries that were not even our own, where we weren't allowed to even go to school, and no policemen patrolled except those who came looking to exploit us because they knew there was nowhere we could go for help. You see us as swamp things who've crawled from the anonymous parts of crowded continents, you see us as sooty nothings, you don't see us, but we can build from scratch and it can be so big and good you can't ignore it.

To Aimal, a baby son is jet fuel applied to a drive that already burned white-hot.

It's no longer enough just to prove he is better than the traffic boss, better than Muqim, or Fatima's dad, the ophthalmologist, and all the American soldiers who tried to drive him off his own roads. Now he has to save his children from growing up like he did. After Yusuf, he has to work even harder.

When he is home, he is down in the basement with his six big-screen monitors forcing his company's name into every crevice of the internet. Or he and Samie are up on the roof in harnesses filling in for the no-shows.

He makes more and more. He buys his wife an Infiniti to drive the first kid and then all the kids around in. He buys a house in a desirable subdivision with plenty of room for as much plastic flotsam as the kids on YouTube have. He spends nearly every waking moment on the roof with the laborers, driving around making deals, or taking his employees out to Korean barbecue.

And he realizes too late that in trying to make sure his children aren't deprived of a childhood like he was, he's deprived them of a father.

Now that he sees what he's done, he'd happily walk off the job if given the choice. Give it all to Samie, leave the business. Go the other way. Make them all poor just for the chance to take his kids trick-or-treating.

He's almost never home. When he has time for leisure, he's out with the guys from work. He plays big buy-in poker with owners on the construction circuit. His wife, so resilient for so long, willing to leave her family and travel across the world to support her new husband, is patient and supportive until something cracks and she isn't anymore. He makes her feel foolish for thinking he's cheating, right up until someone tells her he's been cheating.

She's been deprived of the livable parts of life in Canada, but there's no charge you can levy at someone for stealing that. Instead, she levies all the others: rape, attempted murder, assault, aggravated battery. She files an affidavit that says her union with Aimal was a forced marriage. It's strange when he shows me the document. If it was a forced marriage, I'd been a witness. Riding in the back of the Just Married car, trying not to fall asleep while up front they whispered to each other like grown-ups.

———

THE CHARGES ARE SERIOUS, AS SERIOUS AS IT GETS. THERE ISN'T much evidence, so they can't hold him, but the charges are severe enough that the Crown takes them seriously. Canada seems inclined to see merit in the testimony of an Afghan woman, a class so long silenced.

The protests of an Afghan man are a different matter. Until a case can be heard by the courts, for the protection of his family, Aimal is prevented by bail order from seeing them. He can speak with his wife only through lawyers. He can speak to his children only when his wife permits it, which she refuses to do. A bail order restricts his movements to a prescribed list of locations and prevents him from traveling without the presence of a "surety," a companion who can be fined if Aimal breaks the rules.

A month passes during which Aimal is not allowed to see his children. He doesn't know how he survives it. Two months, six months. He know that in a child's eyes, that's forever. He's rendered them fatherless. It breaks him apart. He begins to spiral.

He tries to distract himself with new business ideas. With Samie's kids, with going to his favorite restaurants and charming the staff. He drinks and drinks. Bottles of Hennessy and the bright-blue one he sees at the LCBO near the checkout. He drink, and drinks, and sometimes, half a bottle deep, he calls the cops and asks to be put through to the officer who handles his wife's case, takes a swig, lets it burn, and unleashes into the receiver. Not all brown men are wife beaters; not all Afghan men hate women. *How dare you keep me from my children?* It doesn't help his case.

Once, he rises in the middle of the night and heads east in the GMC. Along Lake Ontario toward Niagara Falls, swerving over the line, running on the shoulder, hoping other headlights will avoid him. He has an idea of what he'll do when he gets there. When he arrives at the waterfall, he looks out on the misting drop. A big cold inhale drawing him in. Maybe it's time. He wobbles, takes a step forward, and hears Yusuf. "Daddy," Yusuf's voice says from nowhere. "I need you. I need you, Daddy." His son, the one who made him a dad. He doesn't jump; he somehow makes it home.

He doesn't hide how close he is to the edge. Samie can see what's happening. Samie's wife gets it too in the wise, quiet way she has. She hand-braids a bracelet for Aimal with the children's names, just in case Yusuf's voice isn't there to save him and also so there won't be a next time. So that he has to see their names on his wrist when he lifts his drinking hand.

Samie knows Aimal is trying to destroy himself. Samie holds Aimal's shoulder and says, "Brother, my kids could use some time with their uncle." So Aimal starts borrowing them to remember what it's like to be in the vicinity of innocence, and for those slanted milliseconds when the light hits a certain way and you mistake someone else's child for your own.

Samie's daughter, just learning words for people who aren't Mom and Dad, gives Aimal his newest name: "Grandpa." He takes it.

ON HALLOWEEN, HE DAMN NEAR BUYS THE SUPERMARKET OUT OF candy. Enough sugar to keep the kids up for a week and bankrupt Samie at the dentist, but Samie pretends to be fine with it. Aimal forgets the term "trick-or-treating," and when he thinks of it—kids with candy— he thinks of Chuck E. Cheese because to him it sounds the same, or maybe because the jingle has hooked itself into his brain. *Where a kid can be a kid!*

He thinks of a word, *churi*, which means "theft," so when he tries to ask if he can take Samie's kids trick-or-treating, what comes out is a jangling of half-words from different languages: "Can I take them Chucky-churi?"

Samie says, "Can you do *what*?"

Aimal is confused. He's getting confused more easily. His memory gutters between English and Dari. The temperature drops, and now it's *cholly*—another hybrid word that's close to "chilly" but doesn't mean anything, in either language. Often, the words he uses have just enough of each to be meaningless in both, like he's sliding into the cracks be- tween two moving continents and is forgetting, and is being forgotten.

CHAPTER 12

SUMMER 2021

Todos Santos, Mexico

I WAS ON A KIND OF PILGRIMAGE. SOUTH AND WEST TO MEXICO, and the western side of the Baja peninsula. My attempt to reconcile with a sister who had once been my best editor, my fiercest protector. Who pummeled a Montana bully for picking on me when I was in second grade. I'd been determined to keep the family illness from rifting us apart, and I'd failed. We'd just moved my mother on to the rest of her life, but there had been screaming, months of accusations, a new mistrust. The sense in each of us of having been undermined by the other. Each of us pure of motive and selfless, the other self-serving.

My sister had a small hotel there, a kind of inn for an emergent species she called the digital nomad, and a second life in the town around it. I was working on a manuscript, the fact-checking phase of an *Atlantic* article, and a film project. Probably already too much. I was working on a micro-budget film loosely based on my first book. About Marefat, Afghanistan's first coed school, as students and teachers there looked toward a total troop withdrawal I was trying to warn readers about, but wasn't sure would actually ever happen.

But I had traveled mostly to be around my sister and her daughter, my wild-haired niece. I was there because it's hard for me, like it's hard for many, to express the most important things to the most important people. Taking two flights during a pandemic was my way of saying, "I'm here. Let's try to let things heal." She looked at me one morning in her borrowed car, driving down a dirt road, and said she understood why I'd come.

But I didn't end up getting to spend time with her, or her child.

We'd just entered this new family moment, still learning choreography with a role unfilled. Stumbling around, trying to find the right mix of sadness, alcohol, and laughter. And just as my mother went behind the locked doors, a crisis milestone inside our family, outside it, out in the world, the American president had announced the full US troop withdrawal.

I began to worry for my friends there. Only a low-level worry, barely even worry, more like interest, more like attention. The Marefat school served the country's most vulnerable, visible minority group. If the Taliban took over, these friends would be in grave danger, but the Taliban would never take over, so it was just unease.

I had a friend who was more concerned, though. Bella Pollen, a brilliant writer, a funny, irreverent, and quietly, deeply humanitarian booster of the school. She thought we should be proactive. She said, in conversations studded with mutual writerly jealousy and off-color jokes, that it might be wise to find jobs outside Afghanistan for our more vulnerable friends. Just in case. She was overreacting, but it felt like it couldn't hurt. The school's headmaster, Aziz, who I'd written about, who I'd worked with in a half dozen different ways, was on the kill lists. If the Taliban ever did take over, he'd be first in line for retribution. Aziz was a public opponent of Taliban ideology, a proponent of coeducation, an ethnic minority, a religious minority, and a Shia, whereas the Taliban are Sunni. Perhaps most of all, Aziz had guided his school into vigorous cooperation with the Americans. He checked all the wrong boxes.

I spent much of the spring and early summer falling further behind on deadlines and working with Bella, then Bella and her friend Christa, and finally Bella and Christa and Christa's mother, Baroness Frances D'Souza. A graduate student named Justin Hefter, whose only link to the family was having met Aziz's son Abuzar in San Francisco once or twice, but who learned of the effort and somehow immediately rearranged his whole life to support it. Justin's friend Mark Donig, a corporate lawyer whose Zoom backgrounds kept changing, night in New York to day in Israel to some other exotic locale, but who seemed to always be awake.

We spoke with asylum attorneys and networks built for threatened scholars. We emailed universities and think tanks that might like having Aziz in the building. We learned the intricacies of arcane visa processes. We raised some money. We absorbed a new glossary of terms we never wanted to learn: "SIV," a type of immigrant visa for people who were supposed to be but didn't actually seem to be considered "special" for having helped our military; "humanitarian parole," a term excavated, bandied about, and then rejected, a way to quickly get people out of danger and into the United States even before they were fully vetted; and "AMCITS," for when you didn't have time to say "American citizens" but wanted people to know you had responsibilities more important than Afghan people.

On the ground, Aziz continued his work. On calls, he was hopeful; from the ground, the picture was fine. Even once America left, the Afghan security forces were unified and up to the task of defending the country. Aziz was in no rush. And an international trip would be inconvenient for his family. He had young kids; he had older kids starting careers; most of all, his wife was nine months' pregnant. He was touched that foreigners were mobilizing on his behalf, and he agreed that it wouldn't hurt to get passports for those of his family members who didn't yet have them. But he wasn't worried.

By the time I arrived in Mexico in July, things already seemed more grim. The push to set up interesting opportunities for Aziz was becoming a more urgent push to get him out. We'd moved too slowly.

Troops were packing up. Aid organizations were beginning to pack up. The threat of a Taliban advance became more real. Afghans trying to get visas so they could leave the country began to line up in larger and larger numbers outside embassies with smaller and smaller staffs. Doors were beginning to shut.

On calls to Afghanistan, we urged Aziz to hurry up with the family's passports. Bella and Christa began looking into backup plans, even though Aziz promised he'd have passports in hand tomorrow, then next

week, then all that was left was biometrics and they had someone helping, and then it was simply too late.

Lines at the passport office in Kabul grew, the backlog piled up, the
office ran out of the materials to make passport books.

By my first few days at my sister's inn, it was obvious to Bella and
me and the new Impromptu Team that we were going to have to get the
family out of the country without visas. Or even passports.

Well-meaning institutions from USC to UConn to the London
School of Economics bent over backward trying to scurry up positions
and funding for a headmaster who, while inspiring and gifted, had
little formal education, no papers, no real prospect of getting papers,
and a large family to support. Professors roused deans from their summer vacations to plot new routes through old bureaucracies even before Afghanistan became major news and well before helping Afghans
was fashionable. For the brief moments I could pay attention, it was
a heady thing to witness, one of the purest things I'd seen in all the
residue from war I was beginning to sift through. As best I could tell,
people wanted to help because they wanted to help.

They just couldn't. Few universities knew how to get visas from
countries without functioning embassies. There was no playbook for
this. Friends reached out to me with ideas that would never work.
We tilled contacts at the United Nations to see if we could get the
family declared refugees; we sent letters to people with gaudy multi-
hyphenated titles at the State Department. We called congresspeople
who assigned us their most nimble aides; we called retired ambassadors, current ambassadors, baronesses, lords, and speakers of various
houses. A conspiracy of powerful people who all wanted to help this
one family exit, it was just that none of them quite knew how to do so.
We had senators sending letters to the secretary of state about Aziz,
governors writing panicky letters and copying the president. A country was beginning to collapse, the people we were most connected to
were the most at risk, and as the storm bore down, the bridges were
crumbling. We had once worried this would be another Vietnam. In
my book about Aziz and his school, I'd made a big thing of that picture,

how I'd assigned myself the task of capturing my generation's version of an American helicopter lifting off a roof in Saigon, leaving a line of people who helped us and needed to get out, but there isn't enough room.

We'd worried that would happen again.

But it was worse. It felt like that same photo without the helicopter. At least in Vietnam, the American government had plans in place to evacuate tens of thousands of Vietnamese people at risk because they were on our side. This time, there was no plan we could see. It seemed hardly anyone in the government had even considered that hundreds of thousands of people would be trying to get out. It first felt like the government wasn't helping, then began to feel like the government was working against us. We were in the midst of a cabinet-level self-soothe. The White House seemed to be telling itself this wouldn't be that bad, the country would not collapse, we've made the right decision, and we can't allow a run on the exits.

The troop withdrawal accelerated. The Taliban started taking outlying cities.

On Zoom calls with the Impromptu Team trying to evacuate Aziz, we began to entertain wild ideas. Christa had a gift for making connections with people none of us would think of—she'd linked up with a supporter of the school who was in the "security business" and had access to a private jet and a team of mercenaries able to get creative with paperwork.

Did we have the cash?

Could we get it to them?

Could we trust them? Did we have a choice?

Land borders were closing, but maybe an overland hustle to Pakistan was still possible with the right connections.

And then we simply ran out of time.

The Taliban took Herat, a major city. We never thought that would happen.

They got closer to Kabul. We had to face the fact that we'd likely missed the chance to evacuate Aziz's family legally.

More US troops left. The Taliban drew closer to Kabul.

US Embassy personnel now fully abandoned the embassy compound, and what was left of the US diplomatic mission in Afghanistan was now a "dislocated" embassy operating from inside the airport compound.

The airport compound became a garrison. The last thing the US military would be allowed to do was secure the airport until it had guaranteed passage for at least its own people, and then it would let go even of that.

Now we knew we had to get Aziz's family into that airport compound before the Taliban found him. Whatever it took.

But we didn't know who was in charge. No one knew. Even the people inside the airport compound didn't know who was in charge of the airport compound.

The situation had deteriorated so fast, it was so disorganized, that the US State Department and different branches of the military all seemed to have authority over some corner of the compound, but none seemed to know where its own authority ended and another agency's began, and it kept changing anyway.

Each member of the Impromptu Team chased down leads. All of us spent hours piecing together new plans and finding creative ways to make contact with our own country's armed forces, private security groups, politicians. Justin wondered why everyone was focusing on just one airport entrance and plied his own new on-the-ground contacts for other routes. Bella and Christa managed to get through to the British military garrisoned on the ground in Kabul, the British Special Forces, and then even more mercenary groups. They had members of Parliament trying to call in favors on behalf of this one special family; there was just no one to call. Plans stalled out; plans moved to near success—the family names on a manifest, the family's names added to some promising lists—and then collapsed as something shifted again. Insurance companies underwriting the flights out of Kabul got skittish, flights were canceled, the helpful chief of some fiefdom or another on the ground lost control of it. Highly placed people lent their focus to our family, then withdrew it to pursue a route out for some other desperate friend. We felt foolish, we felt purpose, we half-knew we were tilting at windmills, but it felt better than too squarely facing our failure.

Through Trudy Rubin, world affairs columnist for my hometown *Philadelphia Inquirer* and longtime supporter of Aziz, and through Joe, the CEO from my Constitution Center days who'd visited the school with me and met Aziz during our trip to Afghanistan, we learned about an unlikely potential savior. A wealthy American businessman with high-level contacts in foreign governments and in the US Senate was organizing a large charter flight to Rwanda. There were rumors that it would include visas for everyone onboard. I was given his contact information; we composed a letter to him explaining why Aziz and his family deserved to be on that flight. He agreed, told me I just had to coordinate with an Afghan woman on the ground for whom the charter was booked. She was trying to usher the girls from her boarding school to safety, and as she hustled across Kabul, she and I sent encrypted messages back and forth. But I did something wrong, I overstepped, and I received a fiery email from the American businessman telling me the seats were no longer available, Aziz's family was on their own, and not only that, I had jeopardized the entire flight for dozens of girls.

More troops left. More cities fell to the Taliban. I began receiving messages through every single service I had an account on. Everyone was desperate to get out, or to get someone they knew out, and everyone in the country seemed to know how to reach me.

The Taliban reached the outskirts of Kabul. That meant one of two things for Aziz's family: either it was too late for them to get to the airport, or if it wasn't, it was about to be. The Taliban would be in the city within days, maybe within hours. Either way, the family couldn't stay in their house. Too many people knew where it was. They packed their bags, just one each, and then all of them—Aziz and his pregnant wife, their four daughters, and their son—said good-bye to their home forever.

They drove across the city to a safe house in Kabul, where they would hide, indefinitely, and hope that we found a way to get them out.

A feverish back-and-forth began. Simin, one of Aziz's daughters with him in Kabul, sent updates to Abuzar, his eldest son, who was living in San Francisco and who forwarded the updates to the Zoom we were now almost constantly on. I passed the twice-removed updates on the family status to Joe, who had been trying to help engineer a calmer exit through his impressive network of friends. He passed my updates from a safe house in Kabul, via San Francisco, via Mexico, to a national security aide in the office of a senator Joe had managed to get invested in the cause, who was, in turn, liaising with an intelligence source all the way back in Kabul inside the airport compound. A giant loop of communication started at Aziz's undisclosed hiding place in Kabul, pinged around the globe, and ended just a few miles from Aziz, back in Kabul, somewhere inside that airport compound.

The intelligence source would—he told the senator's aide, who told Joe, who told me—secure the family entry into the airport, if they got themselves there. *But*, the source said, time was of the essence. The latest was that the Taliban would be *in* the city within hours.

I passed the update on to the Zoom call, and Abuzar in San Francisco passed it to the Kabul safe house: it was time to decide if they were going to make a run for it.

While they debated inside the safe house, the intelligence source passed another update down the line: the Taliban were now just outside the city. If Aziz's family was going to make a run for it, they had to go *now*. It was happening faster than expected. They had minutes to leave. They had to start destroying documents right now, anything that might identify them, or us. They began trying to memorize phone numbers so they could begin deleting them, since phone numbers could link them to Westerners.

Then another message from the intelligence source inside the airport compound: the Taliban had breached the city limits. They were now in Kabul. It was over. The family had to stay in hiding. If they tried to make a run for it now, they'd be exposed and would likely run right into the Taliban. We were too late.

I faked positivity while telling the Impromptu Team we had to call it off. "Tell your dad to sit tight," I said. "They need to stay in hiding. We have to reevaluate."

There was confusion on the screen. Abuzar was holding a cell phone. "Wait," he said. "Wait . . . but they already left."

CHAPTER 13

AUGUST 15, 2021

Todos Santos, Mexico

I PACED THE ROOM AT THE INN AND TRIED TO IMAGINE WHERE exactly the family was.

Aziz, his children, and his wife somewhere out on the road in Kabul, hurrying toward an airport they still didn't have a way into. The Taliban were moving into the city all around them.

It was early morning there, predawn. In Washington, it was nearing the end of the business day. I had just triggered a potentially ruinous miscommunication, and as the clock wound down, I was running out of ways to correct it.

From Philadelphia, Joe tried to raise the senator's aide before Official Washington shut down for the night. The aide had proven himself dedicated to the family's safety, remarkably so, considering that neither he nor the senator had ever met Aziz, and there were trapped Americans the senator's office was also working to rescue.

But we couldn't expect a senator's aide to stay up all night. I didn't have a direct line to his intelligence contact inside the airport. I'd just placed an entire family's survival on the shoulders of a Senate staffer whose many official and even constitutional obligations—and whose duty to constituents—did not include this.

Once again, as the family snuck across a city the Taliban were filtering into, Joe got the senator's aide on the phone. He promised he'd try the intelligence contact again to relay my message: despite advice that it was no longer safe to move, the family had moved. We needed to know which airport entrance they should head for and how exactly to get them in.

The family was outside, exposed, moving across Kabul in the dark. Simin whispered into her phone, and her brother in San Francisco updated all of us: Bella and Christa in England, Justin in Boston, me in Mexico, and Mark wherever Mark was.

In Kabul, Simin heard gunshots near them; there was yelling. They turned a corner and saw men with long beards and Kalashnikovs.

Somewhere out there, Simin whispered to Abuzar that they were getting close to the airport. There were more and more Talibs. Simin said they hadn't been spotted yet. Or at least it seemed that way; it was hard to tell. It was still dark there. The family was almost at the airport gates.

On my computer screen, Abuzar raised his head from his phone and looked at me. "Where exactly in the airport is this guy going to be?"

I was still trying to find out. I called Joe again; Joe called the senator's aide.

The family got closer to the airport.

I closed my eyes and willed this mysterious contact inside the airport to come back online. But it was out of my reach; there was nothing I could do. I distracted myself by writing to powerful people whose emails I'd poached over the previous months. To John Allen, a retired four-star Marine general who commanded NATO coalition forces in Afghanistan a few years before:

> FYI ATM the family is making a move on the North Gate/ Abbey gate. They're outside trying to get in. Rumors that their hiding spot was compromised, Talibs going door to door. Not sure how reliable it was but they made a judgement call. We're working on people trying to help them get inside. If there's someone you may happen to know inside the airport who can help get them in, please call me.

I hit send.

A sound from my computer. Abuzar in San Francisco: "Jeff, they're a few minutes from the airport. Where's the guy?"

I called Joe again: "Where's the guy?"

Joe: "I'm finding out."

Abuzar: "Jeff, my family's almost there. Where is this guy?"

To Joe: "Joe, where's the guy? They're almost there. They're exposed."

Joe: "I'm finding out."

A moment passed. I wrote another email to General Allen with a link that connected directly to Simin's phone, somewhere in the city, near the airport.

> *This is their exact live location, . . . And if their phone dies it's here: 34.57228992846665, 69.222805747858. This is probably one of those make-or-break moments.*

I didn't even add my name.

On my laptop screen, Abuzar ducked down to speak with Simin.

Then he looked up, looked at me, and made eye contact that was as entreating as a screen allows. "They're there. They're at the airport. My sister is saying there are gunmen all around. She thinks they're Taliban. Taliban is all around. Jeff . . . *where is the guy?*"

I looked away from him and called Joe one more time. One more time I willed good news to materialize, the senator's aide telling Joe someone was there, in front of the airport, smiling and waving the family in.

Joe came back on the line. He didn't say anything at first. He just let out a long, pained sigh.

On my computer screen, Abuzar was still staring at me, trying to hold it together, his sister, out in the falling city, on the phone in his hand. "They're at the gate. They're surrounded by Talibs. Where is he? Where's your guy?"

I looked away. "He's just—he's not there. No one is there. No one is coming to help."

WE STAYED UP ALL NIGHT TRACKING THE FAMILY. ALL OF US WILLING them back through the city unscathed, even when there was now no other way to put it: Kabul had fallen.

With Talibs celebrating, shooting at the sky and cheering, Simin managed to lead her family back into their hiding place unnoticed. But now that the Taliban were taking over, it seemed the only way to get the family to the airport was an armed military escort. I asked General Allen what felt like an insane question: how could we, a few amateurs on laptops, activate the US military on our behalf?

He took the question seriously. He couldn't order military assets around, he said, nor would it be appropriate for a retired general to even ask a favor like that of active-duty military in the midst of a crisis. He was deferential to soldiers on the ground and wouldn't risk creating any more pressure.

But he wanted to help.

He wrote back to me explaining how it would have to work. I had to get the secretary of defense to tell the general in charge of CENTCOM to dispatch a unit from the airport compound in Kabul out to get Aziz. In order to get the secretary of defense to take that action for this one family, I needed to get the State Department to make a request of the Pentagon.

We needed to rethink this.

Team members plied contacts, Joe plied contacts, we tried to get letters to the right people to put the right pieces in place for a US or British military operation, but the idea of either military going out to get Aziz's family felt, even to me in my sleep-deprived state, like fantasy. I read back over General Allen's email trying to ply it for hidden meaning. He'd named some of the most powerful people in the American government, as if I were on a first-name basis with them, as if I myself might wield the American military apparatus as I saw fit. Is that what it had come to? Such disorganization that forces on the ground were looking for amateurs on Zoom in hotel rooms for guidance? I kept looking back to that email, trying to decide whether Allen was really helping me to get the Pentagon working for Aziz, or trying to show me why I shouldn't even try.

Things went wrong. Wires got crossed. While in hiding the family received a call from an unknown but authoritative-sounding party, saying they needed to leave immediately and head for the Serena, an upscale and well-protected hotel in Kabul. But there was conflicting information about whether the Serena was a late holdout from the Taliban or now fully in their hands.

Now the family was in hiding, with Taliban all around, but none of us knew what, exactly, Kabul falling to the Taliban meant for Aziz. Would they murder him and his family on sight, as Hazaras, heathens, critics of theirs? Would they try to show a milder face at first? We didn't know; most Afghans didn't know. Afghans surged toward the airport and massed at the gates, thousands of them trying to get in.

Then, another night, another near disaster.

An evening we had no operation planned, so I tried to finally catch up on sleep. I went to bed at around the same time the people around me went to bed, which now felt foreign, an undeserved luxury.

I awoke in the middle of the night and felt a presence in the room. I heard a breath; I thought I was imagining things. My eyes resolved, and I saw my sister's dog, muzzle leaned on the bed and not barking, not moving, just staring.

I rose, opened the computer, and saw that the Impromptu Team was on a Zoom call because of a frantic operation that had launched at the last minute after a tip someone received that, like mine, turned out to be a mirage. In Kabul the family was hustling through the dark again, somehow making it past distracted Talibs again, only to get stuck, exposed, just outside the airport with no way in. The family was crushed in the throng of bodies, and one of Aziz's daughters had trouble breathing, felt sick, and then fainted, collapsing on Simin's shoulder.

———

AND THAT, FOR ME, WAS IT: WAKING TO AN OPERATION ALREADY HUR-tling toward disaster jolted me. I'd begun the season of Afghanistan's collapse burnt out, went deeper into exhaustion, and kept finding adulterants to prevent the engine from seizing up, but something about seeing a family marching to their likely demise a second time turned a dial in me to manic. The last shot of adrenaline coursed across my brain and squeegeed away worry. I was alone in the middle of the night. I was ecstatic. I was unconcerned. I was excited. If the family survived tonight, they were going to get out. We were going to do it. I was going to do it. I understood I would not sleep until the family was out. A plan formed in my head. Dots connected. If we were going to send them again across a city that had now fully fallen to the Taliban, we needed a plan that could survive failure. We didn't need a plan; we needed three plans, four. We needed fail-safes. Redundancy. Multiple layers of redundancy. Redundant redundancy. We needed to assume any information we built a plan around was outdated. Powerful people from all over the world were now trying to get people they cared about out of the country but were succeeding only by chance. The airport was overrun; planes were taking off with the lucky few who'd been allowed into the airport, and with the unlucky few who hadn't been allowed in but who had burrowed their way in somehow anyway and stormed the tarmac, who were filmed clinging to wings and then being flung thousands of meters to their deaths. Reports emerged of others grasping to landing gear and being crushed when it retracted or freezing and suffocating when the aircraft reached altitude. The reports only made the airport harder to get into. There was a new slang term for the random-chance arrangements that allowed some people to get into the airport compound when so many couldn't: "drug deals." Informal, on-the-spot arrangements.

We needed those too.

We needed to seed the ground for Simin to make a "drug deal" if our plan failed.

By sunup, I was working furiously. Typing furiously, thumbing a BlackBerry furiously, alone in a room neglecting my sister's half-mastiff, who looked at me with what I could've sworn was concern and whose whole body swayed with delight when I glanced up from my laptop for even a second. I flew through old messages, mining for leads I might've missed but could now use, drawing it all to me. Earlier, in the midst of our failed months of bureaucratic wrangling, I'd begun, as a form of procrastination, responding to messages from friends who sent ideas I knew would never work. One had come from, of all people, a screen-writer in Los Angeles:

> *I saw your Instagram about US/NATO contacts at the airport. Are you sorted with this? Will go full HAM and call in every favor I can in an attempt to signal blast/find this. Let me know and I will make this my priority ASAP.*
>
> *Obviously thinking of you and your people. Hope you're doing okay.*

A screenwriter sitting in a Hollywood home office wouldn't have use-ful contacts, but now I said "Sure" because at least I knew not to be dis-appointed when his offer didn't pan out. The screenwriter introduced me by email to another friend, a former naval intelligence officer now work-ing for the Treasury. In London, of all places. Distant from the action, but something in his reply signaled he might know more than I'd expected:

> *Let me just say that I'm not super optimistic in the near term, given scenes at the airport. But I'll see what I can do of course.*

He and I began to talk. Other members of the Impromptu Team be-gan to talk with him too. He said he was connected to some people on the ground. He might be able to link us to a small team of Marines operating off the books. They might be able to get the family from their safe house to the airport, through a city now mostly controlled by the Taliban. It seemed incomplete, a little fantastical, but promising. It felt like our plan A.

I wrote to General Allen. I had no business corresponding directly with him or calling him by his first name, as I'd started to do, but I'd lost all semblance of deference. He was still adamant about not pro-jecting authority over anyone on the ground, and he said I should follow that example. "We do not want to be a 7,000-mile screwdriver." You don't succeed in a chaotic environment by trying to make calls from abroad—you put the people on the ground in positions to make calls on their own. I thought, *Aha. Drug deals.* Quietly, he said, he still wanted to help. And he had a new idea. He asked for the documentation we had of the family—photos and national ID cards—and promised to get back to me. He had a line inside the dislocated US embassy.

He got back to me:

> *Jeff, please tell Aziz that an American from the embassy . . . is likely to text or call him on WhatsApp. He needs to be watching/listening for it. It's 0200 in Kabul.*

We had a second layer of redundancy. If plan A with the Treasury officer and the Marines failed, the family might still have a chance to get into the airport compound because the State Department official inside the airport compound was now on the lookout for them.

We were getting close. Pieces were lining up.

I thought we needed at least one more backup plan before sending the family on another run. I had visions of Aziz's daughter fainting at the gates again, a stampede, his wife crushed. The unborn baby hurt in the chaos. None of these things worried me; they were simply eventualities to avoid. This was not a family of people I loved anymore; they'd become objects in need of logistical consideration, a new clinical outlook only occasionally broken when their faces flashed up at me while sending scans of theirs IDs to some official or another. Between calls and messages to the different pieces of our now rapidly developing plan, I wrote messages directly to Aziz and Simin. We'd all been reluctant to communicate with them during the most kinetic moments, instead keeping a single uncluttered channel between Aziz's daughter in Kabul and son in San Francisco. Now, as they waited, Aziz, Simin, and I exchanged funny, heartfelt, occasionally just foolish messages. They both had a durable capacity for humor and mischief, even amid new rumors that the Taliban were going door to door, looking for people like them.

We tried to make each other smile.

But even those exchanges came from a mechanical part of me that registered morale as an important precondition for success. I sent dirty jokes to Aziz and irreverent ones to his daughter. I laughed at their messages and felt a threatening swell of love for them. Then I expelled it, and the family ceased being human beings I cared about again. They resolved back to numbers on an actuarial table, odds to manage.

The Impromptu Team worked on our third layer of redundancy for the next run at the airport. We didn't say it, but we all knew: this would probably be the last chance.

I spoke with a married couple who knew Aziz and had worked for years in the country. They were watching in horror at what was happening in Afghanistan, and while they too were concerned for dozens or maybe hundreds of other people, including the president of the country, they agreed to do whatever they could to help. And they had a key contact—they were friendly with another general, the one in charge of the US Army's position inside the airport compound.

I sent a zip file with the family's documentation to the couple, the couple forwarded it to the general inside the airport compound, and they reported back that the general had confirmed receipt: the US Army now had the family's identification. The US Army was aware that Aziz would be making a run for the airport in the next few hours.

We would never hear from the general. But his men, too, would be looking out for Aziz.

CHAPTER 14

AUGUST 17, 2021

Todos Santos, Mexico

Now there was a lull, as evening turned to night in Mexico. I thought about all the Afghans I wasn't helping because I'd become almost obsessively focused on just one family. I thought of Aimal. He had family and friends in Afghanistan; surely he was desperate to get them out, but of all the people I was hearing from, all the requests for help, I hadn't heard from him.

Since it felt like the Impromptu Team's plan for Aziz was in place, there was, for the moment, little to do besides wait until just before dawn on the ground, when the family would emerge from their hiding place again and make another break for the airport compound.

For the first time in what felt like years, I had a moment to myself. Justin and other team members hung on a Zoom call to troubleshoot minor details, but I was mostly there because we were maybe about to send people to some violent end, and we needed to somehow be together in space. Things were, for the moment, calm. Simin sounded good on the phone. She seemed capable of the weight. At least, as capable as a twenty-three-year-old could be when she's become responsible for the survival of her whole large family. Her father the target, her pregnant mother, her youngest sister, who fainted last time.

She seemed up for it. Or she gave the right signs to let us hope she was up for it.

Soon, she would receive a call from a Marine. The Marine would not identify himself but would give her a code word. She would use the code word to lead her family through a series of checkpoints. She would have to negotiate the crossing of a line held by the Taliban. That would be hairy. There was now no way across the city to the airport compound without crossing at least one Taliban checkpoint, where the Marines and the Taliban now stood just meters from one another—some temporary agreement having emerged between them.

If that part of the plan held, the Marines would escort the family to the airport gates and, we were told, through them. If something went wrong, we had our redundancy. We'd seeded the preconditions, I thought, for Simin to improvise a "drug deal." Now, on the ground, there were multiple parties invested in getting the family onto the airport compound. There were Marines outside it invested in getting them in, soldiers in the Army instructed by their commander to look out for the family, and at least one highly placed member of the diplomatic corps inside looking out for them too.

If things changed—if one or even two of the plans fell through—there was still a chance that the family would see, or be seen by, *someone* who'd seen their documents, could spot them among the crowd, and who had the power to help them get through.

In Kabul, in their hiding place, they rested.

In New England, San Francisco, and London, Impromptu Team members waited.

And in Mexico, I was now in one of the peculiar moments that for the previous few weeks would simply tumble out of a day at me. Time to rest would emerge like a nervous animal, and I would try to seize it, bracing for the call that would scare it away. I'd become incapable of planning downtime. I hadn't known I needed to. In the lulls, my mind stayed at high RPM, and I was still at speed when my father called.

He was full of his own concern for Aziz and wanted to know the latest. I recited the whole elaborate ballet we had planned with the former commander of NATO forces in Afghanistan, code words and a team of Marines, negotiations with the Taliban, the two-star general inside the airport, the Treasury officer, and the acting political director of the dislocated US embassy. I told him all of it while pacing the room, hardly pausing for breath. He listened to the whole thing, and when he spoke, his voice faltered. He was unsettled.

We hung up, and I knew what he was thinking without him having to say it. I knew he could hear it in my voice. *I* could hear it in my voice. The plan I'd just outlined seemed fantastical. It sounded hallucinatory. It was a flight of ideas. It seemed I didn't have a firm grip on reality. I sounded like I was maybe unwell.

Aimal called just then, during that same lull. As if he'd sensed me thinking about him, or that somewhere out in the ether, his friend was beginning to vibrate at an unstable frequency. We hadn't spoken in a while, so he unleashed a full traditional religious greeting, *As Salaam Alaikum Wa Rahmat Allahi Wa Barkatuh!* "Peace be upon you and Mercy of Allah and His Blessings," and then he laughed. "Taliban is in control now, so we speak like this!"

He couldn't believe I was in Mexico: he was planning to come to Mexico with his business partner for a break. He sounded upbeat, in good spirits at first. He feigned anger at the Canadian prime minister, who'd just promised to help Afghans fleeing the Taliban. "This mother-fucker says he gives twenty thousand visas for Afghan refugees. Now everyone calling *me*! *I'm* not prime minister! I'm just roofer!" He said people were asking him for my phone number too, but he was refusing to give it. He shared rumors he'd heard from Afghanistan; he told me what he thought would happen next. He said that most Taliban came from mountains and valleys, so they were horny. He said it was going to be bad "especially for younger female. No one's looking for my mother. But they're looking for young girls." He'd heard of people who weren't Taliban pretending to be Taliban in order to kidnap women. He was especially worried about two young workers he'd just hired for his women's empowerment and vegetable-oil outfit in Afghanistan. He was worried that he'd set them up as the face of an organization the Taliban wouldn't like, plus they were attractive and bound to catch the eye of some sex-starved Talib from the hills. "They're Kim Kardashian of Afghanistan. They're biggest trouble; something happen because I put them in that position."

He said he was thinking of ways to help, and at that point I could feel the conversation tipping in the direction it did with every Afghan over the past weeks, with everyone who had even an interest in Afghanistan. That part of the conversation where I'm asked, as I was continually asking others, for help. The *Et tu, Brutus?* moment when the people you think are your friends are revealed to be desperate and to have a burden for you to take. The small beat of silence, his interest piqued, his sense that I might have a way to help the people he cared about. And with a cause like this, when it really could be life and death, no burden was too big to hand over. Aimal cleared his throat, and as I braced for the uncomfortable part of the conversation, I heard a shift on the phone.

He sighed, made a joke. He changed the subject.

I should have just offered. I should have reached out and reeled him back, offered to help however I could, as he would've done for me. Instead, I let the silence sit and checked the clock—still a little time before our operation in Kabul was set to begin—and Aimal filled the silence with an idea he wanted to share. We should do a book together now, he said, one we'd long talked of doing. Maybe now was the time. Not *now*, but when the dust had settled, when—*if*—all our people were safe. He talked of the message he'd want it to have, both of us now distracting ourselves from the betrayal he'd just let me commit. He was philosophical, generous. He made me laugh. He talked about what he'd want to tell about his own rise, fall, and rise again. What he thought would be comforting to others, stigmas he wanted to address. "When you don't make money, you always try to hide yourself. When people have no dignity, they always try to hide. Then only once you have something, you say, 'That wasn't a shame; that was something everyone goes through!'"

He brought up Fatima, the Dutch girl we'd gone on a date with. "I know Fatima really liked me. We had something." I pictured that day.

Bounding up rocks in the Salang Pass, all of us arrested and brought to kneel before the police. What was going on there now? Were Talibs now perched on those same rocks, firing at the sky? He brought up his own purpose on Earth. "I'm here to be nice, smile and laugh, and leave."

We spoke like that for a while until he started apologizing for talking too much. "OK, Jaff. I don't want I should take your time." I said no problem, not a bother. I didn't tell him my cheeks hurt from smiling for nearly thirty minutes straight at his stories and jokes—that it'd been the only relief I'd had for weeks. He said he'd been drinking a little and that's what had made him talkative. I didn't think anything of it. We wished each other luck on our respective extractions. We promised to speak again soon.

A few hours later, I was back on Zoom, watching and listening in real time with the Impromptu Team members scattered across the world, but tiled neatly on my screen, as Aziz's family made one more try for the airport compound.

———

THERE WAS A MOMENT, IN THE MIDDLE OF THE NIGHT, WHEN THEY went dark.

Simin stopped communicating right around the time they were supposed to pass the Taliban checkpoint.

I lay on my stomach in my room, chin in my palms like at a Girl Scout slumber party, because I'd been sitting so much for days. It felt good letting my ass have some blood flow while I willed the family across to safety.

In Mexico it was dead quiet outside, but inside my little dome it was vivid and brilliant. The fire of eight souls connected by internet, a furnace of vigilant, nervous energy on its thousandth consecutive hour. In my own mind, still ignited to redline speed by the real-life thriller playing out on my computer screen, a fission happening. Some chemical integrity beginning to break down inside me, lighter elements flung off like shrapnel, to lodge in soft tissue and start some toxic process I couldn't yet see.

We'd been tracking the family by GPS, but soon after linking with the team of Marines, they'd had to turn their phones off and remove the SIM cards. Now we didn't know where they were. Justin, the graduate student, tried to assuage the rest of us. From Boston, he began superimposing paths over maps and sending screenshots to show us where the family could be. They had been going this fast, in that direction, maybe where they are is *here*.

The plan involved cooperation from the Taliban, but really only contact with one Talib, and Taliban control was only a day or two old, so no one knew what to expect from them. Summary execution? Chivalry? Protection for an expectant mother?

Surely they weren't organized enough for all of them to be carrying around a kill list and recognize they'd just found one of their Most Wanted.

Were they?

I tried to distract myself by checking other unrelated messages. But all of them, on every platform, were from people asking for my help getting out of Afghanistan before they were murdered with their families.

While we waited, I felt shame for the time I'd spent trying to help just one family. Shame for the time I'd spent not trying to help anyone. Then shame for the time I *had* spent trying to help, and not reconciling with my sister. All this time ignoring my niece, just then in the midst of a summer of trauma surrounding unreliable men in her life. In my mind, feelings arose, battled, retreated, arose again. Resentment, then grace for being able to play this role, then accusation: all these Afghans were exaggerating. It wasn't that bad. They were firing off requests without knowing how it affected me. I felt self-pity. Some of the sturdiest people I'd known now released jabbering, incoherent requests. Everyone was being reduced.

I aimed my attention back to the screen. Each member of the Impromptu Team pretending to be occupied with other tasks, in the middle of the night, so we wouldn't have to talk about the fact that we may have just sent a family to their deaths.

On the screen, faces tilted, murmuring to people offscreen. A chorus of low tones as we waited. All of us pretending not to be worried.

Then, after long, silent moments, Abuzar's voice from San Francisco crackled through the computer speakers.

"They're in!"

We hesitated, careful not to celebrate prematurely.

They're in *where*, exactly? Are we certain? *All* the way in? No fresh, unseen gauntlet they still have to run?

Then we whooped. I got up to use the bathroom for the first time in a century. Pictures came in of the family collapsed in airport chairs. Aziz looking happy, the kids looking mischievous and wired, the wife looking miserable. They were safe. We didn't know where they'd go from there, but they were in the airport. They'd be flown to some country or another that wasn't Afghanistan, and that's all that mattered. We were allowed relief; we congratulated ourselves. Hadn't we just saved the founder of the country's first coeducational school? We sat in front of each other for ten minutes, put our palms on our faces, and said, "Oh my God, oh my God." We tried to sit in that fragile moment, holding it like a delicate thing in our hands, before it broke open and spilled the notion we were all trying to hold at bay. *Yes, Aziz is safe. His family is safe.*

The rest of the students and teachers were not.

———

THE MISSION CONTINUED.

After three months trying to get Aziz out, we took fifteen minutes to bask.

Before the sun came up, we were already talking about what we owed the rest of the school, now that we'd helped deprive it of a leader. For the rest of the students, time was running out. The Taliban were all over Kabul. The last of the US troops were due to be gone in five days. I slept for a few hours, tried to take an evening with my family, my sister Margot being interviewed as an inspiring female entrepreneur by a design magazine, and I'd just sat down to dinner with them when a message came in from General Allen. It was addressed to two former ambassadors and, somehow, to me too. I ordered a drink and tried to think of an endearing story to tell about Margot. I looked at my screen under the table and read.

> *The troop retrograde has now begun. Troops are flowing out.*
> *Processing of Afghans will effectively cease shortly to ensure as*
> *many AMCITS get out as possible. POTUS decision means*
> *we're out entirely sometime on the 31st. As boots on ground*
> *shrink, capacity to process and provide security diminishes*
> *dramatically. Troops will have to shift to securing our getting*
> *out. There will be a cross over point when no more Afghans go*
> *out . . . only AMCITs and troops and equipment. Highly likely*
> *not all Americans will get out. Our troops and State on the*
> *ground at the airport headed for an impossible situation.*
>
> *My point . . . there are only hours to make the Marefat extract*
> *work.*

I left the dinner. We surged forward with wild, sleep-deprived plans.

Abuzar managed to get a successful trial lawyer on board with the Impromptu Team. She was a fresh epinephrine shot that jacked us back up; upright, wild, and focused again. Aziz's daughter-in-law took on the burden of coordinating the girls on the ground, as did an old friend of mine from the university, and his wife.

We raised money and negotiated the purchase of a bank-repo military transport plane. We would hire a crew to duck in under the radar, land under cover of darkness in a field outside of Kabul, and pick up a group of at-risk girls.

But we nixed the idea when Aziz, now safely in a military camp in Qatar, said an operation like that would put the people left behind at even greater risk than they already were.

We were promised entry for a few dozen girls via bus to the Kabul airport gate one morning, only to lose faith in the plan and call it off. Then we negotiated complex feelings of relief when a bomb detonated at the crowded airport gate right where the bus would have passed, and we heard thirteen US service members and 170 Afghans were killed, but not our girls.

We chartered a plane from a businessman we half-trusted to fly out of a smaller city called Mazar-i-Sharif. We played God, picking favorites for the limited seats, and made the people we'd chosen promise not to tell anyone they were going, not even their families. We sent them north by road, through dozens of Taliban checkpoints, only to find we couldn't get them into that airport either, couldn't send them enough money to stay put because the country was being sanctioned, had to turn them around, send them back through dozens of checkpoints. Back to Kabul to work things out with the families we'd made them abandon.

Nothing worked. My energy faded. Everything aggravated me. I flung dirty looks at people talking too loudly or too quietly. I felt murderous toward people scraping their chairs back from tables. Unclear text messages were crimes against humanity. My reservoir of adrenaline flagged, or it had long since flagged and I couldn't ignore it anymore. Then Aimal called. He and Samie were coming to Mexico. He'd been inundated with evacuation efforts too, and he mentioned something about problems in his family life. He needed a getaway. We would try to meet up. What a crazy thing, to meet and have it not be in his old country or his new one, not in his or in mine. I'd go meet him when he arrived; we'd drink and party and retire to his room to continue our different evacuation efforts. We hung up.

The Impromptu Team simply didn't stop. I grew more easily disoriented. I was having a hard time keeping up with which list of girls was supposed to go to what potential savior. I made mistakes that filtered upstream and became mistakes made by important people who were doing us favors. I confused lists and caused diplomats to send incorrect letters. I was angry and tired. I was mad at everyone. Why should this be my job? I was resentful of other members of the Impromptu Team for continuing to put so much time into this; I desperately needed other members of the Impromptu Team to continue putting so much time into this. I couldn't bear the constant calls and messages from them. I desperately needed to be free of them; I desperately needed to feel a part of them. I was in love with this effort and being poisoned by it. I was beginning to split.

I messed up more spreadsheets. I confused names, and sent the wrong lists to people. I couldn't keep it all straight. The need was endless. The girls were stuck. People heard I'd helped Aziz, and more requests came in, but almost nothing from our one successful mission was relevant anymore. Afghanistan was no longer solid land; it was a constantly shifting ocean, changing so quickly that a helpful contact from a moment ago was now irrelevant and miles away from any possible doorway.

My father flew down to Mexico to surprise my sister for her fortieth birthday. We gathered at a seaside restaurant to drink mezcalitas and chase my niece around the beach, but I was on the phone the entire time, shooing children away so I could hear Afghanistan.

The director and producer of the film loosely based on my book about this very school flew down so we could plan the beginning of production, but I spent no time with them either. I felt sorry for myself, felt embarrassed for feeling sorry for myself, given what people on the ground were contending with, then felt sorry for myself anyway.

And angry. Hadn't I brought this on myself?

Dozens of still new, desperate requests came in, every single day. I'd written one book about the school there, a book few people in my own country read, but it was beginning to feel like every school-age kid in Afghanistan knew about it and could find a way to reach me.

I woke one morning to 185 new message threads. Each one an entirely new request. Aziz had accidentally shared some of our phone numbers publicly, including mine, so whoever didn't already have it did now. I spent a day moving through each message, telling each person "No, I'm sorry, I know you're scared, I know you're in danger, I feel for you, but I can't help you."

A day spent falling behind on our efforts to move the group we had decided we actually might be able to help.

Aimal called again. He was in Mexico. I was in Mexico. I hadn't managed to pull myself from the phone long enough to make it across the tiny sliver of the country to him. He'd circled the world, and I couldn't even cross the room. I realized I hadn't exactly invited him to where I was, either. I would not see him. He must've heard something in my voice because he shifted from humor to concern. He said I needed to make time to separate myself from it all. "Please be realistic about what you can achieve. You are Jaff. I am Aimal. We are not Jesus or Muhammad."

CHAPTER 15

1177 AD

ABOUT A THOUSAND YEARS AGO, A PERSIAN WRITER NAMED FARĪD ud-Dīn Attar completed an epic poem titled *Manṭiq-uṭ-ṭayr*, "The Conference of the Birds." It told the story of a flock, thousands strong, gathering to choose a new leader.

The birds are told that to choose their leader, they should consult the "Simorgh," a revered, phoenix-like creature, and they set off in their thousands on an epic quest.

Along the way to find the Simorgh, they face many tests. The journey is full of tribulation. They must cross seven mountains and valleys, each requiring mastery of some task or the acquisition of some profound knowledge. To cross one, the birds must release their worldly desires. For another, they must learn to embrace love and relinquish reason.

Another obstacle is named for a perhaps untranslatable word, which mixes knowledge, gnosis, insight into mystery. It also happens to be the word that Aziz used to name his school, Marefat.

As the birds in the poem continue their journey, some perish, others give up, and by the end, of the thousands who began, only thirty remain after crossing the final mountain and valley to see the Simorgh.

But the Simorgh isn't where he's supposed to be.

They've come all this way and lost so much, and it's all for nothing. Nothing lies at the end of their journey. No wisdom or reward awaits them. All they find is a small lake.

It's only when the birds amble up to the water and look in that they find what they are looking for. They see no mythical creature; there is no Simorgh.

What they see instead is their own reflection and, with it, the realization: *morgh*, by itself, means "bird." And *si* means "thirty." What the birds see at the end of their journey, when they look into the water, is "thirty birds." They see themselves. There is no divine creature there. Or, more precisely, the divine creature is *them*. And the wisdom they sought lay not in some sacred being, but in themselves, and their journey.

When members of the Impromptu Team realized we were going to need money to resettle the girls, perhaps millions of dollars, and that it was hard to raise money without a name, it was in this poem that we sought one. We thought about simply calling ourselves the Conference of the Birds. We thought about drawing a name from some feature of the story. We thought about calling ourselves Seven Mountains, but that kind of sounded like a rehab clinic, or Seven Valleys, but that sounded even more like a rehab clinic. We settled, in the end, on the 30 Birds Foundation. It was apt, for the obvious association with flight, but it was more than that. Like the birds in the poem, the girls we tried to help were actually doing most of the work themselves. They ordered themselves into groups, coordinated on the ground, somehow kept track of one another, and protected information without a single leak.

And it was apt also because like the birds in the poem, they were not seeking new wisdom; they were carrying it within them. The school, hope, growth, the future of a country—none of it was gone, we were trying to say. It was just stored in the minds of travelers. The Impromptu Team became the 30 Birds Foundation. Later came a debut on CNN, Christiane Amanpour interviewing Simin by phone, her face a postage stamp in the corner of the screen because she was now stuck on a base in Quantico, Virginia, and Abuzar calling in from a studio in San Francisco. A segment titled "How a Secret Network Helped Evacuate Hundreds of Afghans." It showed footage of them, many of them schoolgirls who marched across a technically closed border into Pakistan, thanks to a route Bella had somehow opened through a contact she'd made with exactly the right Pakistani government official. Footage rolled of girls landing in Canada, a city called Saskatoon, of all places, "The Paris of the Prairies," where they were welcomed. At the airport a policeman who'd served with the Canadian military in Afghanistan was waiting for them, with a tiny Afghan flag and a welcome sign.

But that was only half the group; the others were still getting ready to make their own crossing into Pakistan. And then there were the dozens of others I'd made promises to who were still in Afghanistan, and not on any helpful list I could access.

We pressed on.

But it was around that time, as I was beginning to split apart, that I realized I was missing my mother's last lucid months. I flew back to Philadelphia so I was now close to her, but I never saw her. She was disappearing, dormant and confined in her confusing new home. In the last moments when my mother was my mother, I abandoned her. I slipped out from under a family burden and let it crush down on my father, my sisters. Then I realized what I'd done and tried to return, backing out of evacuation efforts and letting that burden crush down on teammates. I let everyone down everywhere. I couldn't decide where to aim my fading attention. The pressure to choose right was massive, existential, because a new sense was settling in, a sense that no matter how things were going on any given day, something invisible was slipping away, something precious and irreplaceable. I was leaking some vital substance that, once lost, couldn't be recovered. At first just an ambient sense, until I understood that this thing beginning to feel so excruciatingly scarce, always, was *time*. A feeling, an obsession, that time was running out. Time to reconcile with my mother, time to be with a family that felt like it was crashing through atmosphere and breaking up. Time to get Afghan girls to safety, time to hit rapidly approaching book deadlines that felt alternately frivolous and like the last bastion of self. Choosing right was crucial because choosing wrong was not a correctable error. A sense of dread leaked into every porous part of life. A feeling that sometimes made sense and often didn't, sometimes felt obvious and often materialized as if wormholed in from an unseen corner of the universe, this feeling that for some important thing, for everything, I was too late.

I fell behind on book projects while trying to help the 30 Birds Foundation; I fell behind on 30 Birds while trying to make progress on books. Messages from Taliban-occupied Afghanistan came in on every single messaging platform, the phone in my pocket a nuclear fuel rod flinging off all the unhelpful isotopes, a block of poison that went everywhere with me. When I came back to evacuations, to the daily calls and constant messages, I felt useless. Everyone was working hard to help a group of girls stuck in limbo in Pakistan, giving up progress on work and time with family. Why did I deserve to be an exception? I weakened more. I was beginning to seize up, the propeller slowing. A blackened engine sputtering, coughing up the last of its life and flaming out.

And then I went into a tailspin.

CHAPTER 16

SEPTEMBER 3, 2021

Canada

AIMAL AND SAMIE GET BACK FROM MEXICO FEELING AS RELAXED as possible, given the circumstances. Aimal still fielding constant calls from friends asking for his help getting out of Afghanistan, and the absence from his kids still twists up his gut. But he's managing. Mostly, he's worried about me. He isn't disappointed we'd been in the same country without getting together so much as he's troubled. He feels it's a sign I need help. He decides to start calling, trying to make sure I do something fun. He urges me to relax. He senses I might be overdoing it. He feels the least he can do is withhold my number from all his Afghan friends, who are constantly asking him to connect them with Jaff. They can think he was an asshole; that's fine. The one thing he knows he can do for a friend is make sure he doesn't add to the burden.

Then everything changes. It's Aimal's niece. She calls from back home saying the Taliban are now taking young women like her out to rape them. She's hysterical. "Uncle, please, I don't wanna get raped; I don't deserve to get raped!"

Aimal loses control. She tells him she'd hidden herself, but sooner or later they'll find her. He doesn't know what to do. He has to help, but how can he help? He breaks his rule.

He calls me, and when he can't reach me, he leaves a message: "I don't care what the bill . . . you have to call for me. Please don't bring your brother down. Give me favor. I don't care about the guys. Let

291

the guys die. But she's my niece, she's 18 years old kid, I don't want—brother, please, push your buttons. I don't care how you push, push it hard; I need to pull her out."

He doesn't know what I can do. Maybe nothing, but he's desperate. He needs to do something; he's never been good at sitting still. But what's there to do? What can he do from here? *From here.*

He leaves me another message. "I'm heading out . . . your brother's heading out to Afghanistan. I will *fight* the Taliban. Maybe the US left, run away. Canada left, run away, but I'm not gonna run away from my niece. If they gonna kill me, I would *willingly* to leave my blood for my family. And if you're my brother, you don't let me down. No one's listening. For fucking sake they think they gonna come and they gonna go for welfare. I'm *willingly* to pay for my family; you know me. But at this point I'm getting way emotional; I cannot lose my niece. To go under the hand of the Taliban, to get rape. It's so painful. I cannot tolerate; I don't know how the fuck I'm gonna put myself to Afghanistan, but please, brother, pull out my niece; that's your niece as well. Your niece is being almost getting rape."

By the time he's done, he's so worked up he figures maybe he *will* just go. From a frenzy of emotion to a crazy idea, from a crazy idea to something actually worth considering. People are being flung from planes trying to get out of Kabul, people are being blown up at the airport, and now he has to find a way *in*. So he'll find a way. If anyone can, he knows he can. He books a flight to Qatar, from Qatar to Uzbekistan. It hardly registers that he still isn't officially allowed to travel alone. He isn't about to put someone else at risk by dragging them to Afghanistan. He packs a few things without thinking and leaves.

CHAPTER 17

SEPTEMBER 11, 2021

Philadelphia

I GOT AIMAL'S MESSAGE AND DIDN'T KNOW WHAT TO DO. THE MESsage was ranting; it was madness. I'd never heard him like that. I avoided him. It was easy to do; my little team had our daily, sometimes twice-daily calls.

But I couldn't avoid him forever, and finally, an unforgivable week after his desperate call, I called back.

The line connected, but Aimal's voice sounded off. A little higher than usual, a little faster, the English better. It wasn't him.

"He left his phone with me." It was Samie.

"Where is he?"

"Yeah, man, he went to Afghanistan."

CHAPTER 18

SEPTEMBER 13, 2021

Termez–Hairatan Checkpoint, near Balkh, Afghanistan

HE LEAVES HIS PHONE BEHIND SO THAT WHEN THE TALIBS STOP and search him, there will be no connections to the West. He lands in Tashkent and gets a ticket on a puddle jumper to Termez, where a sea of people are trying to get from Afghanistan into Uzbekistan. He slips by the other way.

He finds his way to the northern city of Mazar-i-Sharif, bundles himself in tribal clothing, and hires a car down to Kabul.

He has to pass through another Taliban checkpoint every hour, but he makes it all the way into Taliban-controlled Kabul unscathed. It looks exactly the same since he left, but in some ways totally different. He doesn't know what he's expecting. He's a man in a turban, and he gets some second looks—his beard's only a few days old—but the Talibs mostly leave him be: they still seem as surprised as everyone else that they run the country now.

He finds his niece, and once he has her in his sights and knows she'll be OK, he finally calms down. Away from her, he could picture the worst. Now that she's there, in front of him, he knows he can keep her safe. And while he's here, he has others to look after.

He manages to get the *National Geographic* people to help his mother because in his absence, his company here signed a contract to help their journalists operate in the country.

He gets the women's empowerment sisters into the airport compound. Once inside, they're herded onto one of the planes shuttling refugees to Qatar, then flown from Qatar to a US Army base in, of all places, Wisconsin. He doesn't know anything about Wisconsin other than it's in America. They're safe, but even though they're out of danger and Aimal himself isn't, he worries about them. Neither is very comfortable speaking English, and once they're in Wisconsin, they have a hard time staying in contact.

Even sitting in Kabul plotting an escape with his niece, he still feels the women's empowerment sisters are suffering an ordeal that's his fault. He put them at the front of his organization, and he feels he owes them more than just safety; he owes them some level of comfort. He figures it's worth the risk of logging on to Facebook. He sends his American friend a message. Then he takes his niece and plans a secret route back up to the north, across the border into Uzbekistan. He rents her a house and leaves her with enough money to look after herself, at least until things settle down.

CHAPTER 19

SEPTEMBER 13, 2021

Philadelphia

ANOTHER MESSAGE FROM AIMAL, SEEKING A SMALL FAVOR FOR the women's empowerment sisters. "Can you send a SIM card or number at this address? Please, brother, as soon if you could arrange. I'll sent you the money coz she need a USA phone number with internet. Thanks, I'll call you tomorrow once I'm out back of the sheet hole." He sent a photo of some torn scrap paper with a handwritten address. He seemed fine now. Some relief there, but I wasn't fine.

I fell further behind on deadlines. Editors treated me with unexpected patience. My short-term memory stopped working—clogged or overwhelmed because I was trying to stay connected to a thousand unstable atoms, incoming signals from groups in various kinds of crises that didn't honor any schedule or time zone. Messages that seemed desperate and urgent even when they weren't. I lost the ability to discern between the two; everything seemed like a fire.

CHAPTER 20

NOVEMBER 2021

Canada

AFTER HIS IMPULSIVE TRIP TO AFGHANISTAN IN THE MIDST OF THE Taliban takeover, Aimal comes back to Canada and tries to catch up on business. He can't stop thinking about the people he's evacuated. The protective instinct has fired back on, the radar screen in his head with blinking dots. The women's empowerment sisters he believes he put at risk, the family members and friends and all the life rafts he'd loaded up and shoved off, all his people in their various unfinished escapes.

The sisters, stuck on an army base in Wisconsin, weigh on him. Now that they have SIM cards and phone credit, they call him all the time, asking when they're going to be let off this base. Where they'll be sent, what's next for them. How can he know? They're safe but speak as if in this camp, on this base, they're prisoners.

The older sister calls to say they're being shipped off. Sent to Tennessee, has he heard of it?

They've been given a bedbug-infested motel room in Nashville and the phone number of a coordinator who is supposed to help them get settled, but the coordinator never answers the phone. Or maybe the sisters are too intimidated to try the number; either way, they're alone. They can't speak the language, and it's his fault they had to leave their country. He has to go help. Again, he'll travel alone. He has a business to run, he's just catching up on jobs, and he's not about to take his co-owner away from work too.

297

He breaks the Crown's terms a second time.

In Nashville he takes the sisters to a municipal office building that can help them get working papers. They go to meet the head of the office that resettles immigrants, and Aimal tries to charm a woman behind the desk so she'll look out for them. He takes the girls out on the town. He gives them a credit card with a $25,000 limit and tells them to spend it all. He speaks to them in their language and takes them on road trips, and once they seem comfortable, like they have enough optimism to last them at least a few months settling into their new life in America, he flies back to Canada so he can finally start carrying his weight again at the company.

Samie picks him up from the airport, and they go straight to their jobsites. An entire workday passes, and at dinnertime he still hasn't even showered since America. They drive back to Samie's house so Aimal can see Samie's kids and pick up his truck.

He leaves, done with a long day, a long few months, finally done with all his round-the-world travel. Finally some moments alone. A long night of sleep. He just needs a shower and one night to put Afghanistan and its whole chaotic aftermath behind him. Then he'll be ready. A full partner to Samie again, and maybe he'll find a way to make some overtures to his wife. Maybe Samie can be an intermediary—she still trusts Samie—and he'll find some way to see the kids again. *The kids*. The chaos of his collapsing country has been a partial distraction, but it's now been most of a year since he's even laid eyes on his own children. He has to try hard not to think of them, but of course it's impossible.

He looks out the window. He turns the radio up. He's almost home, a few minutes from his bed, when lights exploded in his rearview. A police car. He slows down, but he wasn't speeding. Then another car, then seven more: they'd been waiting for him. A dozen police cars coming at him from all angles. The first officer reaches the window, and Aimal nods at the battalion of cops surrounding him. "Who am I, Osama bin Laden?"

"Where are you going?"

"To my lawyer's office." He's allowed to travel alone to meetings with his lawyer. The officer disappears. Aimal calls his lawyer, the officer comes back, and Aimal puts the phone on speaker.

"He's coming for an appointment with me," the lawyer says. The officer ignores the phone.

"We're taking you in. We're not supposed to fall for that anymore."

Aimal sighs. He knows what will happen now. He'll do a few days as the lawyer sorts it out and charges him a small fortune, plus bail. He'll spend a night in the police station, maybe a little more while the paperwork is arranged, and *then* he'll have his shower, his own bed for a day or two, and be back up on the roof.

But this time it's different. A bail hearing in which the Crown asks Samie, "What's Aimal worth to you?" Samie answers honestly: "Millions." He means it both literally and because the two are as good as family. How do you put a price tag on family? But it's the wrong answer. To the Crown, it means Aimal has too much sway over the person who's supposed to make sure he behaves.

And that is obvious.

When Aimal left the country to save his niece, he broke the rules. No one stopped him.

When he did it again to help the women's empowerment sisters in Nashville because the American government couldn't, and because the American government was proving itself totally unprepared for the surge of refugees it had just caused, Aimal broke the rules again.

They ask Aimal's younger brother, who had shown up with clothing disheveled and eyes bloodshot, if he has the money to guarantee his brother won't break the rules again. Sure, why not? I can get it. They ask where he can get it from. Well, he says, I'll just borrow it from Aimal.

The Crown denies bail. Aimal's influence over his community is too big for the "surety" system to work. He's remanded until such time as they can establish how to make sure that he abides by the terms of his bail order.

Aimal, in other words, is going to jail.

CHAPTER 21

DECEMBER 2021

Philadelphia

I couldn't remember names; I couldn't remember tasks. Three words into a sentence, I couldn't remember why I'd started talking. My ability to function around people ground to a halt, took extraordinary effort, like moving a boulder out of the way just to muster some grunt of a hello. Matching the blasting steam engine in my head with the movement of air through my diaphragm and the flexing of an embouchure—having a conversation—required impossible coordination, landing a triple axel in a hurricane. How had I ever done it? Applying my mind to words in polite society, or even with family, was like trying to time the landing onto a full-speed treadmill. The risk of being flung against the wall, embarrassment and pain, shame for having broken whatever I crashed into.

I couldn't muster the effort to speak; I couldn't bear receding into silence. I wanted to be left alone; I needed attention. The thought of doing anything—eating, dressing, moving, sleeping, waking up—made me physically ill and sent panic through my limbs, wild electricity in my elbows and fingers. The thought of sitting still did too. My meds were adjusted. Doubled, tripled, halved. I calmed down, but it was an illusion, a circadian lull, and then the flames came back. My father had me make cocktails. He said they were really good, asked me to have one, asked me to have two, asked me to stop drinking. I wandered onto the roof of his house and then the roof of my apartment, which was three floors up. I laughed. I came down. I drove a little faster than I should've. I noticed sturdy-looking trees. I called my mom.

"Remember to do something fun for yourself every day." Locked away, but had she ever been so comforting? A lifeline, a connection, some frizzled frequency of hope. God, she really did know me, and stripped of pretense by rotting coils in her brain, there was love. She asked what I was working on. I told her about the book, the biography of a bomb. She made a noise. "Remember to do something fun for yourself."

Loss was everywhere. A pandemic that started out feeling like it affected everyone but me now felt like it affected nobody the way it did me. Community exploded. I couldn't find friends; I couldn't even picture them. I was lost in self-absorption. Everyone was experiencing loss, but I felt alone with mine. A mother, a plan, youth, friends. I'd lost a country. My first war zone. I'd gone with a bit of a sense to help and mostly to extract, to feel adrenaline, sex, violence. I'd gone with a death wish, and I'd fallen in love. Not with girls—though I did that too; I always did, even if they didn't always know—but with a school, a community, perhaps most of all with Aimal and everything he stood for. Can you fall in love with a country? If it's a place you despise, can't stand, are compelled to return to, what is that but family? I'd lost that too. I'd lost a war. For my whole long catalog of mental health struggles—my deep, monstrous depressions, obsessions, wild ion storms of panic—I was certain that trauma wasn't one of them. War is hell, but I'd sailed through all my wars without injury. It was the end of one that did me in.

Now there was guilt. What had I done? I'd landed in a country a decade and change before with a swell of artless, adolescent vigor, of appetite. I'd affected the people who assembled to help me; I'd pushed their faces into trauma that they, unlike me, couldn't just leave. Only now, as a hundred messages of fresh despair met me every night before trying to sleep, was I paying any kind of price. I'd gone as a journalist, not a soldier, not a gun for hire, certain that this meant my hands were clean. I hadn't fired a weapon there, so how could I injure people? I'd injured people. I'd written a book exposing the inner thoughts of people from a traumatized community, of a thirteen-year-old girl who'd watched bombs kill classmates. I'd made her recount the moments, then made her recount them again so I could get the details just right, and then showed her to the world as if saving her. The cover of that book was a photo of a different girl, one I hadn't even bothered to meet, plucked from a group picture of a morning lineup and turned into a micro-celebrity in her community, whether she wanted that or not. A girl who would be how old now? Who was how old then? A girl who was gone now. A classmate of hers told me, matter of factly, in the midst of the evacuations, that she was blown up, my cover girl, some years ago.

I'd sat with Aimal the first time I visited him in Canada, sitting with him and his Christians, and he told a story about visiting a morgue with me. His version of the story. He told it in a major key at first, bragging about how fearless and crazy his American friend was, but the room went quiet, and he stopped smiling. For a moment, maybe the only moment, he didn't know what to say. Started speaking then stopped, like he'd forgotten the point. Then he said he had nightmares about that day. It haunted him all the time.

I hadn't fired a gun into a crowd of civilians, hadn't ordered a drone strike on a gathering of insurgents that turned out to just be the groom's half of a wedding party, but now I saw that what I had done wasn't much better.

I carried around a backpack of pills. I realized that I was grieving at the exact wrong time. I ignored my mom. I stopped visiting. I called her again. Again, she asked what I was working on, and this time the question leveled me. How had it taken this long to realize that "What are you working on?" was cover for "What do you do for work?" A step or two from "Who are you?"

She made her voice sweet. "Remember to do something fun for yourself every day."

I got on some 30 Birds Zoom calls and made inappropriate jokes even though speaking twisted my gut. The team members laughed, exclaimed how happy they were to see me, acted like I hadn't gone months without contributing a single thing; they were all love. I needed them; I needed to be free. I couldn't see an exit.

CHAPTER 22

JANUARY 2022

Toronto East Detention Centre
"The East"

They book him and put him in the "Dark Hole" so fast it's as if the whole system was waiting for this. The segregation unit, some bogus excuse or another for why they have to keep him isolated for seventeen days like he's some kind of cannibal, a danger to the most dangerous men. He should be at home, he should be at some mild facility near his house, near his ex-wife, near the venues of the extraordinary crimes she accused him of.

Instead he's here, unconvicted but in prison. "The East," not a place for victims of misunderstanding. The East is for people who knew what they were doing. Not in some breezy suburban complex, but a hard place for the city's worst, a half-hour from the Toronto Blue Jays. A place for murderers and gangbangers serving life sentences, but it's Aimal frog-marched into isolation.

He can't quite believe he's here. How easy it was for them to do this to him. A single hearing, a few wrong answers, he slips and tilts right out of his life. He's always been able to manipulate the system, but this time everything together was too much. Weakened, tired, and traveling around the world to save people he owed. The miles piled up, and he let down his guard. Here he is, let out every 48 for a shower, and otherwise alone, only two moldering old airport thrillers to keep him company. He's skirted bombings, shootings, warlord feuds, and terrorist-recruiting attempts, but following a bond order after the collapse of a country proved too much. The collapse of a country and also, perhaps, a family.

And still. Prison. The system is rigged against him. The system is racist. Easy for detectives and judges to line up against a brown man with a Muslim name.

He deserves this. The system should listen to women. Look at his country, after all.

The system should consider that men tell the truth sometimes too. In his country, if a woman behaved like his wife had here . . . you wouldn't want to see that. They'd tear her head off and throw it to the neighbors. He'd said that once, right to her face. She took it as a threat. How could she think he meant it?

How could she not?

Only a small man beats his wife. Was he small? He'd ignored her, disappeared, barely helped with the kids, had he changed a diaper? He removed her from her family and then cheated; he had her stand up and cook for his friends while she recovered from a C-section and his friends just sat on their asses. *That's abuse. That counts; I did abuse her.*

He doesn't know how he feels, or he's sure how he feels, and then it changes.

What is he doing here?

He knows. It's the officer he used to call up drunk and insult. The one who has it in for him. She orchestrated this. She received his Hennessy-scented screeds and had her revenge, somehow.

They booked him and put him in the Dark Hole. How did they do that so fast? He has nothing to do but argue with himself, that and the airport thrillers.

He's finally moved out of isolation. A correctional officer addresses him like a booking agent: "We're putting you in protective custody." A few minutes out of segregation and Aimal is already getting a read on this place. PC is for pedophiles and rapists. PC is "protection" from other prisoners taking punishment into their own hands.

Well, if there were real pedophiles and rapists, he'd have a hard time keeping his fists to himself. "Put me in GP."

"Some of the people on the range there are pretty hard."

"Yah, brother, look at my name. What, they grew up with pistols? I grew up with RPGs."

"Suit yourself."

Qaf, Yeh, Ghani . . . now, the ultimate invisible puzzle to solve. He has to identify the power structure, and he finds it isn't hard. The players are easy to see; he reads their pressure points. Even from his cell he can see who to concentrate on.

Mo, a giant of a man, and Nice, who is nice to Aimal it seems because Aimal has a Muslim name but is not strictly speaking the nicest person generally. And H, the leader, in for who knows how long after a handful of murders. H is king of the castle, that's clear. Aimal knows the type. He can see it in the bearing, the body language he learned to read when he was driving people he couldn't really speak with around Kabul. H needs to be respected but not fawned over. H controls phone time. H controls the real estate too, the going rate for the good cells, and oversees the weed distribution. Drugs smuggled into prison in orifices Aimal prefers not to think about. Sometimes the whole range is pungent. There are no lighters, but the inmates are like him, finding angles everywhere. For rolling papers they repurpose cafeteria sugar packets. For fire they pull the nose-holding wire from COVID facemasks, loop it around a battery from the TV remote, send sparks into toilet paper, and light their joints.

H controls the price of toilet booze. Sealed plastic bags of cleaning solvent and sugar from the cafeteria, tied to strings and dropped into the toilet like bait. Flushed down to ferment while hiding in pipes.

Aimal learns the intricacies. Phone time is currency. Cells toward the outside of the range are the worst. Closer to outside so they're cold. The inside cells are warmer, and if you crane your neck, you can see the TV even during lockdown. He watches the Super Bowl from his cell, trying to follow the rules of the game, and feels some comfort thinking of the time I came to see him and brought a tiny Eagles jersey for Yusuf.

He was only just born then. The roofing business just starting. Wasn't that when they'd sat over the liquor, Aimal tired and happy, asking me if he should really go ahead and launch a company doing roofing, Yusuf tumbling around at their ankles?

How big is Yusuf now? Aimal hasn't seen him in eight months. Aimal wonders how long it takes for a child to forget a father's face. And where was his wife in that memory?

Will his daughter know him at all? His daughter, you love all your children the same, but she's the real miracle. How had she come from *him*? What more proof of a higher power than that Aimal, even having traveled through his damaged past, could still create a being like her?

And his youngest child, named for the oldest prophet. The child he hardly knows. Maybe now, here, since he doesn't know his son, Aimal can at least get to know his namesake.

———

"Unless they spare me from hellfire like God spared Isaac from Abraham," the man across his cell says. A married professor from Oman who'd taken up with a student, ran into her ex one night. Some dumb fight broke out, and the professor threw a punch. Some freak valence knocked the man toward the sidewalk, hitting his head just so and paralyzing him. Attempted murder, the book came down. The professor was a gentle soul but slave to his pecker like the rest of us, and Aimal likes him. Aimal learns that being Muslim is a good thing in The East. Believers here stick with each other. There seems to be no better armor than Islam. Why *not* pray?

With the professor coaching him up—wiser than Aimal but not as loud, not as fast—Aimal begins spouting little wisdoms from the Quran. He recites duas that the professor had just recited to him. Other Muslims ask him one day to lead prayers. *Him*, sinner of sinners, leading the faithful of Range A4A. "Taliban," they call him, and he doesn't mind even though the Taliban is kind of why he's here. He knows a nickname is a good sign. He turns around one day and realizes he's the sheikh.

Nice shouts down from the second-floor cells, "Will you guys shut up? They're praying," and even H raises his hand to quiet the inmates. Aimal nods, winks, and begins the prayers.

He begins leading the prayers just as he's realizing he has no idea what Islam is. He knows what he learned as a kid from the foreign NGO. He knows the whole Holy Book. He's memorized much of it. But he's memorized it in Arabic, and he doesn't speak Arabic. He knows the way the words curl in his mouth, but he doesn't know what they mean. Like most of his friends back home—a choir member chanting in a dead language. He has never read from a Quran translated into a language he actually understands. It's a prison in Canada where he first learns what he never learned in an Islamic republic. Now, at thirty-six, he reads the Holy Book, and it blows him away. How beautiful it is! How gentle and wise his prophet was, *all* the prophets were!

How soothing and lovely that none denied the others. Christians and Jews are his siblings. He begins to think of the Almighty as a parent, the prophets as just nannies. If a brother is cared for by one nanny and a sister by another, do they take the nannies' last names? No! Their parents are still their parents! We are the same! He feels tingling down his skin. Little hairs stand up.

He dreams of his foreigners, the friends he's now more forcefully removed from but feels even closer to. He has a dream about me in which I'm flying away as some kind of bird. An eagle? He believes he knows what it means. Maybe it's corny, but you can't control your dreams, can you? Something about too much expectation on a free spirit, that's what he thinks.

And in the morning, he does what he needs to do to make prison submit, as he did in the drought land of his birth, the war zone it became, in the mass of the cold country he fled to.

——

IN H HE SEES A MAN WHO LIKES RESPECT BUT IS DISGUSTED BY THE syrupy, wheedling weakness others try. You have to show that you know he's the boss but that you yourself are no pushover. Respect, not fear.

Aimal approaches him with élan. "Hey, you're H. I'm gonna make a call, yeah?" The gang leader is impressed.

Aimal joins a poker game and uses an old move. He loses big on purpose, and when one of the players says, "You owe me $1,500, so how are you going to pay?," he already knows his next move.

"Don't worry, brother. Tell me who on the outside to send to."

Down on the range: "H, I'm gonna make a call."

"You kidding. *Again?* All right, go ahead." He calls Samie, and Samie wires money to the winner's email address. Samie is as attentive to Aimal as Aimal has ever been to a client, and more responsive than any inmate's girlfriend. On the range, word spreads that Aimal can make things happen. Samie keeps the business running and Aimal's canteen topped up so he always has candy and chips to pay for a haircut or phone time. And when the gentle professor with the iron fist says he hasn't spoken to his family back in Oman in months, Aimal pays forward the favor he received when he first landed in Canada and the friendly Black man dialed an international number and let him speak to me. Aimal works it out with H, makes sure phone credit is lined up, raps on the professor's cell, and says, "OK, Haji. Go call your family."

CHAPTER 23

FEBRUARY 2022

Philadelphia

I WASN'T TAKING CALLS. I WASN'T TALKING TO ANYONE; I COULDN'T. I hadn't heard from Aimal, and I hadn't checked in. I didn't bother trying to reach him until one of the women's empowerment sisters sent me a message asking if I knew anything about his whereabouts.

Even then, I didn't pay it all that much mind. I knew Aimal was fine; he was always fine.

And then that started to break down. Through my storm, a new worry. I called his brothers; I called Samie. I pieced together what was going on with him. They each had enough information that together I got the whole grim picture, and when I did, there was a glowing seed of dread. That this might be it, the thing he doesn't come back from. I knew just enough from his other short stints in jail. The day or two he told me he had to endure while accusations were sculpted and pruned to fit forms, forms that made their electronic march through chambers and courts, and Aimal waited, being degraded by arrogant guards. I knew enough to see that those earlier stints drove his eyes down and in toward the darkest part of himself, and I knew that the more time he spent there, the harder it was to lift out of it. What would months do?

And I knew that somehow, in a way I couldn't quite describe but felt sure of, I had had a part in it. I'd seeded the trauma that sent him off on these occasional tears toward self-sabotage. I'd stepped off a plane a decade and a half before and turned a smiley kid who glided above the Earth into a collapsing planet of a man with something noxious running toward its core. I saw this only now, but I was too wounded, and maybe he was too, to do anything about it.

I couldn't think of anything I could do to help him get out. I'd asked everyone I knew for favors trying to get a school out of Afghanistan. I felt that no one owed me anymore; I owed everyone now, even if I owed Aimal most.

I tried to go on with life. I tried to nudge along the book we'd talked about. I ducked and scratched and clawed and tried to crawl out from the squall bruising through my nervous system, the total system failure that now had this added to it too. Guilt was a debris picked up and blasted at gale force through my field of vision; it stung badly enough I sometimes had to close my eyes. Guilt for having gone to his country, for hurting him and realizing it too late. For abandoning my teammates and the people they were still trying to rescue. For abandoning my family as I looked over their heads to plan grand gestures for people I didn't know, while somewhere behind me, my mother smiled and disappeared.

——

When I learned Aimal had finally been let out of jail, I limped back up to Canada to see him. We talked only briefly first. He was wearing a LoJack-type tracker bolted to his ankle as part of the terms of his release. The government's way of making sure he didn't violate his bail again, and didn't go anywhere near his wife. And when we spoke, there was a hitch in his voice. He said the ankle monitor conflicted with the phone signal in some unnatural way. It did something to him. Talking on the phone caused him physical pain, so he said we'd catch up when I was there and we could go on a drive together. He made me promise to send him my flight information. One last time, he insisted on picking me up.

This time, I put my foot down. It was finally too much. He wasn't allowed to travel alone to the airport, he'd just been in jail for almost three months, and now the government knew exactly where he was all the time.

"Don't worry," he said. "Then I send Samie to get you."

I winced. Samie, who was now trying to keep Aimal out of jail while running the whole business with Aimal still at half-capacity and the specter of a more permanent absence looming over them.

Still, I knew I wasn't going to win the argument, and keeping Aimal on the phone was, apparently, actually hurting him.

"Fine," I said. "Tell Samie that to pay him back for the time he loses coming to the airport, I'll put on a harness and go up on the roof."

"Oh, no," Aimal said. His voice became serious. "There is requirement to be on roof you have to be six feet tall." I heard Samie's laugh in the background.

"You motherfucker," I said, and I smiled for the first time in a long time.

CHAPTER 24

MARCH 4, 2022

Canada

WHEN I ARRIVED AT THE AIRPORT IN TORONTO, SAMIE WASN'T there. Aimal was.

I nearly yelled at him. He said don't worry; he'd figured out a workaround: we were working on a book together, weren't we? That counted as "work," and the government allowed him to move around the province if it was for work. He led me out to his parking spot, untangled a charging cable, and plugged himself into the truck. "Yah, Jaff, can you please to send email for me?" He handed me his phone and dictated a message. Where he was, where he was going, when he'd be there, and who he was with. A constant test: the Crown looking for cracks between what his messages said and what the ankle monitor did.

But as we drove, he actually seemed calm. Like some roiling thing inside him had settled. He told me he had met a professor from Oman in prison and how much of a shock it was to read scripture in a language he understood. "Abraham didn't have Denali. He didn't have cake. This system made us robot, always money first. Internally I always want to be rich guy. Now I want to be rich in my heart. *Internally* I want to be rich. Yah, Jaff, I'm getting there. I need to focus on me."

He said maybe being locked away for so long was actually good for him. "It taught me about patience. Not rushing, because things work out in the end. People waited for me. Right now I'm loaded for work for months. We don't even have time to cash check." He described a feeling he got reading scripture for the first time in a language he knew.

Little hairs standing up. "Ah, what's it called." I realized he was talking about goose bumps. "Goose bumps." He smiled. "Yah, Jaff." He rolled up his sleeves and touched his arms. "Now I have goose bumps thinking about having goose bumps."

Samie met us back at the office. He was in a less introspective mood. I could see the exhaustion on his face. His whole patient family had been tested by Aimal's conflict. Aimal told me on the drive how remarkably dedicated Samie had been. Feeding the canteen and doing favors on the outside for family members of convicts so Aimal could pick his way through the prison's social scaffolding. Samie managing the lawyer, keeping the business running, making sure Aimal's kids and their mother were looked after while Aimal couldn't, trying to keep a line of communication to her open.

So when I arrived for that last trip, Samie and possibly Aimal too, were scheming on some kind of détente between Aimal and his wife. They couldn't go on like this, that much was obvious to all of them, and the business couldn't either. She wouldn't go near Aimal but still sometimes talked to Samie because he was always even-keeled and responsible, so Samie thought there was a chance he could get the two of them in the room together, without lawyers, and settle this once and for all. It sounded like fantasy to me, given all that had transpired. The threats, the months in prison, how dug in they both were. How much they'd spent on lawyers.

But that was part of it. They saw lawyers as thriving on the conflict, the arms dealers of domestic resentment. They saw the police as nursing a vendetta against Aimal, and his wife as exploited more than protected by them. So where did that leave things? The only people whose interests lay in ending the fight were the primary combatants. But they needed to understand each other. They needed at least to speak with each other.

It would be risky. Samie and Aimal talked it out in front of me. Aimal wasn't allowed to go near her because she'd told the police she didn't feel safe around him. She told Samie she worried that if the police found out she was talking to him, he could get in trouble, but she could too.

Would they see her as someone willing to do whatever it took to resolve conflict, or would they just see her as a liar? Could they make trouble for her and the kids?

But mostly, no matter how badly she wanted to resolve the conflict, she didn't want to see Aimal. And that, it turned out, is where I came in.

A FEW DAYS AFTER I ARRIVED, AIMAL GAVE ME HIS TRUCK, AND I spent most of the day in a hotel room working while he and Samie went around to jobsites. In the afternoon, Aimal called asking if I wanted to come by the office around 4 p.m. I drove over, and Samie laid out a plan: he had invited Aimal's wife over. She thought she was just meeting with Samie, but I would be there too. Aimal would be hanging around somewhere nearby, and Samie would try to convince her that, since I was there, nothing bad could happen. Surely, Aimal wouldn't misbehave with his American guest keeping an eye on things.

Before I could argue, or even knew what I should be arguing, there was a knock on the office door. She was here. Samie answered, Aimal slipped out past her to yield the room, the first time they'd seen each other in nearly a year. She looked rattled for a moment, but she recovered and greeted me as if I were a welcomed guest arriving in her home after a long journey, not part of what felt even to me like a bit of an ambush.

Samie pulled out a chair for her, sat down, and began his pitch. I was trying to decide whether I should pretend to pay attention or pretend not to pay attention. Samie ran through all the obvious things: "This is bad for you both, bad for the kids, and all this money on lawyers," while I thought, *And who are you to be telling her this, Samie! And then, Actually, who better than the guy who's managed to keep his own family together while keeping a company afloat and his business partner alive inside a prison surrounded by convicted murderers?* She nodded along, none of this new to her; she seemed to genuinely want this to be over. It looked as though the only barrier was really that she didn't trust Aimal. Samie commiserated: "I'm tired of taking care of this guy!" And she laughed:

"How do you think I feel?" Then they laughed together and looked at me as though I also shared custody over this man-child of theirs, so I tried to shrug in an unreadable way because for me until now it had always felt like the opposite.

At that moment, Samie skewed toward pushy. "So can I go get Aimal? He's outside; I'm sure he's not far. Let me just go get him." She balked. "You have nothing to worry about. Jeff will stay. Aimal won't pull any shit."

She seemed to soften, just a little, but still had a concern. Either her last true objection to seeing him, or maybe a made-up excuse to cut this plan off at the knees. "The ankle monitor of his, can't it listen?"

Samie had an answer for that.

So out went Samie, and in came Aimal with a shoved-down grin again, more guilty than mischievous. Looking at his wife for the first time in nine months.

He kept a respectful distance. Samie was knocking around downstairs, and he reappeared with a bright-red mop bucket full of water. Aimal took off his left shoe and sock, and I sat there trying not to laugh as he plopped his bare foot with the ankle monitor into the water because they figured if the ankle monitor could listen, water would muffle the sound, and they began to talk. Two hours like that, maybe more, wearing a bright red bucket as a left shoe, as if this were some slapstick sitcom and not a man trying to reel back the tragedy he'd unleashed on his life.

Aimal was overenergized, at stake was the chance to see his kids again, and I could see that old instinct firing on. Fight, flight, freeze, and, for him, *talk*. He was a man granted a last chance to save himself, an open look at the goal with time running out. And he was choking. I knew he couldn't help it. The pressure was getting to him, and when backed into a corner, when desperate and when lives were on the line, Aimal *talked*. He'd almost always been able to talk himself out of mortal threats. He'd talked himself out of danger in prison, talked himself out of a Taliban attack, and talked me out of arrests. This, to him, was the most important crisis yet, and he couldn't talk his way out of it. He wouldn't shut up. He wouldn't let her get a word in. He was panicking, slipping, lecturing her about how his past made him this way, how he'd give her anything she wanted and how he was good for it, how he was a motherfucker, he knew that, and she could recant her testimony and this would all be fine. I touched his knee to slow him down, but he just kept going, Samie said, "Will you shut the fuck up, Aimal?" But even when he tried, he couldn't, it was painful to be a part of, I wished there was some way I could do what he'd always done for me, but he wouldn't shut up. I could see her feeling the crazy coming off him. He'd had his chance, and I knew he blew it.

CHAPTER 25

MARCH 8, 2022

Canada

THE NEXT MORNING, AIMAL IS AWAKENED BY A CALL AT 7 A.M.

She asks him where he is because she wants to bring some of his clothes back to him. A bad sign? A good sign? A permanent cleaving, dividing the last of their belongings?

Or maybe progress, since it means she's still willing to at least briefly be in the same space as him. Maybe a sign that the mop-bucket summit didn't go as badly as it seemed. They agree to meet at the office, neutral territory.

But when she shows up, there's something else. He can hardly believe it: from her car a child tumbles out with a swollen shape and a rhythm to his movements Aimal recognizes. The child screams, "Papaaa!" Eyes bulging like behind them a mind is trying to process something too big to comprehend. His son, but larger. The last Aimal saw him, Yusuf knew only a few words, still pointed and wailed. Now, there he is, running toward Aimal, then stopping to prepare a full proper sentence. "Daddy, can I hug you?"

And Aimal feels he can weep right there.

Yusuf pulls back and looks at the office. "Daddy, is this where you live?"

CHAPTER 26

APRIL 2022

I LEFT AIMAL DURING A TURNING POINT. AT LEAST, IT LOOKED like one, like a child running into his father's arms announced the office as a kind of demilitarized zone. It wouldn't last, the conflict too deep-rooted and too well-attended to expire after one good breakthrough. But for a time, Aimal and his ex-wife became something like amicable co-parents. He saw all three of his children almost every day. His wife began doing some work for the company, keeping things organized around the office. When I talked to Aimal on the phone, she was laughing in the background. She and I could joke, and I didn't feel disloyal. She went to the Crown and said she didn't want to proceed with a trial, and without their key witness, they dropped the charges. I hoped—*I thought*—she felt secure now.

I allowed myself to laugh at how it'd turned out. "I'm a free man now!" Aimal sounded happy on the phone, not giddy but good enough, and one by one, I heard about all the people he was trying to get to safety reaching their destinations too. The women's empowerment sisters were comfortable, more or less, in Nashville. Though they, like thousands and thousands of other Afghans flung asunder by the chaotic end to America's longest war, had a long way to go before feeling anything resembling the comfort of a home. Aimal's mother finally made it to Canada, where she lived in a house he arranged for her, and she saw her grandkids all the time.

Meanwhile, on the phone he told me that another immigrant on the Guelph construction circuit, a Russian friend of his, had developed a terminal heart condition and decided as a last act to share his prized possession, his home, and offered to sell it to Aimal for well under market value. Aimal told me he took one look at the yard, pictured his kids running through sprinklers and kicking soccer balls, and accepted. It felt to me that he'd managed to put roofs over the heads of the most important people in his life now, along with, of course, his hundreds of paying customers. The business was thriving too. His reputation was strong enough to survive a few absent months. I could always hear that when I'd drive around with him in Canada, listening to him talk to his workers and his customers. A boss who gets up on the roof with you and pays more than the others. To customers, a roofer who's slick but not as slick as the worst. It helped that his mind, though dulled by war trauma and then family trauma, was still—I could hear it—sharper than most. He could still see things others didn't, play the little puzzles unseen to everyone else. And it helped, perhaps most of all, that he had a partner in crime—a friend, another brother, really—who was always there for him, never wavered, the two bound together as if there were some cord formed in the country where a part of them both would always remain. Samie never once left his side. From my perspective, it seemed that here in this clean little corner of North America, for just a moment, there was a version of what winning looks like.

TOO LATE, 2022

WRITERS WHO GO TO WAR ZONES TEND NOT TO BE SUPPORTIVE of war, though we might be accused of having a kind of chemical dependence on it. A hatred and a need for it. The White House press-pool reporter holding her nose and giving column inches to a president whose misdeeds move newspapers and pay salaries, the tabloid star letting the paparazzi catch a bad side and staying relevant. Some of us see the horrors and want to warn others; some of us see the horrors and want to undo the airbrushed parts of recruiting posters. To show the cold unshiny innards of war.

Some of us are just doing a job, some of us are after glory, and I suppose for most of us it's some cocktail of it all. And while we're at it, some of us care for the people schlepping us along on our adventures, and some of us are in touch with the harm we can cause if we're not careful or humble. Some of us come to see that only when it's too late.

Once, back in college, I heard a reporter describe what it was like to cover a mass shooting that had happened at an Amish schoolhouse. A ferocious anomaly in a culture foreign to her. She said something like, "It was just horrible; your instincts as a human are to leave these poor people alone, you don't want to bother them, but you have to." And I remember thinking, "Do you?" We convince ourselves of our own indispensable work, and it licenses us to do things that cause their own trauma. But rarely are we—or at least, rarely am I—writing about something that will immediately save lives. I have never exposed the poisoning of a water supply or unmasked a mass murderer before the killing could continue. I *have* tried to bring readers to wars and crises I believed they didn't know or care enough about, but even when I've been comfortable in my motives, those adventures have exacted a toll on the people I've asked to help me. I haven't just covered injury; I have injured the people who've been my sources and my support staff, my translators and drivers. And of course, in one case, the person who was all of those things.

———

NEVER DID I LICENSE MYSELF MORE FULLY THAN I DID IN AFGHANI-stan. I was part of a civilizing force, I was there to spread forwardness and capture backwardness, and rarely was other people's privacy, or their pain, really my concern, except as a symbol of some exceptional trend. Oppression of women, oppression of minorities, the savagery of a class that can strap bombs to themselves and walk into city parks. I was there to listen, but I rarely hung around long enough to listen. I can speak really only for myself, but I don't think it's a coincidence that people like me who went there to explain didn't really understand, and that the war my country led a coalition into ended with such a spectacular and tragic display of collective misunderstanding.

I don't think war, no matter how it's entered, is predestined to end a certain way. If war can ever be justified, then even justified wars can end badly, can end worse than wars started with weaker reasoning. Colonial-ists slicing through communities can stumble into a few contributions; humanitarians can break things. The war in Afghanistan wasn't predes-tined to end the way it did, though perhaps a tragic end was foreseeable once it became clear that it began without enough understanding. Not enough humility, not enough knowledge, and we didn't realize the scale or nature of the impact we were having until it was too late.

It's of course too late to undo the calamitous end to our adventure in Afghanistan. But perhaps it's not too late for all wars, or for all conflicts tempting us toward war. And for those of us involved in planning them, fighting them, trying to prevent them—in documenting them—perhaps one humble goal can be simply to listen. There's a saying I heard once from Aziz, the headmaster who appears in both this book and my first one, which I heard again and again throughout the writing and rewriting of this book. Mostly, it was applied to the impossible-seeming feats necessary to get people out of the country as the war came to its disastrous end and every door slammed shut. It often felt like what we were trying to do was not just difficult but literally impossible, that we were trying to move mountains. And I kept hearing the headmaster teasing me, trying it in Dari first. *Koh ba koh na mi rasad; Adam ba adam mi rasad.* "Mountains cannot move together," he'd translate, since he always had to translate. "But a person can move to another person."

Perhaps, in the end, that's what war reporting should strive to do. Not just interview survivors, or catalog who did what to whom, but to collapse the gap in understanding. We talk of sources and subjects and objects and characters, and these categories are of course also people. It's a person standing by the wreckage with a mic in her face, interviewed, thanked, and left alone, to cancel her afternoon plans because as of just now her living room is empty.

We tend not to look behind at the rest of a life, the whole of a life. The afters and befores, and if we did, we might know what we're getting ourselves into and what impact we might ourselves be having. We might know what we're doing, we might do it better, we might decide not to do it. We can shrink the distance between us if we acknowledge that it exists. We might learn more, and share more, so the next two countries can avoid suffering next time. Or so at least two people can.

A NOTE ON SOURCES

The preponderance of material in this book comes from interviews; from, where applicable, my own memory; and from documentation, contracts, contemporaneous notes, or other records that Aimal or I kept.

Although I owe a large debt to many scholars and writers for their wisdom and reflections on the period and on Afghanistan, there are several sources worth noting explicitly, since I used specific details I found only in those works. Those include:

Douglas A. Blackmon. *Slavery by Another Name*. New York: Anchor, 2009.

Rahim Faiez. "Afghanistan Hires Tribesman to Secure Polls." Associated Press, August 11, 2009.

Rod Nordland. "Working to Help a Haven for Afghan Women Blossom." *New York Times*, June 20, 2010.

Amit R. Paley. "Iraqis Joining Insurgency Less for Cause Than Cash." *Washington Post*, November 20, 2007.

David Remnick. *Reporting*. New York: Knopf Doubleday, 2006.

Mark Tran. "Afghanistan Calls for Media Blackout Ahead of Election." *Guardian*, August 18, 2009.

Lawrence Wright. *The Looming Tower*. New York: Vintage, 2006.

ACKNOWLEDGMENTS

Authors often acknowledge their families, but I don't think anyone has ever had as much of a reason for gratitude to family as I have to mine. Thank you, Dad, Margot, and Jenna for your patience with me over the years, for reading endless messy drafts, and for taking on so much of the burden during family crises.

Thanks to Mom, for handling illness with grace. For the years you spent celebrating us for traveling out of our comfort zones and bringing friendships back. Thank you for sending me west. I love you.

To the 30 Birds team: you've become my family as well. You are extraordinary people, even aside from this thing we've found ourselves buried in. A group of talented speakers, presenters, filmmakers, writers, and storytellers. The 30 Birds story has been and will be told in better and more comprehensive form elsewhere. There will be a better representation of the thousands upon thousands of hours each of you put in. The long, tense, sleepless nights and the sacrifice of health, wealth, time with family, and (in Bella's case) personal hygiene. All the more generous for the fact that at key moments, you were there, picking up one another's slack, and in many cases mine. You continue to awe me, but your being there when I stumbled is a demonstration of the sacrifice, I suppose, that made the alchemy work. Thank you to all of Saskatoon, Saskatchewan, for bringing our community into yours.

To name names: Thank you, Bella Pollen, a professional idol of mine, a collaborator, a hero, and an indispensable source of support. As a writer, she could, and will, tell stories like this in ways that make the rest of us jealous. Instead, she saw a need before I did and then simply never stopped. Steering us collectively, and me personally, around more icebergs than I can even remember. Justin Hefter, a model human being. Brilliant, tireless, generous, and a true man of action. Our conscience and our steam engine. Mark Donig, a scholar and a gentleman, a chess master, but one who will stay up all night before a full day of work making sure the pieces are arranged, just so, to help deserving people he doesn't even know, and then to disappear before the victory lap, because his gifts are needed elsewhere.

Abuzar and Tahera: I see you, and I know you've made even more sacrifices than most of us will ever know. Mohammad and Manizha, my brother and sister among so many new brothers and sisters. I love you guys. Jennifer Selendy, an angel who put us on her back when we most needed it: a conscience, a taurine drink, and an absolute powerhouse.

Christa, a beautiful soul, somehow also a brilliant writer, who spent so long in the trenches, made personal connections with everyone who needed it, and was always there to right the ship when it threatened to tip.

And to all the girls in Saskatoon and those of you on your way, who did all the real work, while the rest of us bit our nails behind computer screens.

Thanks to the unnamed governors, senators, congressmen and congresswomen, ambassadors, generals and soldiers, Republicans, Democrats, and hippies who refused to claim credit. It took a collective failure of the American government to reveal to me how many deeply good people there are inside of it.

Thanks to David Larabell. A guardian and a friend and a brother, who never withdrew even when it was hard to be my friend. It's an insult to call you a miraculous agent. To Michelle Weiner and Jamie Stockton, who've done extraordinary things. I remember four-country phone calls into war zones, just to make sure fighters featured in stories weren't getting short shrift. All the unnecessary but deeply appreciated gestures.

Thanks to Ben Kalin. The world's most adaptable, indefatigable fact-checker, who quickly realized that this book needed much more than just fact-checking. Thanks for being a conscience, for handling every difficulty a book can throw at you with such grace and tact, and for being an extra editorial eye. If there are mistakes in this book, it's because I did everything I could to make your job harder.

To Ben Adams: patient, wise, brilliant, and supportive. There is simply no one better. Ben and the rest of the PublicAffairs team, who showed nothing but support even when this book required accommodation after accommodation. Thanks for your uncanny bedside manner, which is of course why this book is here, but also why it ever had a chance of working. Thanks to the ineffable Melissa Veronesi for nimble field marshaling, handling every variable I threw at you with aplomb and a clever new work-around.

Thanks to Donald Pharr for applying the kind of talent, experience, sensitivity, and effort typically reserved for titans of literature. If this book works at all, it's because it was saved by you.

Thanks to my endlessly patient and supportive friends. Gene and Juice, Durve, Sly, #2— the rest of you know who you are, but your nicknames aren't as cool. Thanks to you all for having my back so many times and in such exceptional ways. And what can anyone say about Kathy Gilsinan? A treasured source of commiseration, support, advice, reassurance, and all the other things that a friend needs but a writer needs even more. The doubt monster is real, but sometimes looks a little smaller when viewed through two sets of eyes.

Thank you to Melissa Rudderham, who looked after me and helped me stay safe and also stay productive in so many ways. To Obaid Nejati, a boss and a friend who was perfectly protective. To Hugh Allen, who on several occasions made the seemingly impossible suddenly seem possible.

Thanks to Steve Landrigan, an early supporter who helped in incalculable ways, and to Qais Akbar Omar. I met them on literally my first day in Afghanistan, and they have remained steadfast sources of support, of fact-checking, of quiet, innovative ways of helping, and of that barbed kind of brotherly love. To Nasim Fekrat, whom I've known forever, it seems, and who has helped my family when my family needed it most.

To Aziz Royesh: my father, brother, friend, and perhaps most of all, my teacher, always.

Thanks to Trudy Rubin, a hero and mentor, who has always lent me her reputation and connected me to just the right person at just the right time, and who has quietly modeled how to be both a writer and an actor, even during the most horrifying times.

To those early people who helped give me the little nudges along on the path. Thank you, Richard Hart, for patiently starting my career, and Eric Gillin, for steering me through the first months of trying to be a war correspondent. To Ken Rogerson, who was simply always there with guidance, encouragement, and wisdom. To Bob Bliwise, who carved out the first venues for me and showed me that I could maybe do this. To Doug Blackmon, for letting me write my book.

Thanks to Sammy Heller, who read an early draft of this and took care to strike the perfect balance between suggestions for a draft that really needed it and encouragement for a person who did. A new and constant source of both editorial and emotional support.

To Liz Butler, who's read so much and who has kept me at least within view of sanity, and who won't stop showing me what's possible. To Jessica Chappell, a godsend who has gone miles above and beyond.

Thank you to Howard and Mary Hurtig, who have looked after my family in ways both extraordinary and quiet, and who somehow made the connection that led to my first home in Kabul.

To Rory and Shoshana Stewart, who gave me that home during my very first weeks in the country back in 2007 and asked for nothing in return. And who gave me my only exercise—I haven't forgotten those Frisbee games.

To Muqim Jamshady and Afghan Logistics: your cars kept me safe and mobile, and you are the reason I ever met Aimal in the first place.

And, last, thank you, Aimal. For keeping me alive and for helping me in more ways than even a book can account for. You've gone to extraordinary lengths to look after those you care about, and there is a list as long as another book of extraordinary things you've done just for me. And after all that, thank you, brother, for showing me it's OK to open up. For putting the idea in my head for years, this idea of telling our story—your story—and then being so generous with it.

JONAH G VAN BEMMELEN

JEFFREY E. STERN is an award-winning journalist and author. Stern has written three books, including *The 15:17 to Paris*, which was turned into a major motion picture by Clint Eastwood and Warner Brothers, and *The Last Thousand*, which received an honorable mention for Best Book of the Year by *Library Journal*. He has reported from Yemen, Iraq, Afghanistan, Guantanamo Bay, Kashmir, the epicenter of the West African Ebola outbreak, and Oklahoma's death row. His work has appeared in the *New York Times Magazine, Vanity Fair, Atlantic*, and other outlets. In 2019 he received the Overseas Press Club award for the best human rights reporting in any medium and the Amnesty International award for foreign reporting.

PublicAffairs is a publishing house founded in 1997. It is a tribute to the standards, values, and flair of three persons who have served as mentors to countless reporters, writers, editors, and book people of all kinds, including me.

I. F. STONE, proprietor of *I. F. Stone's Weekly*, combined a commitment to the First Amendment with entrepreneurial zeal and reporting skill and became one of the great independent journalists in American history. At the age of eighty, Izzy published *The Trial of Socrates*, which was a national bestseller. He wrote the book after he taught himself ancient Greek.

BENJAMIN C. BRADLEE was for nearly thirty years the charismatic editorial leader of *The Washington Post*. It was Ben who gave the *Post* the range and courage to pursue such historic issues as Watergate. He supported his reporters with a tenacity that made them fearless and it is no accident that so many became authors of influential, best-selling books.

ROBERT L. BERNSTEIN, the chief executive of Random House for more than a quarter century, guided one of the nation's premier publishing houses. Bob was personally responsible for many books of political dissent and argument that challenged tyranny around the globe. He is also the founder and longtime chair of Human Rights Watch, one of the most respected human rights organizations in the world.

·   ·   ·

For fifty years, the banner of Public Affairs Press was carried by its owner Morris B. Schnapper, who published Gandhi, Nasser, Toynbee, Truman, and about 1,500 other authors. In 1983, Schnapper was described by *The Washington Post* as "a redoubtable gadfly." His legacy will endure in the books to come.

Peter Osnos, *Founder*